ADVANCED PRAISE

"*Boss Brooks* is a stunning story, beautifully told, of a family's search for the truth in a web of crimes from nearly a century ago. It is one of the finest true crime stories I have ever read and shows the courage it takes to seek redemption for the acts of our ancestors. This story will haunt you. And it will give you hope."

—PHILIP LEE WILLIAMS, author of twenty-one books
and member of the Georgia Writers Hall of Fame

"Told like a true crime novel, the suspense in *Boss Brooks* builds with every page. With pitch-perfect prose and superior investigative reporting, the story of a man with two headstones unfolds with the ease of a fine silk blanket uncovering the who, what, when, and why a man would fake his own death, leaving his beloved family on the brink of destitution, only to start over with another. Equal parts intriguing and infuriating, Boss Brooks ultimately leaves the reader not only satisfied with its message of forgiveness but thirsting for more."

—LISA PATTON, bestselling author of *Whistlin' Dixie in a Nor'easter*

"Family trees are bound to have some tangled roots, but the story that unwinds in the pages of *Boss Brooks* keeps getting better, in the way only a true story can. Turner and Alligood have connected century-old dots, revealing a powerful picture of the cost of family secrets. If you've got one buried, let the light shine in."

—DEMETRIA KALODIMOS, executive producer of *The Nashville Banner*

DO NOTHING SECRETLY;
FOR TIME SEES AND
HEARS ALL THINGS,
AND DISCLOSES ALL.
—SOPHOCLES

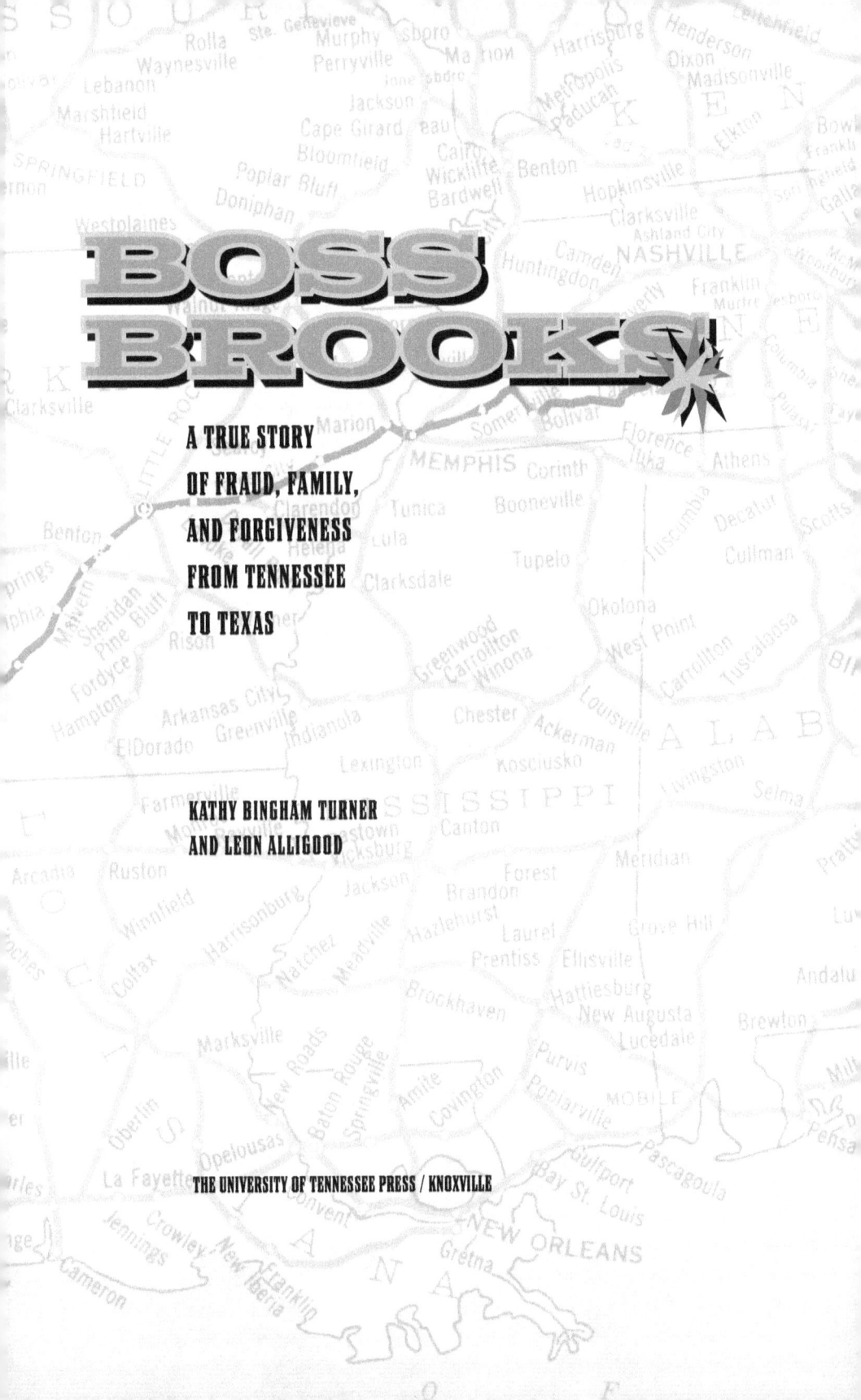

BOSS BROOKS

A TRUE STORY
OF FRAUD, FAMILY,
AND FORGIVENESS
FROM TENNESSEE
TO TEXAS

KATHY BINGHAM TURNER
AND LEON ALLIGOOD

THE UNIVERSITY OF TENNESSEE PRESS / KNOXVILLE

KATHY BINGHAM TURNER

I dedicate this book to three major influences on my life. They are no longer on this earth but will live eternally in these pages.

My grandmother, Mary Louise Brooks Bingham, who exhibited extraordinary strength

My father, Lytle Brooks Bingham, who had the gift of grace and forgiveness

My brother, Lytle Stephen Bingham, who set a standard of the highest integrity

And, to our Bingham and Brooks families and future descendants

LEON ALLIGOOD

To my grandparents, Arthur and Marie Alligood and Hubert and Ruth Hiers

They made my childhood memorable

CONTENTS

ILLUSTRATIONS

MAPS

ACKNOWLEDGMENTS

Telling the story of Boss Brooks has not been a solitary affair. As this narrative moved toward publication the authors were assisted by many people.

Chief among the contributors were the children of Marvin Lester Brooks: Sue Crow, Freddie Brooks, Bobbie Ann Williams, and Sonny Brooks. Their willingness to offer comprehensive remembrances of their father and their desire to learn of his early life in Tennessee enriched the manuscript. Sadly, Sue Crow did not survive to see this book published. She died in February 2025 and was buried in Sherwood Cemetery.

Attorney John J. Ross of Savannah, Tennessee, allowed access to the papers of his grandfather Elijah W. Ross, who represented the Hardin County Bank in the insurance trials of 1932. Without the attorney's view of the legal maneuverings found in this trove of information (kept secure all these decades in a safe, no less), the resulting manuscript would lack many telling details that make this story so unique. To have access to this material was a storyteller's dream.

In like measure, the authors are indebted to various archives. The Tennessee State Library and Archives provided transcripts of the insurance cases heard in the State Appeals Court and the Supreme Court of Tennessee. Hardin County clerk and master Martha Smith retrieved boxes of documents related to the Chancery Court trials of May 1932. Vital information was also rendered by the Baylor Collections of Political Materials at Baylor University and by the Western Kentucky University Archives.

Gratitude is also due to the helpful staffs at the Hardin County Library in Savannah, Tennessee, and the Jackson-Madison County Library in Jackson, Tennessee. We also thank the Hardin County Historical Society for providing period photos of Saltillo and Savannah.

Several individuals were especially helpful as we followed the Boss Brooks trail.

Roger Gant, a third-generation caretaker of Shady Grove Cemetery, was a repository of enlightening information. His genealogical knowledge of Saltillo families was invaluable, and he was an eager advocate for a deep telling of the Boss story. If he could not answer a question, he knew where to find the answer.

Hugh Berryman, now retired as a professor of forensic anthropology at Middle Tennessee State University, provided an extensive review of cadaver decay and his thoughts on the difficulties of exhuming a body. We are indebted to his scholarship.

Regarding our understanding of tuberculosis diagnosis and treatment in the 1920s and 1930s, thanks are given to two physicians: Dr. Yasmine Ali, a cardiologist who is an assistant clinical professor at Vanderbilt University in addition to being an author; and Dr. Jon Warkentin, TB Control Program Officer with the Tennessee Department of Health.

We offer kudos to Leigh Melton Singleton for the appealing design of the Boss Brooks family tree and for maps of Saltillo, Tennessee, and Sherwood, Texas.

Caleb Knies brought our attention to the insurance cases heard by the Supreme Court of Tennessee. At the time, he was working at the Tennessee State Library and Archives while completing a doctorate in history at MTSU. He now teaches American history at Tennessee State University in Nashville.

Charles Watlington of Jackson, Tennessee, is due thanks for information about his grandfather and father, who discovered Boss's burning car in 1931.

From Kathy Bingham Turner:
I thank Judith Willis, a cousin, for her role as "soul sister" during this journey, providing detailed family history and photos, as well as emotional support. Her broad knowledge of Saltillo connections—who's related to whom— was invaluable.

I also cherish the enthusiastic support of other Bingham relatives in my pursuit of truth about the events of 1931.

My friends Nancy Harris, Michael Gardner, and Bill Brennan provided critical support during the ups and downs of writing the book. I treasure their unwavering advocacy for this project. Many other friends offered encouragement and served as sounding boards as the structure of the story came together. A special nod goes to Lisa Patton, who was piqued by the Boss Brooks story early in the research and who offered advice and wisdom that was welcomed.

My brother, Steve, was a significant contributor to our research, providing clarity and enhancing understanding of several aspects of the story. Sadly, he has since passed away, but he eagerly listened as I read the manuscript to him during his last days. I believe he found comfort from it.

To my son, Harrison. As always, your positive nature and encouragement have meant so much.

To my husband, Greg. Thanks for understanding the importance of this journey, for your unwavering support and especially for generously allowing another man (Boss) in my life for the past thirteen years.

From Leon Alligood:

I am indebted to many friends who offered writing advice and motivation. Tony Kessler lent his prodigious copyediting skills, deleting many unneeded commas and offering helpful notes. Keith Ryan Cartwright was a stalwart encourager during our search for a publishing home. Greg Pitts, director of the School of Journalism and Strategic Media during much of my tenure at MTSU, was an enthusiastic supporter of the Boss Brooks story. So was my longtime writing buddy and fellow newspaper colleague Ken Beck. I am grateful to all for their support.

To my former students: thanks for listening to me share this story (many times) through the years.

To my wife, Bertie, and my family: thanks for always believing in me, even when I didn't believe in myself.

Finally, the authors are appreciative to the University of Tennessee Press for publishing the Boss Brooks story. We were told many times the path to publishing depended upon finding the one editor who believed in our story as much as we did. Thomas Wells was that person for us. We are grateful to him and his excellent staff for this opportunity to tell a most interesting story from Tennessee to Texas and (hopefully) beyond.

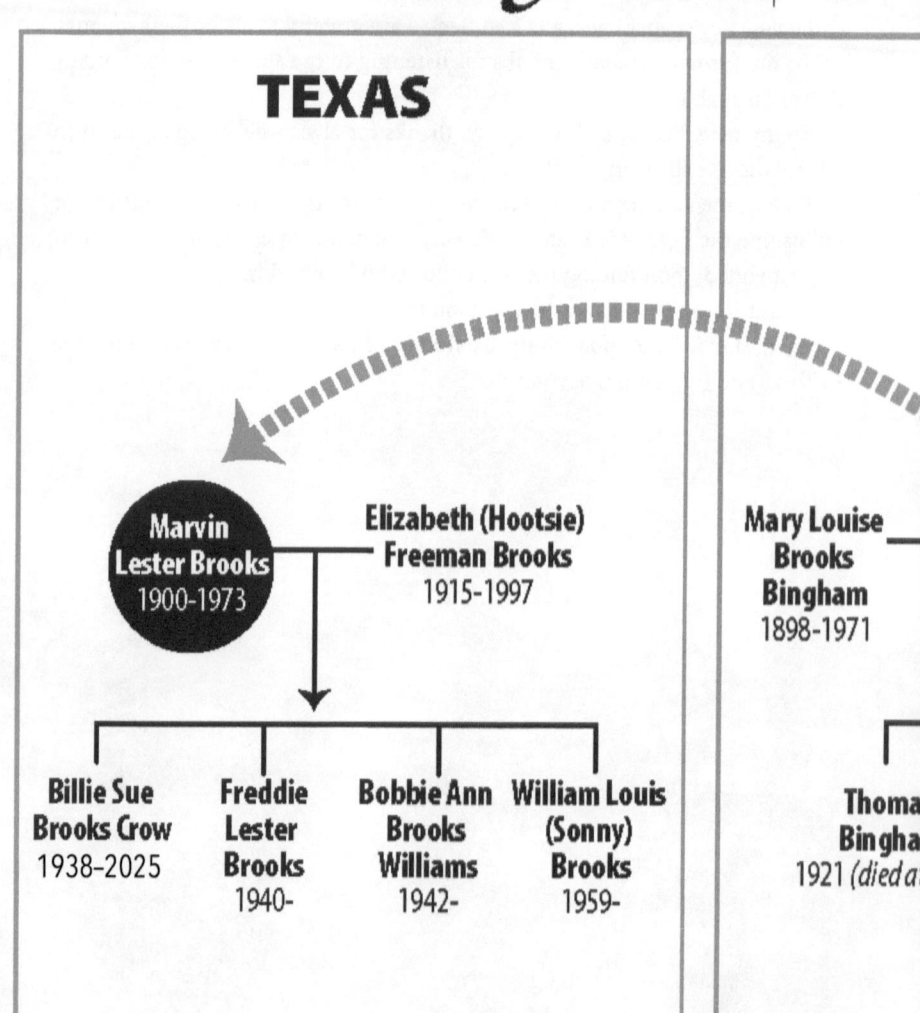

TEXAS

Marvin Lester Brooks 1900-1973

Elizabeth (Hootsie) Freeman Brooks 1915-1997

Mary Louise Brooks Bingham 1898-1971

Billie Sue Brooks Crow 1938-2025

Freddie Lester Brooks 1940-

Bobbie Ann Brooks Williams 1942-

William Louis (Sonny) Brooks 1959-

Thomas Bingham 1921 *(died at*

s Family Tree

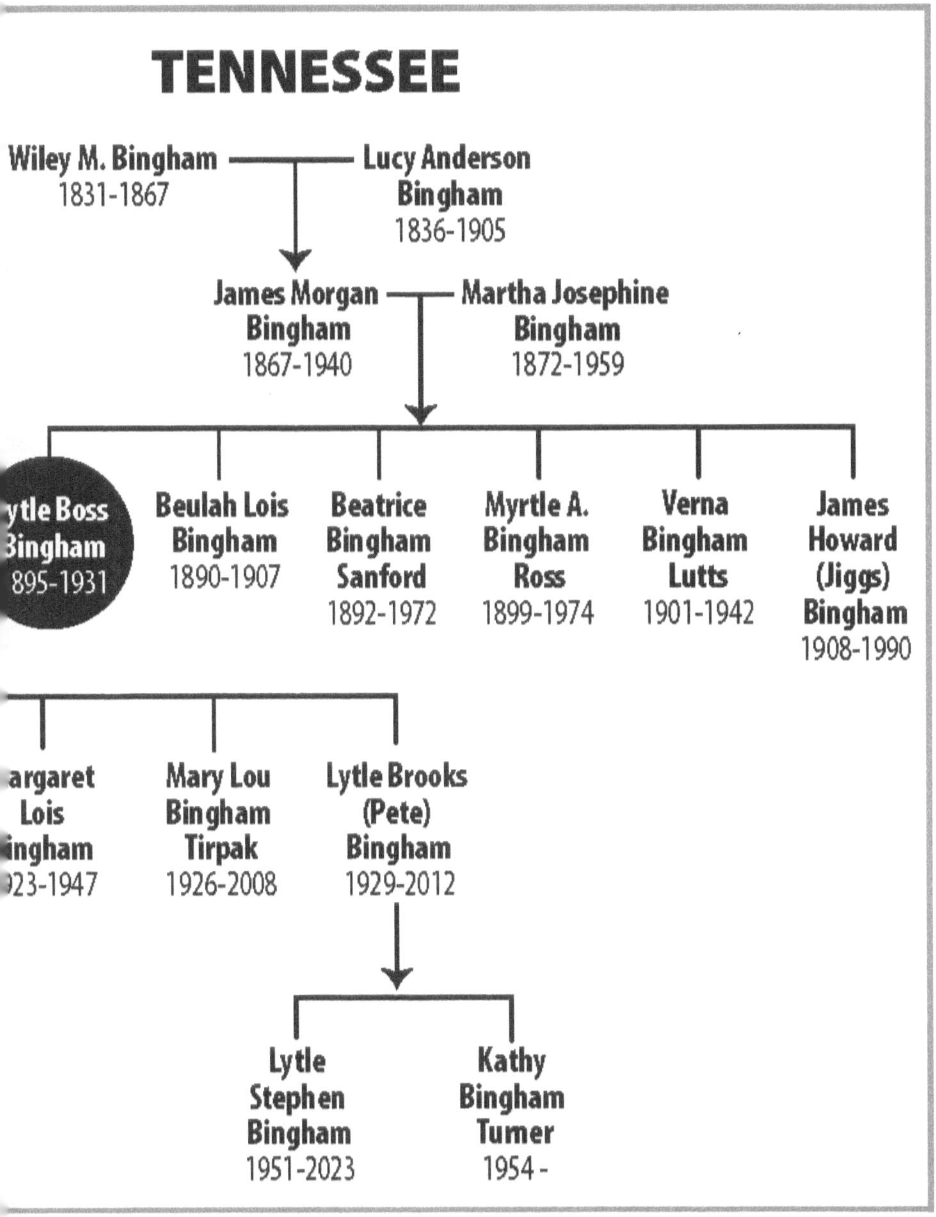

TENNESSEE

Wiley M. Bingham ——— Lucy Anderson
1831-1867   Bingham
                    1836-1905

James Morgan ——— Martha Josephine
   Bingham   Bingham
   1867-1940   1872-1959

| ytle Boss Bingham 895-1931 | Beulah Lois Bingham 1890-1907 | Beatrice Bingham Sanford 1892-1972 | Myrtle A. Bingham Ross 1899-1974 | Verna Bingham Lutts 1901-1942 | James Howard (Jiggs) Bingham 1908-1990 |

| argaret Lois ingham 23-1947 | Mary Lou Bingham Tirpak 1926-2008 | Lytle Brooks (Pete) Bingham 1929-2012 |

| Lytle Stephen Bingham 1951-2023 | Kathy Bingham Turner 1954 - |

THE WORST PART

Had anyone been watching from the woods surrounding the graveyard, the men at work on that cold January night would have appeared industrious, such was their apparent dedication to the task at hand. But their reason for being in Shady Grove Cemetery after dark was not the product of rational thought.

Illuminated by the twin shafts of a car's headlights, shovels sliced into the moist ground and were lifted in a slow arc. Scoop by scoop, the dark Tennessee soil was removed. The men labored despite an inhospitable wind, their exhaling breaths a mist that appeared and disappeared in front of their strained faces. The inky blackness surrounding them was thick with foul weather; sleet and snow were expected before daybreak.[1] One fact was clear: no one participating in this macabre scene wanted to be here in the light of day. They remained alert for passersby, unlikely on such a spiteful night as this, but nevertheless kept an eye on the dirt drive leading into the field of tombstones. None of the men wanted to explain this enterprise because, after all, grave snatching was against the laws of Tennessee, not to mention a startling contradiction to the lives of good and decent men.

And they were good and decent men. Weren't they?

That was a question to be pondered for the remainder of their lives.

Watching this spectacle unfold on his behalf was Lytle Boss Bingham, the affable head cashier of Hardin County Bank. At 35, he was well-known to the citizens of Saltillo, a small town on the west bank of the Tennessee River, positioned at the point of a bend on the broad waterway. Boss, as he was called by all, had worked at the bank for nearly fifteen years, rising in 1928 to the top post, just as the American economy was teetering toward disaster. As the fat palm of the Depression bore down on his beloved town, the suffering to come was evident, yet customers—his friends and neighbors—and the bank's board of directors trusted him to steer them clear of financial ruin.

On this count Boss Bingham failed. After learning an auditor was coming to investigate a shortage, Boss knew his day of dread had begun. Compounding his problems at the bank, Boss suffered from tuberculosis and had been advised by his physician, Dr. Luther A. Parker, who was also the president of the bank board, to seek a drier climate or risk death. For more than a week Boss had been too ill to report for work, and now he was leaving Saltillo.

Earlier in the day he wrote a letter of explanation to Dr. Parker, a letter that in coming years would be continuously parsed to determine the head cashier's motives. Then Boss and his younger brother, Howard, made their way to Shady Grove. Boss was going to fake his death. For that, a body was needed.

The men grunted to lift spades of dirt as the hole grew deeper. Putting a casket into the ground was a simple task compared to excavating one already entombed by several hundred pounds of West Tennessee soil. The task was even more a challenge when the dirt was extracted shovelfuls at a time. The wind howled, whipping blasts of frigid air through the oaks and hickories, their branches swaying over the men like shamans in a trance.

Without a doubt no one present at this unbecoming scene wished to be there. However, circumstances had forced their hands. The bank would soon be deemed insolvent. If nothing was done, investigators would ask questions, seek indictments, bring jail sentences and ruination to families whose roots, like the Binghams, were firmly planted in the river town.

What happened on this bitter January evening would never be forgotten, nor spoken of, at least not in public. Those who were at the cemetery, and those who aided Boss's getaway in other ways, made a pact to remain silent, taking their secret to the graves. Ironically, a few would be buried at Shady Grove in the decades to come.

Boss, meanwhile, became a man with two tombstones, one in Tennessee, another in West Texas, where he settled after hastily leaving Saltillo.

Unlike his friends who accompanied him to the graveyard that night, Boss couldn't keep the secret. After a stroke nearly killed him in 1971, he confessed to his Texas family what had transpired before and after that cold winter's night forty years earlier. The reverberations of his revelation were felt soon enough by Tennessee kin.

But that would come years later in this story.

First, the repugnant business in the cemetery had to be concluded. The hole deepened and the shoveling men sank into the ground. After hours of digging, one of the spades struck something solid. Those present on that terrible night paused to look at one another, gauging each other's resolve.

The worst part was about to begin.[2]

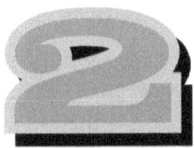

SOARING WEST

MAY 4, 2015, BOSS/BROOKS

My fellow passengers on the flight from Dallas to San Angelo were an interesting mix of people: oil company men, dressed in jeans, T-shirts and dusty boots, headed back to the fracking fields of West Texas; a woman with a fidgety young son going home after a visit with relatives in Louisiana; a cluster of servicemen returning for duty at Goodfellow Air Force Base, where members of all service branches studied cryptology, the art of deciphering secrets.[1]

And there's me, on a deciphering mission of my own.

I sat forward of the wing, watching through the window as the plane bulldozed through white clouds. When I departed Nashville, the weather was hot for early May, but coming out of an exceptionally snowy winter, the warm spell felt good to the bones. Awaiting me in West Texas was a front of howling winds streaming down from the Rockies, the kind that swept tumbleweed across dusty rangelands, but were also capable of producing thunderstorms and possibly tornadoes. Following the rain, the temperature was expected to rise into the nineties.

I did not know what to expect on this trip, for more reasons than Mother Nature and I was apprehensive. Too unsettled to read, I stared out the window. Occasionally, there was an opening in the clouds, and I saw the ground transforming by the mile, the dark green of East Texas yielding to lighter hues until the earth turned a pale palette: hills the color of aged parchment and fields striped with crops: cotton, corn and wheat, among others.

Rivers, whose names were unknown to me, appeared like ribbons fallen from a little girl's hair. The channels of dark water twisted and turned, sometimes almost doubling back on themselves. I followed their curves until our flight path veered away and they disappeared into the horizon, only to have another unknown river catch my eye.

The jet cruised at 23,000 feet, retracing the journey of my paternal grandfather, whom I never met, but whose absence in my life created an emptiness I sought to fill. Now retired, there was time to pursue his past. I spent thirty-eight years in the human resources department of Gannett, owner of Nashville's largest daily, *The Tennessean*. At the age of twenty-one, I entered the newspaper's 1100 Broadway office, several blocks east of Music Row, to begin work. I was the least senior person in the office, but I learned the job, I liked the people and I stayed until retirement in 2014. When I exited I was head of the department.

During my decades at the newspaper, I developed a nose for news. Consequently, when I examined my grandfather's story, I was surprised by how little I knew. What began in my last two years of employment as idle curiosity became an obsession. I immersed myself in genealogical research and quizzing relatives. I wanted to uncover the complicated truth about my grandfather, a man who faked his death and got away with it.

By the time Lytle Boss Bingham was born in 1895, the oldest son of a farming couple, the Binghams had been raising crops in the bottomlands of the Tennessee River for three-quarters of a century. Boss was a farmer but exhibited a talent for mathematics. After high school he spent a year in business school and returned to work at Hardin County Bank as assistant cashier while he farmed on the side. He married his sweetheart, Mary Louise Brooks, in 1916 and over the next fifteen years they had four children. The oldest, a boy named James Thomas, died shortly after birth, most likely to delivery complications. The next two children were girls, Margaret Lois and Mary Lou. Their baby brother, the youngest, was my father, Lytle Brooks Bingham, who inherited his father's forename. Brooks was his mother's maiden name.

My dad was two when his father disappeared from Saltillo on January 14, 1931. Boss told my grandmother he must attend to banking business out of town. He disappeared into the night. My grandmother, my aunts and my father never saw him again.

The following morning his black Chevy coupe was found consumed by fire on a state highway several miles south of Jackson, Tennessee.[2] Deputies found one occupant, burned beyond recognition. Several of my grandfather's closest friends identified the charred corpse as that of their banker and Sunday school director at Sulphur Well Church.[3] That was enough for the county coroner, who was also a funeral director, to issue a death certificate for Lytle Boss Bingham. A day later, a funeral was held in Shady Grove Cemetery and, after some months, a headstone bearing only my grandfather's name, the year of his birth (1895) and the year of his death (1931) was erected.[4]

When I was a child, I was told this narrative of my grandfather's death, but the story was a lie, a web of obfuscation spun by my grandmother and others. The truth is my grandfather did not die in a fiery crash in 1931. The charred body found in his burned car was not him, but a stolen cadaver.

I now know my beloved grandmother, a steadfast woman of prayer who memorized many Bible verses, helped in no small way to perpetuate this deceit, as well as to commit insurance fraud. In court appearances resulting from lawsuits filed against life insurance companies, my grandmother raised her hand to swear the truth and testified her husband was dead, when she knew he was alive.[5] With the help of family members and friends in Saltillo, and a considerable measure of luck, Boss Bingham successfully convinced the world he was no longer alive.

Among his family, neighbors and even many of the bank depositors who lost all they had during those fragile years of the Depression, Boss was described "as a fine man," an individual of purpose, possessing integrity and honor. He was a man, many suggested, who would sacrifice himself for the greater good. By others, however, he was portrayed as an absconder. Some depositors who lost their savings viewed him "as a damn crook."

I spent years reconciling these contradictory descriptions about the grandfather I didn't know and the actions of my grandmother, whom I knew very well. Or thought I did.

My questions led to more inquiries, but my quest to define my grandfather was not always welcomed, not only from relatives but from others in Hardin County who mythologized my grandfather. He was remembered either as a cashier who cashed in, at the bank's expense, or as a hero of the Depression for refusing to foreclose on dozens of farms and homes belonging to his family and friends. My search for truth has been as frustrating as it has been exhilarating and exhausting. For every definitive answer found, new questions emerged.

I could not find all the answers in Tennessee. That's why I was on a plane soaring over the Lone Star State following the route Boss began in the winter of 1931. My eventual destination is the dusty town of Sherwood, Texas, a short drive west of San Angelo. This is where my grandfather fashioned a new identity,

Marvin Lester Brooks.[6] This is where he recuperated from tuberculosis, camping beside a creek for more than a year, where he bought a farm and raised cotton, where he waved at neighbors as he passed by in his pickup and where he was so highly regarded by voters that he was elected to the Irion County Commission for three consecutive terms.

Sherwood is where he met and married another woman, with whom he had four children.[7] My Texas family. They awaited my arrival, prepared to share their father's life: where he lived, worked and where he died a second time. On this journey, I will visit my grandfather's grave and touch the tombstone that marks his real final resting place.

As the state of Texas slipped beneath me, I questioned if I was prepared to interrogate the children of my grandfather's second life. I'm conflicted because the man they refer to as "Dad" is the same man who abandoned my father and his two sisters, the grandfather who never bounced me on his knee. And, most significantly, he was the husband my dear grandmother lost forever.

Yet, I looked forward to getting to know these new relatives. I wanted to hear their stories of my lost grandfather: what made him laugh, the nature of his disposition, his thoughts on living a double life. I was curious if I recognized traits of my Tennessee relatives in the Texas siblings. In the sons, would I see my father? I anticipated sharing their memories so I might feel connected to this man who thoroughly disrupted my family.

So many questions to ask; so much to understand.

If I had been a curious child, I might have asked my grandmother about my grandfather's simple headstone at Shady Grove Cemetery. Unlike other grave markers, where loved ones were remembered with engraved words of endearment, the upright slab marking my grandfather's grave stood practically mute. In recent years I have come to understand that the simple marker represented a loose thread in the fabric of my family's history.

And now was the time to pull that thread.

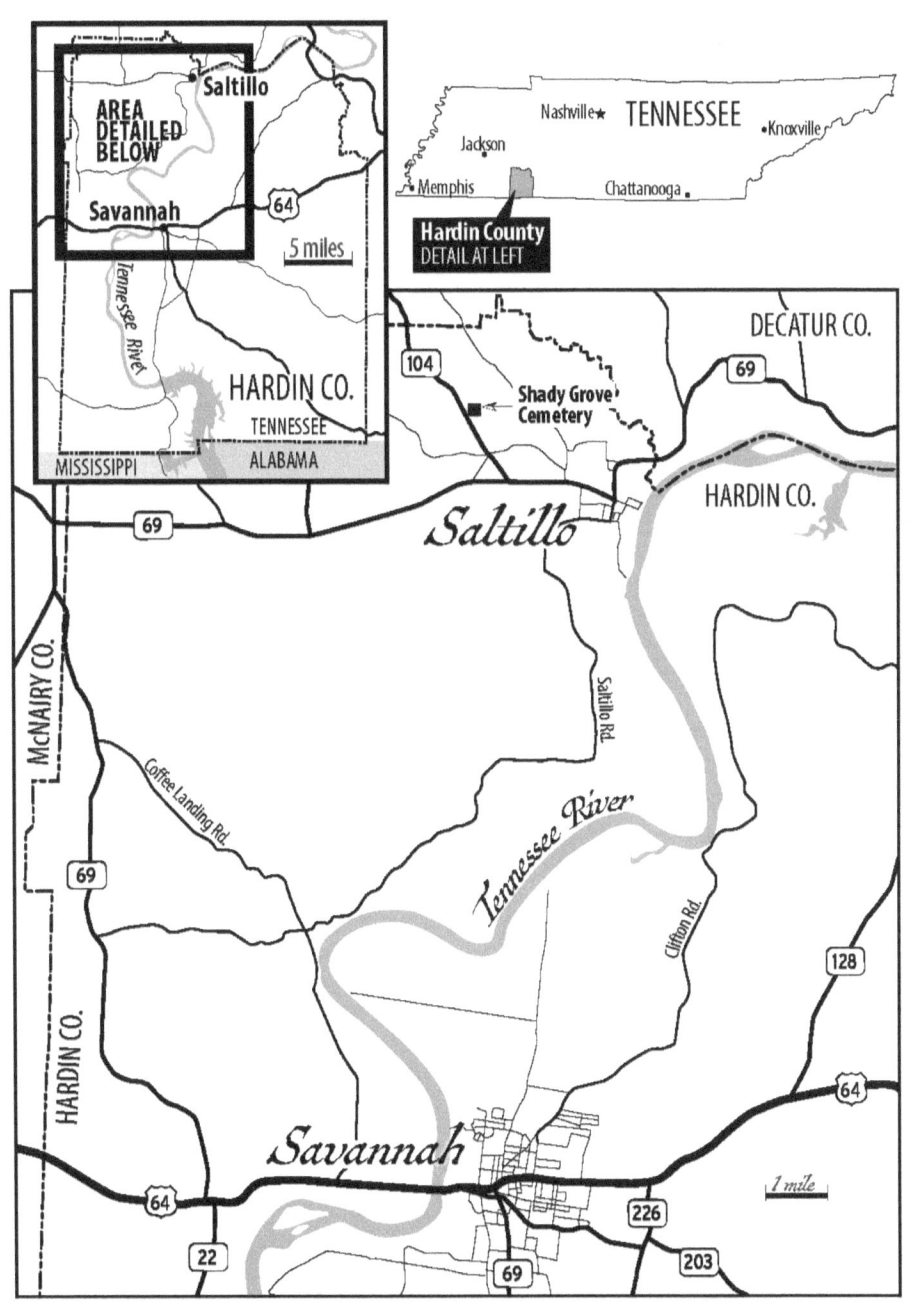

THE LIE

When white men settled Hardin County in the early nineteenth century they discovered a land flush with flora and fauna.[1] Old-growth forests abounded, pines one hundred-foot tall and stands of red oak, chestnut, and hickory so large at their bases that three adults couldn't connect hands around the trees. Beneath their canopies, the woods teemed with wildlife: turkeys, white-tailed deer, foxes, bobcats, panthers, even black bears and red wolves. Tributaries flowing into the Tennessee River were home to significant populations of beaver and otter, and the area was prized by regional Native American tribes as a hunting ground.

The county was named for Joseph Hardin Sr., an officer in the Continental Army who led troops at King's Mountain and other battles during the Revolutionary War.[2] Following the conflict, he was granted three thousand acres near the river, which at the time was considered frontier territory. When borders for the new county were drawn, Hardin became its name.

Boss's great-great-grandfather, Alexander Bingham, along with his wife, who had the unusual name of Barbery, and brother, Isaac, arrived at the backwoods outpost known as Davy's Landing in the 1820s.[3] This was Alexander's final stop in a string of hop-scotch moves made during the previous decade.[4] The village was renamed Saltillo in 1849 by returning veterans of the Mexican American

War, which ended the previous year.[5] Saltillo is the name of a city in northeastern Mexico, two hundred miles from Laredo, Texas.

Alexander Bingham had seven children with Barbery. The father and two of his teenaged sons, Wylie and Calvin, cleared land, built a log house, and raised crops in the fertile bottomland. They fished in the river and killed game in the thick woods. However, after Barbery died in 1844, Alexander, then forty-one, married a woman seventeen years his junior. In 1855, Wylie and Calvin Bingham rebuked their father's younger bride by moving their families to join other relatives in Arkansas. Numerous uncles, aunts and cousins had established land claims in Calhoun County, Arkansas, deep in the southern portion of the state.

Nothing good came of the move. Calvin, apparently a rolling stone, soon left the Arkansas frontier for an even wilder frontier in Texas, where he died in 1857 at the age of twenty-four.

Meanwhile, Wylie, my great-great grandfather, died a decade later under a veil of mystery. Family lore has his demise chalked up to one of three causes. Typhoid was to blame by some, but, considering the lack of medical care available, he could have succumbed to any number of maladies. The second possible cause was murder, perhaps related to his service as a Confederate private in the Fourth Regiment of the Arkansas Infantry. Emotions ran high during the post–Civil War years as Reconstruction brought transformative changes, and it's believed by some that Wylie, who was in his mid to late thirties, may have found himself facing the business end of a long gun.

The third possible cause of Wylie's demise, according to another family story, is that he disappeared of his own volition, abandoning his wife and five sons. This is the most disconcerting to me. Not to place too fine a point on it, but did these two men, Wylie and his future grandson, Boss, share an instinct to flee when life got messy?

Another commonality was noted. Both had tombstones at Shady Grove Cemetery, but neither man was buried there.[6] Unlike my grandfather, who was buried in Texas, no one in my family knows where Wylie was interred. His tombstone in Shady Grove serves only as a memorial.

There's no doubt that Wylie's widow, Lucy Anderson Bingham, met with hard times due to her husband's absence. She had five sons, ages one to fourteen. Even with the help of her husband's relatives, prospects were dim. She sent word to her father in Saltillo, asking if he would move her back to Tennessee. In a week-long journey in the spring of 1868, Abraham Anderson, another whose family were early settlers in Saltillo, and his son, George, drove a team of mules 275 miles to south-central Arkansas.[7] After a few days of rest for man and mules, the meager belongings of his daughter and grandsons were loaded into the wagon, and the sure-footed beasts retraced their steps northeast to Tennessee, the wagon much heavier on the return trek.

My great-grandfather, James Morgan Bingham, was the youngest of the boys, barely eighteen months old on that plodding journey.[8] My direct line ancestor grew up in Saltillo and like his brothers, took up the agrarian life, raising crops and cattle, prospering to the extent Tennessee farmers could expect in those pre-mechanized times. Some years were bountiful, others lean.

In 1889, James Morgan, twenty-one, married a woman named Josie, seventeen at the time, whom he met at Sulphur Well Church. Their first home was a log cabin hewn from trees cut in the woods. The couple had six children, four daughters and two sons. Lytle Boss Bingham, my grandfather, was the eldest of their two sons.[9] By his birth in 1895, the Binghams had established themselves as able farmers, raising crops and a few hogs and cattle, all for their own use.[10] Later, cotton became a money crop.

Much has been made in my family whether Boss was a nickname or a proper name. The answer, based on census records, is he was likely given the name at birth. In the 1900 census, he's listed as "Boss."[11] What remains unclear is why James Morgan and Josie gave him such an unusual name. Were they imbuing their baby boy with the hopeful destiny that he would become a captain of capitalism, a supervisor of many? Regardless, no one ever called him Lytle, not as a youngster in the town's one-room schoolhouse or later as cashier at Hardin County Bank. He introduced himself to strangers as Boss Bingham and his many friends knew him by no other name.

As a child my grandfather proved to be a good reader and a quick study. He enjoyed school and excelled in mathematics. When he announced, at nineteen, his intention to attend Bowling Green Business University, in Bowling Green, Kentucky, some 185 miles to the north, his parents did not oppose the additional study.[12] I assume they scraped together savings, perhaps even sold livestock to afford the seventy-five dollar per semester tuition, just as families save and sacrifice for college today. When he departed Saltillo in the fall of 1914 for Kentucky, the journey may have been his first trip away from home, perhaps even his first train ride.

Bowling Green Business University was a well-known, privately owned institution, matriculating more than a thousand students per semester. Advertisements for the college promised a thorough education in "bookkeeping, banking, penmanship, English grammar, mathematics and spelling."[13]

The private school was founded in 1884 as the Southern Normal School and Business College. In 1907, a coalition of the school's owners and the local citizenry convinced the commonwealth to operate the Normal School, which trained teachers.[14] It later became Western Kentucky University. Meanwhile, the business college became Bowling Green Business University, an institution whose alumni became presidents of railroads, newspaper editors, state and federal judges, and a US Supreme Court justice. One of the most famous alumnus was Cordell Hull of Byrdstown, Tennessee, who was a student at the school in its early years.[15] After graduating in 1887, Hull entered law school. He became a federal judge, a congressman and, most notably, was secretary of state in the Roosevelt administration during World War II.

Boss's ambitions were not as high. If my grandfather was smitten with the larger world found outside Hardin County, he never spoke or wrote of it.

Apparently, he always intended to return to Saltillo following graduation, although, to be sure, it wasn't the best move for career advancement. At the time, the small town had a dozen or so businesses, including several general stores, a livery stable, café, one boarding house, a post office, several churches and a cotton gin.[16] Of the businesses, none required the services of a full-time bookkeeper.

But there was the Hardin County Bank, whose letterhead at the time proudly noted the institution was "capitalized at $25,000."[17] Upon his return to Saltillo, he took the job of assistant cashier. My grandfather believed he could have the best of both worlds, working at the bank, but also being close enough to the farm to raise crops and cattle on the side. Compared to the common ilk of Saltillo, he was an educated man, but he valued rural life and the comfort of being close to his parents, siblings, and many friends.

My grandmother, in no small measure, also played a role in Boss's return to Tennessee.

Mary Louise Brooks, a slender woman with a pretty smile, was two and a half years younger than Boss. She and my grandfather attended the town's only school, and both families were members of Sulphur Well Church, so named because of a nearby spring whose mineral-laced water was said to possess healing properties. After he graduated from business college in the spring of 1915, Boss and Mary's courtship blossomed. By summer they were a pair. By Christmas they were engaged.

They married February 6, 1916, a mild Sunday afternoon, in a small affair at the home of Boss's parents.[18] The newlyweds took no honeymoon, but began preparations for building a house, constructed a short distance away. For fifteen years they lived, by account of family and friends, a contented life, despite hardships. Their firstborn, a son named Thomas, died shortly after birth, but three other children, two daughters and a son, arrived in quick succession.[19]

In my memory, her tall and slim figure always moved with grace, portraying a refinement that belied her rural roots. Her step was swift and her stride always seemed purposeful, moving from one task to another. Spying an offending scrap of lint on a carpet she would kneel to pinch it between fingers and rise to continue her walk through the room, all in one fluid movement.

She wore dresses fitted to the waist with a thin, matching fabric belt or knife-pleated skirts with a blouse featuring a folded back collar. Her few outfits were always clean and starched, with stockings rolled up above her knees and a handkerchief tucked in the belt. Of course, I can't attest for her sense of fashion during the Depression era when much of this story took place. However, I can say I've never seen a photo of her wearing pants, even hoeing in the garden.

She was industrious, always working about the house. I enjoyed laundry day when she threaded wet clothes through the roller-fed "wringer" to squeeze out water. Then I followed her to the clothesline. In the kitchen I watched her make fried fruit pies. They were perfect half-moon pastries filled with whatever fruit was in season, the edges sealed by the tines of a fork. She was a good baker. Inhaling the aroma of her yeast rolls was almost as good as tasting them fresh from the oven. When tomatoes were ripe in the garden, she always canned them whole or squeezed them to make juice.

Her hair was gray and silver when I was a kid, always trimmed short but not enough to affect her natural curls. She only had to run a wet comb from front to back and those beautiful waves fell into perfect position. My dad inherited the same wavy hair. I did not, but I do share her slender feet and long neck.

As a girl I was fascinated by the loose skin on the back of her hands. I pinched the skin to form a row and then used my finger to mow it down. Her fingers were long and slender, but she had big knuckles, as I do, too. To my horror, the skin on the back of my hands is now loose enough for me to pinch and form a row.

During childhood, my grandmother was a force in my life. I called her "grandmother," for that is what she preferred, rather than a pet name popular with southern grandparents. If this implies that she was formal, she may have been, but, to me, I never gave a thought to it.

I was sixteen, a junior in high school and full of youthful ignorance, when my father summoned my brother, Steve, and me to his home in Charleston, Missouri. My beloved grandmother was dying. My father and mother divorced when I was five. Afterward, we lived most of the time with our mother in Savannah, the county seat of Hardin County, but in the summer would spend time with our dad in Missouri. My grandmother would be there to babysit us while my father was at work. In her mid-sixties, grandmother moved full-time to Missouri to live with my father, and it was there, in the latter part of 1970, that she went to the doctor complaining of pain. The diagnosis was terminal cancer.

It was a cold day in February, three months later, that my brother, my mother and I drove 207 miles from Hardin County to the hospital in Cape Girardeau, about a half an hour's drive from Charleston.

We arrived to find a woman in the hospital bed whose name was Mary Louise Bingham, but the withering figure whose wrinkled hand weakly reached out to hold mine did not resemble the cheery woman who guided my hands to knead dough. At times she appeared to know us; other times, we were only shadows. She was my grandmother, but she was not.

We offered goodbyes one by one. First, my mother, followed by my brother, and, finally, me. I stood by her hospital bed, alone in the room with her. It was my time to say farewell, but I inexplicably couldn't give voice to the same three words my mother and brother said to her: "I love you." They wouldn't form in my mouth, and I could not understand why, for I did love this woman.

As a kid I understood my grandmother was a special woman, although if asked why, I would not have been able to explain. Today, I acknowledge her formative influence. She taught me right from wrong. On this point there was no gray, only black and white. She molded my character. I considered her a fountain of wisdom, someone who could solve all manner of tasks with an easygoing spirit combined with no-nonsense determination. Even when I was a little girl, I equated her with gritty perseverance. Standing in her shadow I felt safe. Her love surrounded me and all these years later I still feel her touch on my life. As a youngster I understood the roots of our love stretched to the quicks of our souls.

So why couldn't I say those three words I had whispered in her ear hundreds of times before?

I hurriedly left the hospital room. On the long drive home, my heart flooded with regret long before reaching the Tennessee state line. My love for that woman ran deep. She had always been a balm for my soul. Her hugs, well, her hugs were what I missed most. She often hugged me tightly for no reason except that I was within hugging distance. My decision not to say those words rests as heavy on my heart today as the day I last saw her. The fact she was in a medicated haze and unaware of my omission offered no relief.

She died March 11, 1971, at the age of seventy-two.

Four years later, all I knew of Bingham history was rewritten.

My father summoned me to Missouri again in the summer of 1975, between my junior and senior year of college at Middle Tennessee State University. Turning into the driveway, I noted numerous people, strangers to me, mingling on the lawn, but my father did not introduce me to his visitors. After enveloping me in a hug he led me to the living room where a slide projector was aimed at a wall. He flipped the "ON" switch and a beam of light brought the wall to life.

Faces appeared. Faces of the strangers outside my father's home. Except they were younger. It was a wedding. There was a bride being escorted by a man in his sixties. I turned to my father, who watched the images with a fascination I did not understand. He turned off the machine and faced me.

My father spoke calmly and clearly, so as not to be misunderstood. The older man in the film was his father, Boss Bingham. What his mother, my grandmother, had told him since he was a little boy was not the truth. Boss was not burned alive in a car crash in the winter of 1931. He moved to Texas, changing his last name to Brooks. He married another woman and had four children, two sons and two daughters. The daughters and their husbands were the people I saw when I pulled into the driveway. The women were my father's half sisters, my aunts.

I stammered, trying but failing to understand the magnitude of this revelation.

"Now you can't say a word about this to anyone outside the family," my father warned. I heard him, but failed to comprehend, his heavy words rushing at me. I only caught phrases: "there could be trouble," "people could get arrested," "this is just for us to know."

And that's how I learned that my grandfather, who never rocked me as a baby, or read me a bedtime story, or knew anything about my life, faked his death in 1931 and began a new life in West Texas.

He did so with help from friends, his siblings and my Bible-toting, prayer warrior grandmother, who all conspired in different ways for different reasons to keep Boss Bingham of Saltillo, Tennessee, buried in Shady Grove Cemetery. What happened at Hardin County Bank, where my grandfather was head cashier, was central to why he left Tennessee, but it would be years before I understood all that transpired.

To protect the innocent, The Lie was created by my grandmother and others. Boss's departure was like the plop of a rock in a still pond. Rippling waves affected every Bingham in its path. As the years went by, those co-opted by the falsehood tightened their grip on the family secret. This made their loss even more palpable. Those closest to Boss felt the loss the most. A husband, a father, a brother, a dear friend was gone, but not dead, just not present with them, never to be present with them again. In other words, a death of another kind.

The Lie had to remain unchanged over time, or the scandal would be exposed and more lives ruined. The Lie had to prevail.

And, so it did, until my grandmother died and then my grandfather, a man known by a name other than Boss Bingham, died two years later.

I obeyed my father's admonition never to talk publicly about our family's secret, but after his death in 2012 I resolved to deconstruct The Lie. I missed my father every day, but the "why" of my grandfather's disappearance and its residual effects on my grandmother compelled me to take a closer look.

During summer visits with my grandmother, she sometimes paused while rolling out bread dough or washing the dishes to stare out the kitchen window. I always wondered what she was thinking. Now I believe she may have been imagining another life, one where she and Boss grew old together near the west bank of the Tennessee River, surrounded by grandchildren and great-grandchildren. Her life would have been markedly different had that come to pass.

I never knew my grandmother to be melancholy for very long, which is a surprise after learning how she suffered, both economically and socially, due to my grandfather's disappearance. There was mental suffering, too, knowing the only man she would ever love was also the one who abandoned her and their three children. I knew my grandmother to be an honest woman, but in the insurance trials of 1932 she lied multiple times that her husband was buried in Shady Grove Cemetery. I am certain she carried the guilt on Sundays to church, her refuge of emotional sustenance. Each day she read her well-worn King James Bible, the tissue-thin paper offering a whispered rustle as her fingers turned pages. I hoped she found relief from guilt as the years passed, but of this I am uncertain, and my doubt sometimes enveloped me with grief for this woman I loved so much. She didn't deserve what happened to her.

Perhaps Boss didn't deserve his banishment, too. My family's story is a complicated one, much more complicated than I imagined. I understand why some in my family cautioned that it's best to leave the past in the past.

But I could not, primarily because I couldn't say "I love you" when I left my grandmother's hospital room. I'm still unsure why those words were beyond my will to utter, but I am convinced telling the story of my absent grandfather, and in so doing, telling my grandmother's untold story, will lead to an understanding that the Binghams of Saltillo have craved for a long, long time.

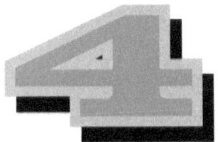

FINDING MY WAY

My Texas relatives were not at the airport in San Angelo to greet me. This was at my behest: I didn't want to be an inconvenience. The directions they provided me didn't appear all that complicated before leaving the car rental lot at San Angelo Regional Airport. Just a short ride on an expressway, then a few turns on county roads and I'd be at the home of Freddie Brooks, my . . . my what? As my grandfather's son and my father's half brother, would he be my uncle or just a relation whose link to me would always require an explanation? This question of familial connection was adding to my apprehension as the low skyline of San Angelo appeared in the rearview mirror of my blue Prius rental and the flat countryside expanded beyond the windshield. I was certain my first turn was accurate but after that the passing landscape of just-planted fields made every mile look the same and the next turns didn't feel right.

I was accustomed to finding my way in Nashville via uniform city blocks. Navigating the wide openness of Texas offered a different challenge because the GPS feature on my phone stopped working. I was looking for FM 765, which in the nomenclature of the Texas Department of Transportation, meant Farm to Market Road 765. Beginning in the late 1930s, Texas began improving rural roads so that farmers and ranchers could more easily transport their crops and cattle to market. However, the system wasn't much help to a Tennessee girl finding her way to relatives she didn't really know.

After driving around until I connected with cell service again, I reached for my phone to call Bobbie. Bobbie Ann Williams was my . . . again, my what? She was Freddie's younger sister and had enthusiastically taken up my cause to write a book about my grandfather's disappearance from Tennessee and his second life in Texas. She wanted answers as much as I did. When I suggested a visit to Texas with the intention to interview the Brooks siblings, she started planning not just a talk session with her sister and brothers, but a three-day tour of all the places my grandfather lived and worked, plus a look at hundreds of family photos. This was exactly what I needed. Now if I could just find Freddie's house.

The call connected, thankfully, and the soft twang of Bobbie's voice filled the car.

With the rental pulled over, I told her what landmarks I could see: signs for a custom saddle shop, a mechanic's garage, and a restaurant.

"I think you've passed by several times already," she said matter-of-factly. "I'll go out and wave." Oriented to the proper direction, my job now was to be on the lookout for a tall woman with ginger hair, standing in the front yard of a home I'd never visited. I hoped that Texas was not a state of "wavers," as is my part of Tennessee, where a drive down a country lane earns a wave at each house if someone's outside.

Then I saw her. She stood half a football field off the roadway at the end of a wide paved drive leading to a single-story brick house framed by large trees. Bobbie's right hand was extended high, the palm rotating back and forth at the wrist in that most human expression of welcome.

I had been found.

By the time the car was parked in the driveway, Bobbie and Freddie were joined by their oldest sibling, Billie Sue Crow. Bobbie was the first to bear hug me, followed by Sue. Freddie's hug was especially tight.

"It's good to see you, girl," he said.

Then he added, "Let's eat."

Maybe it was the long flight, or relief following the frustration of being lost, or I was just happy to finally be in Texas on my Boss mission, but the words "Let's eat" made me realize I was famished. I was ushered into the house where a fish fry with all the fixings—pinto beans, slaw, and sweating glasses of iced tea—was in the final stages of preparation. Freddie, assisted by his wife, Linda, was at the stove, retrieving sizzling filets of catfish from a pan of hot oil and piling them on a platter lined with a split paper sack. An avid fisherman for much of his adult life, Freddie, seventy-four, owned a fish camp on the Rio Grande, a place to which he would sometimes disappear for several days at the time with a buddy or two. Most trips he'd return with enough fish to stock the freezer. This night I was glad the fish took the bait, for the meal was delicious. Over my protest that I was stuffed, my plate was refilled several times.

It was Freddie I was most interested in seeing face-to-face, hoping to recognize elements of Boss that he may have shared with my father. For the most part I was disappointed. Freddie and my dad did not look alike and shared little of their father's features. Given the proper angle and with the light just so, there were similarities, like their broad foreheads, but their faces offered only hints of familial connection. Let me add I was not disappointed with Freddie, just that I was hoping he'd be the spitting image of my grandfather or resemble my father. I sensed he and I were going to get along well. I would learn he was as good a storyteller as he was a fryer of fish. Before dinner was complete, I was anticipating my talk with him.

Bobbie outlined the schedule for my visit. One day was allocated for interviewing the three of them, followed by a time of sifting through a dozen or more photo albums and other family memorabilia stored in shoe boxes and plastic tubs. Another day would be a field trip to Sherwood and Mertzon, small towns west of San Angelo where the siblings grew up. We'd also visit Sonny's place, about an hour's drive farther west. Sonny was much younger than his siblings. Freddie and Sue were already on their own and Bobbie was in high school when he was born. I had seen a few photos of him when he was a child and teenager, but knew little about him, so I was curious to make his acquaintance.

During the meal, I couldn't help but ask questions, and the siblings were more than helpful to give answers in between bites of hush puppies and catfish. The conversation served as my primer on Brooks family history. They told stories of growing up without electricity and how their mother, whose given name was Elizabeth, but everyone called her Hootsie, cooked all the family's meals on a wood-fired stove during their childhood. Soon it was a "remember when" fest for the three of them as one story segued seamlessly to the next. Laughter spilled from the room. I laughed, too, although I didn't always understand the context of stories or know the identity of their many neighbors and friends who played roles in them.

It dawned on me that I wanted to know more about Hootsie, the woman my grandfather chose to spend his life with after he left Tennessee and my grandmother, but I decided to wait until later to inquire deeper. I certainly didn't blame her for marrying my grandfather, but I wondered about her reaction to learning of her husband's previous life.

I confess that at supper and during the conversation that continued afterward, I referred to the trio's dad as "Boss," a faux pas for which I apologized. For them,

"Boss" was a name they learned was associated with their father but was not a name by which they knew him. They explained that most people in their community simply addressed him as "Brooks." Of course, in the family it was different. The girls called him "Daddy." Freddie used the term, "Dad."

I wondered how much Freddie, Sue and Bobbie knew about the failure of Hardin County Bank and how their father's reputation was stained by what happened in January 1931. Prior to the bank's forced closure, L. B. Bingham was a providing husband and father, Sunday school director, successful businessman and farmer, but those superlatives changed after the bank failed.

When my grandfather departed Tennessee, he was forced to reinvent himself. His given name became a liability because that man was dead, so he needed a new identity, with a believable backstory. He was not alone in such an endeavor. In the 1930s, an estimated one and a half million American men abandoned their families.[1] Some were running from the law and needed a new name to avoid trouble. Others, no doubt, just wanted a fresh start. I think my grandfather needed a new identity for both reasons.

By the time he reached the small town of Sayre, Oklahoma, situated on the western boundary of the state, hard against the Texas state line, Boss chose Marvin Lester Brooks as his new name.[2] In so choosing, it's clear his Saltillo family was on his mind. Brooks was my grandmother's maiden name and, also, my father's middle name. Lester was her brother's name. Marvin, I assume, was plucked from thin air. One day he was Boss; the next he was Brooks. His Texas children did not learn until 1972 that the surname they inherited was not his true last name. They were one and the same man, but, as I was to learn in my interviews with the siblings, Boss and Brooks differed in many respects.

Living in an age where individuals go to great lengths to protect their identities, it's hard to imagine that reinventing yourself could be as easy as changing your name, but it was possible in 1931. Driver's licenses didn't feature photos and Social Security cards wouldn't be issued for another five and a half years. In rural areas, birth certificates were often not issued at all. The tools employed in the twenty-first century to prove who we are were not available the year my grandfather disappeared. In that era, identity was based on how convincingly you led others to believe who you were. My grandfather, accustomed through his business dealings to the importance of positive first impressions, put forth his hand to a stranger and said: "My name is Marvin Lester Brooks."

And he became Marvin Lester Brooks.

When the Tennessee native arrived in Sherwood, presenting himself as a ranch hand for hire, his second persona had formed. Soon after, Texas friends reduced his name to Brooks. I'm guessing it wasn't much of a difference for him.

Both names began with the letter "B." Both were one-syllable. Both were easy to remember.

Boss and Brooks. Brooks and Boss.

I sat at the kitchen table enveloped in conversations about one man with two names, two families, two lives, two careers and two death certificates. I knew much about the man from Tennessee and now I was surrounded by the family on the other side of the Boss/Brooks mirror. My mission in Texas was to see my grandfather from that vantage. Guiding me would be the three smiling faces who sat around Freddie's kitchen table, and I was glad for them to lead the way. They already felt like family . . . and they were.

They were my Uncle Freddie and Aunts Sue and Bobbie, tethered to me biologically by a common denominator, their father, my grandfather. That's who they are, it's who I am, plain and simple, no explanation needed.

PROMOTION

BOSS

The body of Robert Hinkle, longtime cashier of Hardin County Bank, was found May 5, 1928, in a garden behind the Main Street home of his sister, less than a half mile from the bank.[1] A hired hand discovered the corpse. The sight of Hinkle's body leaning against a fence post, his chin dipping low, his shirt soaked in blood, the man's hunting shotgun in his lap, offered a bizarre scene that destroyed the reverie of the spring morning.[2] Within minutes, the frightened farm worker was dispatched to town, making a beeline to the combination physician's office and apothecary of Dr. Luther A. Parker, one of two physicians in Saltillo.

The farmhand's stammering words spilled out with the punch of a telegram. Dr. Parker, a portly, broad-shouldered man, absorbed the news and moved to fetch his doctor's bag. He walked out of the office, the farmhand leading the way, with curious onlookers in tow. News, particularly bad news, traveled quickly in the small town.

The physician found the body of his banker and friend, Robert Hinkle, in the condition the rattled farmhand had noted. Parker took in the scene, noting the position of the body. He knelt to examine the single gunshot wound to the chest. Later that morning, he issued a death certificate.[3] Under "cause," the doctor wrote "accidental gun shot." Time of death was listed as 6:15 a.m., but that was likely the time the body was discovered.

Hinkle had been seen in town the previous day by many people, including the doctor, and, of course, my grandfather, who was Hinkle's assistant cashier at the bank. By 1928, Boss had been working at the bank for more than a decade, responsible for waiting on customers, posting deposits and withdrawals, and reconciling the books at the end of each day. Hinkle's primary duties included loan approvals and investing the bank's capital to ensure a profit for stockholders.

On this latter point, that was getting harder and harder to do. Banks across the country were being squeezed by dwindling deposits and loan holders who were slow to pay or couldn't make payments. For a rural institution like Hardin County Bank, whose existence depended largely upon agricultural trade, the boom-and-bust cycles of farming meant operating on narrow margins. By the end of 1927, the selling price of cotton, a primary money crop in Hardin County, dropped precipitously from a high of thirty-eight and a half cents per pound in 1920, just after World War I, to sixteen cents per pound.[4]

Most of the farmers in Saltillo continued to grow crops using mules and horses instead of mechanized machines, employing the same methods established in the previous century, methods that didn't include the rotation of crops or allowing a field to go fallow for a season so that its fertility might be restored. At a time when applications of science to agriculture were raising crop yields and keeping pests at bay in certain parts of the country, such progressive notions went mostly unnoticed in rural Tennessee because these practices required cash.[5] Banks were slow to loan money and many farmers had no savings.

Common practice in good times had the farmer taking out a loan to buy seed and fertilizer in the spring for the upcoming growing season. At harvest time the next autumn, the farmer would pay off the note from proceeds of the crop sale, pocketing the difference as profit. On the eve of the Depression, however, families in Saltillo felt pinched. Many sought loan extensions from the bank. But the worst was yet to come.

My grandfather saw trouble brewing, reading the furrowed faces of his friends and neighbors as they explained their individual dilemmas, but also in his personal finances. He had a mortgage payment just like many of his friends and boll weevils weren't showing favoritism by skipping his cotton fields. Boss also saw apprehension in his supervisor's demeanor. On several occasions, rumors floated through the small town that the bank was broke but Hinkle offered reassurances of the bank's solvency.

The truth was just the opposite.[6] According to records from the State Department of Insurance and Banking, Hardin County Bank had been declining for some time, dropping in value every quarter since early 1923, when the bank's semiannual Statement of Condition reported assets of $173,000. By April 1928, just a month before Hinkle's death, assets had declined to $46,000. In addition, the bank, whose stationary had proudly proclaimed for years that it was "capitalized at $25,000," quietly reduced its capitalization to $15,000 in the fall of 1926.[7] Stockholders, primarily directors of the bank board, cashed out their investments.

Past due loans were also a problem.[8] In the November 1927 report to the state, the bank reported arrearages amounted to $7,900, roughly a third of the loans outstanding.

Several months before the sixty-year-old banker was found dead, Hinkle pulled Boss aside one morning, confiding that over the previous weekend he had moved his wife and four children to Jackson, the largest town in the region, about fifty miles north of Saltillo.[9] He also acknowledged he was selling his fine, large home in Saltillo, across the street from Dr. Parker's residence, and was going to stay at the home of friends during the week, while visiting his family in Jackson on the weekends.

The announcement struck my grandfather as very odd. He couldn't understand why Hinkle would separate himself from his family.[10]

Relocating his family was not Hinkle's only odd action. For several months, the cashier made frequent trips to the First National Bank in Jackson. Small banks required help with administrative duties in this pre-computerized age of banking so rural financial institutions often turned to larger banks for assistance. In addition, small banks deposited the bulk of their funds into larger banks to earn interest.

On April 24, 1928, the board of directors of the Hardin County Bank met in their semiannual session to receive what would be Hinkle's final status report as head cashier.[11] He reported the bank was faring well despite the economic downturn, with assets of $46,080 and no loans past due. This last piece of information was surprising to me because six months earlier, Hinkle reported past due loans of $7,900.

If any of the ten directors or its longtime president, local merchant and farmer, J. H. Craven, questioned the head cashier's report, particularly the miraculous decline in the amount of past due loans, there is no record of it. Perhaps the board felt their confidence in Hinkle to lead the small bank through these turbulent times had been justified. I assume my grandfather attended that gathering but minutes of meetings were lost in the ensuing years so it's unclear. I also don't know for certain what Boss understood about the bank's condition. Common sense would dictate that he must have known the bank's true worth was not as rosy as Hinkle's report, but did he know it was headed for failure?

Here, let me make a few observations about Hinkle, the bank and my grandfather's ascent to the top position.

First, I have doubts about Dr. Parker's conclusion regarding Hinkle's death. Many in town believed Hinkle took his own life, and the story was passed from generation to generation, as it was to me. Common to this storyline is that a forked stick was found near the body, a stick that could have been used to push the trigger if the muzzle had been pointed at Hinkle's chest.[12]

My family's account of Hinkle's last days is largely based on interviews Howard Bingham, Boss's brother, gave to his son, Bill.

Howard was thirteen years younger than my grandfather and in many ways the opposite in personality. His nickname was Jiggs, a reference to one of the main characters in a popular comic strip "Bringing up Father." Howard was born with a grin and zeal for life. Whereas my grandfather was rarely captured by a camera with a smile on his face, Howard was counterpoint to his stoic brother, but the men's devotion to each other was strong as the Tennessee River's current.

In the interview with his son, Howard mentioned a forked stick found by the cashier's body and this story element was also part of my grandfather's narrative told to his Texas daughters more than forty years later as he lay in a hospital bed recuperating from a stroke.[13]

Hinkle's death was reported on the front page of *The Tennessean* but the article did not report the death as anything but a tragedy. The article described him as "one of the wealthiest men in this section, who owns several large plantations on the Tennessee River and was cashier of the Hardin County Bank." [14] The article said Hinkle had gone missing after taking "a hammerless double-barrel shotgun into the garden with him to kill rabbits which had been damaging the plants." The weapon accidentally fired as he was "drawing the gun through a wire fence," the newspaper reported.

After Dr. Parker ruled the death accidental there was no coroner's inquest, nor an autopsy, into the matter. What the doc reported, stood, even if there was talk otherwise.

By all accounts, Hinkle was given a funeral befitting his stature in the community.

The Hinkles came to Saltillo much later than the Binghams but were a family of means. The family patriarch, William F. Hinkle, was born in Kentucky in 1844.[15] After his mother died when he was seven, William Hinkle was sent to school in Louisville which he attended through high school. When his studies at Gettysburg College were interrupted by the Civil War, the elder Hinkle served in a Union infantry unit, receiving a promotion to officer for gallantry at Shiloh, twenty-two miles upriver from Saltillo.[16]

Following the surrender of Confederate forces at Appomattox, William Hinkle departed for Tennessee. Despite the carnage he witnessed at "bloody Shiloh," the region appealed to him. He recognized economic opportunity in Saltillo, perched in the bend of the river, where riverboats could make landings. Shortly after arriving, he met and married a local woman, Martha White. The couple had four children, the oldest being Robert, followed by three daughters.[17] William Hinkle established himself as a teacher, mercantile owner, and postmaster, and was an active churchgoer and Mason. Despite being a former Union officer, he was respected, serving three terms in the Tennessee legislature.

Robert Hinkle patterned his life after his father's: active in community affairs, solid family man and a leadership role in the local bank. As he aged into his fifties, the younger Hinkle resembled his Dad: graying but mostly black hair, with dark eyes and thin lines creasing his forehead.

A week after Robert Hinkle was buried, the board of directors of Hardin County Bank, now led by a new board president, Dr. Parker, unanimously named my grandfather as the new head cashier.[18] How Dr. Parker, who had not previously served on the bank board, came to be a member and new leader of the group, isn't clear in bank records. One month J. H. Craven was president and Hinkle the head cashier; the next month their names were replaced by Parker and my grandfather. In addition, several board members were replaced by new members, all men, of course, in this era of patriarchal privilege.

After taking over the bank, my grandfather made a curious move. Instead of naming a new assistant cashier, Boss hired Jiggs, his brother, to help around the bank.[19] Rather than making him an official employee, Boss paid his brother twenty-five dollars a month from his own salary. This point was made clear by my Great-Uncle Howard's interviews and by my grandfather in telling his story to his Texas daughters.

Why did he enter this unusual arrangement with his younger brother? The simplest and the most rational answer is the bank couldn't afford to hire an assistant but Jiggs, still living at home, needed a job.

As with all things Boss, however, the simplest answer doesn't satisfy. Let's just assume my grandfather's examination of the bank's books left him shaken, understanding his culpability in the bank's impending insolvency. By keeping Jiggs off the bank's official payroll Boss could hopefully isolate his younger brother from possible prosecution. This distinction regarding my great-uncle's duties was explored in numerous court depositions but no certain explanation was ever offered.

I suspect my grandfather, sitting at the large oak desk in the bank, came to rue the day in May when Robert Hinkle went hunting for pesky rabbits, but Boss didn't know just how badly the next year would unfold.

Disaster loomed.[20] Black Tuesday, that awful day in October 1929 was approaching. Titans of Wall Street would soon lose their seats of privilege. Some would leap from the windows of their high-rise offices. There were signs calamity was near. From late 1928 through 1929, the market, driven by zealous speculation and buying on margin, suffered a series of deep losses followed by stratospheric recoveries. The market was not for the faint of heart, but otherwise prudent men and women, including millions of small investors far from the din of the trading floor, were lured by easy money.

The time was coming, and soon, to pay the piper. US banking was about to plummet into the 1930s, creating a period of economic dysfunction that marked generations of Americans to come.

But few were listening to the sounding alarms.

In Saltillo, L. B. Bingham was the boss, a job he'd always wanted.

Now, he was head cashier, attempting to serve depositors and make the board of directors happy. Now it was his role to keep his part of the world, tucked away on a wide loop of the Tennessee River, from disappearing into a maw of despair.

As certain as the river flowed to join the Ohio and then the Mississippi to be mixed with the briny waters of the Gulf of Mexico, destruction in many forms was coming.

How heavy Boss's burden must have been.

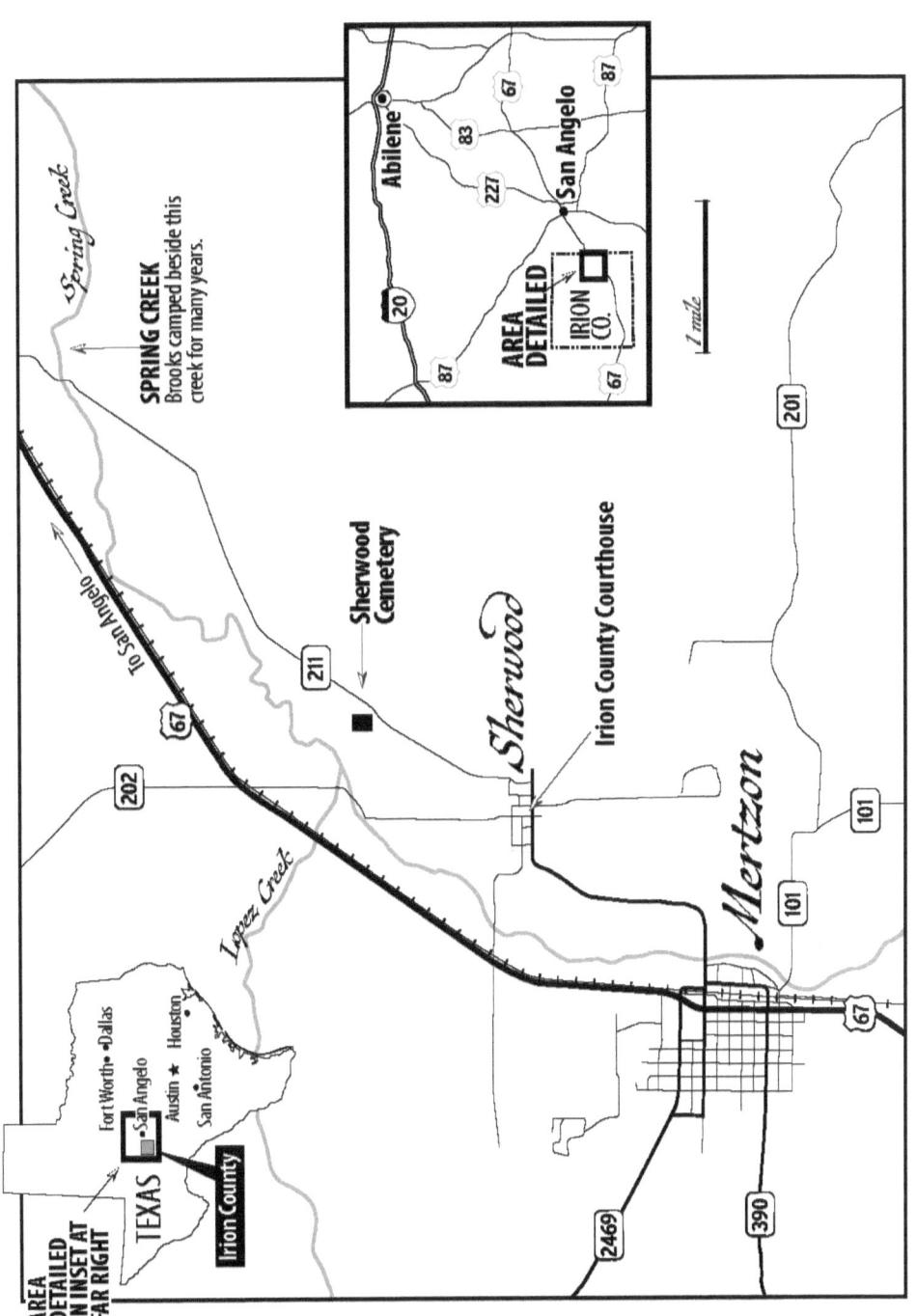

AREA
DETAILED
IN INSET AT
FAR RIGHT

TEXAS

Fort Worth • Dallas
San Angelo
Austin ★ Houston
San Antonio

Irion County

Lopez Creek

202

To San Angelo

67

211

■ Sherwood
Cemetery

Sherwood

Irion County Courthouse

Mertzon

101

101

2469

390

67

201

SPRING CREEK
Brooks camped beside this
creek for many years.

Spring Creek

AREA
DETAILED

IRION
CO.

20

87

67

227

83

67

Abilene

San Angelo

87

1 mile

SINGING HYMNS

MAY 7, 2015: BROOKS

I was awakened by the smell of frying bacon and sausage and chattering voices. My confused brain took a moment to triangulate my position on the globe before recollecting where I was—San Angelo, at the home of Freddie Brooks, the oldest son of my grandfather's Texas offspring. The voices coming from the kitchen were Freddie and his sisters, Sue and Bobbie. Immediately I remembered my mission this sunny day: to interview them.

And that was the figurative splash of water in my face needed to get me on my feet, dashing about the guest bedroom dressing for my morning entrance, my mind racing with a hundred, no, a thousand, possibilities of how this mission of mine could fall apart.

I can't say how many times in the past decade I imagined this day, sitting before my grandfather's Texas-born children, asking question after question after question. When I was a kid, I didn't quiz my grandmother about my grandfather. She didn't talk about him much and the times she did the conversation centered only on what a good man he was. My conversations with my Tennessee cousins over the years were fruitful to a degree, but they, like me, had never met the man. They couldn't describe the timbre of his voice, or know his favorite foods, or even identify the color of his eyes because the few photos we have of him were black-and-white prints.

There was much I wanted to learn about him. Could he sing? Was he a story-teller? Did he have friends? What did they say of him? As a father, was he a disciplinarian? Was he a hard worker? What kind of truck did he drive? What did he do for fun?

Those were the easy questions. I intended to ask others that weren't so easy. Questions about the night he left Saltillo and about digging up the body used to convince authorities he was dead. I wanted to know if my Texas aunts and uncles believed their father was, well, a crook.

Even more than the bank intrigue, I wanted to understand why he never returned to Tennessee, to my beloved grandmother and his three kids. How could I ask that indelicate question?

All my life, Boss was a two-dimensional character, a figure fashioned by family story in the form of a man, but that image, in my mind's eye, was as static as the photo of him taken in the bank before he disappeared from Saltillo. I hoped the words of his Texas children would give definition to the impassive face I studied for so long. If anyone could accomplish this task, it would be the three siblings who waited for me just down the hall. After all Boss, rather Brooks, had told his story directly to them.

I took a deep breath of Texas air infused with the scent of fresh-cooked bacon and walked into the kitchen.

Sue was first to be interviewed. That seemed fitting since she was the oldest of the trio, born in November of 1938. We were in a bedroom at the far end of Freddie's home, a room with shafts of morning light streaming through a pair of windows looking out on the front lawn. She sat in a chair next to the bed, her arms folded across her lap, unsure exactly what one does with their hands while being interviewed. Her hair, streaked with gray, was cut fashionably short on the sides, with the top parted on the left (just as her father parted his hair) and brushed over to form a delicate arch above her wide forehead (another telling nod to her father).

If Sue was anxious, I was a nervous Nellie. I so wanted this to go well.

Her full name was Billie Sue Brooks Warren Burleson Crow, a retired executive secretary and bookkeeper, she said, reciting these particulars into the microphone. Her home was in Brownwood, about one hundred miles to the east of San Angelo. She'd lived there for going on fourteen years. As her name indicated, she's been married and divorced a few times. Asked later about her marital status, she offered a little chuckle and a shrug of her shoulders as if to say: it is what it is.

Freddie and Bobbie called her "Sis" when they were preschoolers. Brooks took to the nickname, too.

"Well, everywhere my daddy went, I went. He always said if he ate a cow turd I would, too," Sue said without so much as a smirk, but only momentarily. Her face melted into a grin, and she chuckled.

"Like I say, I went everywhere he went."

Where they went was Sherwood, Texas, a town of 450 hearty souls making a living in semiarid Irion County.

Because of its size, Texas is a state of geographical extremes.[1] The boast that "everything's big in Texas" is not hype; it's part of the state's history. When Texas was annexed into the Union in 1845 leaders had the option of creating several states out of the 268,581 square miles, but instead chose to make one.

Coming from Tennessee, whose boundaries form a narrow rectangle, bent at angles on the eastern and western borders, I am used to thinking of distances in reference to where I live near Nashville, the state's largest city. Mountain City, on the northeastern border, is a 333-mile drive, while Memphis, the farthest city to the west, is 212 miles. For comparison, Sherwood is 387 miles west of Houston, the largest city in the state. El Paso, situated near at the western edge of the state, is also a drive of 387 miles from Sherwood.

This part of Texas, the Edwards Plateau to be specific, is the southernmost terminus of the Great Plains, which stretch northward in a widening funnel ending in the central provinces of Canada.[2] In the age of the bison, large herds over-wintered on the plateau.

The differences in the homelands where my grandfather established dual careers and lives were readily apparent. Irion County is mostly brown. Hardin County is green.

The bottomland the Binghams farmed in Tennessee was rich in nutrients and conducive to row cropping.[3] Add an average of fifty-two inches of rainfall each year and you can understand why agricultural pursuits drove the region's economic engine.

Farming in Irion County, however, required consideration of two realities: the relative lack of rainfall (eighteen inches annually) and the shallowness of the topsoil, which makes raising crops problematic without irrigation.[4] However, there's enough rainfall to sustain rangeland for grazing cattle and sheep, as evidenced by the numbers of ranches seen while driving the back roads.

Irion County also offered a view from horizon to horizon that's very different from Tennessee. Juniper, mesquite, and brush oak trees painted the landscape in muted colors. Native grasses grew in clumps, and where there's no grass, the khaki-colored soil appeared bare. A third of Irion County's 1,052 square miles were suitable for cropland and the rest was best used for grazing animals.[5] The land Brooks settled near Sherwood, located on the northwestern edge of the Edwards escarpment, was a little better there than average for the region. Irrigation, however, remained a necessity.

Sue married in April of 1956, a month before graduating from high school. She enrolled in business school and in 1959, she and her husband bought land next to Brooks' farm and together, father and daughter, worked side by side raising cotton as a cash crop and corn to feed the livestock. They were also, in large part, subsistence farmers. There were always a few milk cows, a few hogs for slaughtering and a small herd of sheep to browse the pastures. The hard work never bothered her, even as a kid sweating in the heat of summer, she said.

"We had a lot of good times. We'd pick cotton with our neighbors. We all had races and we'd see who could pick the most cotton. One time, Freddie put a big old rock in his sack because he was going to win. Daddy told him that rock does not count. He took the rock out," Sue said, chuckling.

"Daddy would throw in watermelon seed with the cotton seed when he'd plant. Oh, it'd be so good when you'd get to one of those watermelons and break it open. They were orange-meated. Come from Mexico. I've tried and tried to find some more orange-meated watermelons and have never been able to find them," she said.

For Sue, work on the farm came naturally. She arrived home from school one day when she was eight or nine and found no one was present. "I didn't know what to do so I just curled up in the chair with my dog and went to sleep. Well, I woke up and it was getting pretty late. The sun was going down. Mama and Daddy wasn't there. I knew the cows had to be milked so I went out and I got the cows in, and I milked the cows and fed the hogs and was just finishing up when Mama and Daddy came in. Daddy said, 'Boy, I am glad you knew how to do that. That's your job from now on,'" she recalled.

"In high school I'd have rough, rough hands because I'd be having to milk in the morning, and it'd be cold, and my hands would get chapped."

Apparently, Hootsie thought her daughter was becoming too much of a tomboy. "When I got about fourteen, fifteen, well, Mama told me, 'I'm sending you to Aunt Ethel's because Freddie needs to learn to do this stuff.' I stayed up there all summer, took summer classes and got a babysitting job and Freddie had to do all the work," she said, laughing.

"Talk about your daddy. When did you learn of his dual identity?" I asked. It wasn't the smoothest of transitions into the personal territory of the story I had come to hear, but Sue wasn't fazed.

"Well, off and on when we were little kids, they would tell us he had another family that he had left in Tennessee. And, I don't remember him ever showing me those pictures, but Mama would show me. The top dresser in the chest of drawers had these pictures in it," Sue said.

I heard her words, but it took a moment for me to comprehend her meaning. Brooks, the man who carried a secret that could have put him in jail, told his Texas kids about their Tennessee half sisters and half brother and kept photos of them. That goes to answer if he had forgotten my Tennessee aunts and my father. On the cold night he left Saltillo, photos of them were in his pocket. To Sue I may have appeared composed, but my mind was wheeling with emotions and more questions.

Sue made it clear that it was her mother, Hootsie, who most often would show her the fading photos. "And many a time I would walk by there and I would stop and look at those pictures. But we knew from the time we were very small that there was another family."

From this point, Sue took control of the conversation. She knew that I had come to hear what her father confessed in 1971 as he was recuperating from a stroke, and she was ready to tell me.

"He came this way because he had TB, consumption is what they called it at that time. They told him you have consumption. You're not gonna live and in a matter of a few hours . . . he didn't tell me how many hours . . . but in a few hours they cooked up all this and got it set up and carried out and he went off in the car and turned off the road and burned."

"They," she said, were three men.

"Whenever he would say about digging up the grave he would say 'we.' I don't know if he was able to participate or if he was not able to participate, but he said that was the coldest, wettest, soggiest thing he ever saw in his life when they were doing this. And he said that was the stinking-est car he ever saw. He said sometimes, many, many years later, he could still smell that. He told me several times how bad it smelled. I don't know how many miles he had to drive with that body in there, but it was sure making him sick."

"Do you remember him saying who the three men were?" I asked.

"Yeah, he told me who they were. There was a banker, a doctor . . . a banker and a doctor and another man. There were three," she said.

"There was him and three guys and Mary."

Of course, Mary was my grandmother. Sue's mention of her name was a reminder of her direct involvement in her husband's disappearance.

"He said they came to his house. This was all thought up, carried out, everything in a few hours. But I'm sure they convinced him that he was going to die anyway so that would relieve anybody else of wrongdoing. And he told me, Sis I took . . . and he told me how much money that he took from the bank that night," she said.

On the night my grandfather departed Saltillo, he told his brother, Howard, to go to the bank after closing and clear out the cash register. Howard returned with $105 in bills and a small amount of change.

Sue said that her father noted that he had enough in his personal account to cover the unusual withdrawal. "I swear right now that I never saw a penny of any of that other money," Sue quoted her father. "That other money," she said, referred to customers' accounts.

Sue continued, quoting her father: "The main thing I did, and I did it wrong and that's why I paid the price. I loaned the money to these two cotton gins. He said, I saw that their overdrafts were covered as long as I could." Sue said when her father learned that an audit had been ordered, he understood "that something had to be done."

Leaving was the only answer, Sue said.

"He and Mary made a pact that if he did leave that he would write for her, and she would come. But she found out later there was no way that could happen. If she'd ever disappeared from that town there'd be somebody trailing on her."

That was an understatement, of course.[6] My grandfather had purchased numerous life insurance policies amounting to more than $37,000. When my grandmother tried to collect, the insurance companies refused to pay death benefits because they were certain my grandfather was alive. At least two of the insurance companies employed private investigators to find Boss and to monitor my grandmother's movements.

Sue said her father lived with the fear that his Tennessee identity could be uncovered no matter how many years had passed. The closest call, she said, came in the 1950s during Brooks' second term as a county commissioner when he represented the county at a meeting of regional officials in Austin.

A state senator named Dorsey B. Hardeman approached him. "Dorsey B. said, you look familiar," Sue said. "He was trying to remember where he met Daddy and Daddy said, 'No, you have me confused with someone else.'"

Brooks was right to be worried. Hardeman grew up in Henderson, Tennessee, about twenty-nine miles northwest of Saltillo.[7] His father was a Church of Christ minister and one of the founders of Freed-Hardeman University in Henderson. After graduating from Vanderbilt Law School in 1924, Dorsey Hardeman was a prosecutor in Tennessee until 1932 when he moved to San Angelo, where he had relatives, to practice law.[8] Within four years he was elected mayor of the town and went on to serve many terms in the state legislature, both as a representative and a senator.

During his time as a Tennessee prosecutor, Hardeman could have heard about my grandfather's case and the ensuing insurance trials that my grandmother initiated. Nothing in the court records in Tennessee indicated Hardeman's involvement, however. Maybe the state senator did recognize him as someone from Tennessee at that Austin meeting but just couldn't come up with a name. Or maybe Hardeman recognized a touch of Tennessee twang in Brook's accent. Regardless, nothing came of their chance meeting, except resolve from Brooks.

"It scared him, I think," Sue said. "He said he'd never be in the same room again with Dorsey Hardeman."

Although he feared being found out, Sue said her father didn't lead the life of a man carrying an untold burden. "He had his own life. He led his own life. You wouldn't have thought anything was wrong, or he had done anything wrong or anything," Sue said.

"People didn't know what his first name was because everybody just said Brooks and they knew who Brooks was."

Sue said he kept his social life to just a few close friends. An active Mason in Tennessee, Brooks never sought to join a lodge in Texas. "I guess he thought he'd have to tell too much history to get a membership down here," Sue said.

He didn't go to church in Texas, either. In Tennessee he was superintendent of the Sunday school at Sulphur Well Church and was ordained a deacon, along with two other men, about a year before leaving Tennessee. "They are men of affairs and are destined to greatly assist the pastor," a newspaper article reported.[9]

But in Texas my grandfather rarely attended services, his oldest daughter said.

"The only time he would go to church would be when we had something special or something, like baptism or something. He didn't feel like he was worthy to go to church."

Sue said her dad kept in touch with his younger sister, Verna, for several years after he left Tennessee. "You could tell that he was very, very close to Verna. He wrote her a note (telling) where he was, and he had this (post office) box in San Angelo. Every month she would send him money until he got to where he could do a little work. Then he wrote her and told her he could handle it on his own. He never did hear from her after that," she said.

After enrolling in a business school, Sue told Brooks that she was thinking of applying for a job at the local bank. Brooks nixed the idea. "He said, no Sis, I don't want you to go into banking. He says, you're too soft-hearted, you're too much like me. I don't ever want you to go into banking." Recalling her father's gentle, but insistent, admonition, Sue paused for a moment. Then she continued: "So, instead I went into the secretarial and accounting fields."

Sue noted the years she farmed with her dad were one of the most memorable periods of her life. Particularly at irrigation time, which was very hands-on. Water use was regulated, and farmers were given a specific time to divert water from the creek into their planted fields. She and her father would stay up through the night to make sure the crop got a good drink.

"We had seventy-two hours of water rights. All in one row. We'd go out and sit on the bank of the ditch. Take a cover and lay it down in the back of the pickup every once in a while," she remembered.

"Daddy would sit back there and sing, and he enjoyed singing. That was a very special time for me." Brooks, she said, had neither the bright lilt of an Irish tenor nor the thunder of an operatic bass, but he always sang on key and his voice projected, floating above the field as the precious water rushed into the furrows.

A standard from the Baptist hymnal was his favorite, Sue said.

"When he would sing *The Old Rugged Cross*, he had a quiver in his voice. It would chill you it was just so special."

She raised her glasses to wipe away tears that flowed unchecked.

I was crying as well.

The Old Rugged Cross was one of my grandmother's favorite hymns, too.

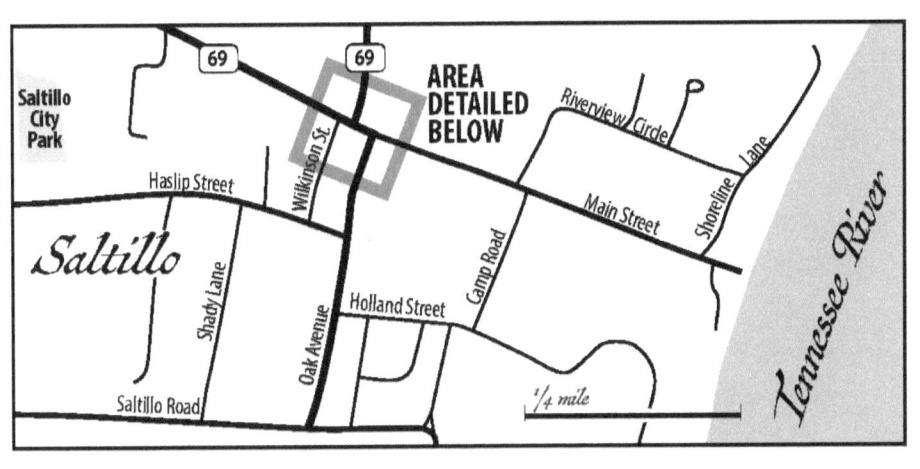

Saltillo

Saltillo City Park

Haslip Street

Shady Lane

Saltillo Road

Oak Avenue

Wilkinson St.

69

69

AREA DETAILED BELOW

Holland Street

Camp Road

Riverview Circle

Main Street

Shoreline Lane

Tennessee River

¼ mile

NORTH

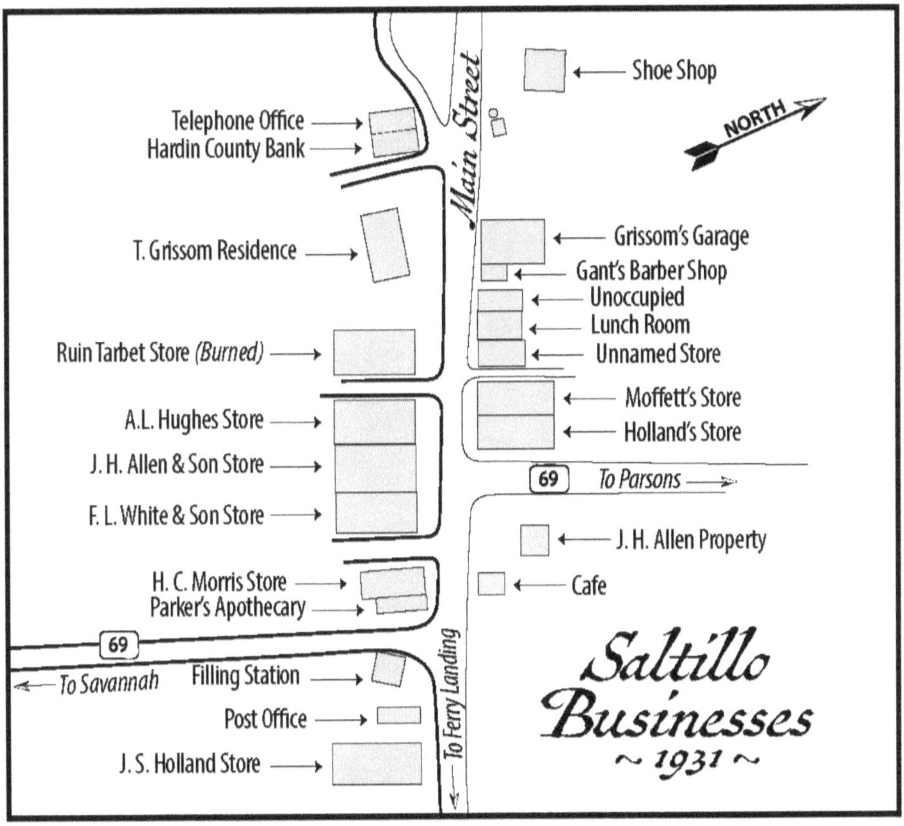

Main Street

Shoe Shop

Telephone Office
Hardin County Bank

Grissom's Garage
Gant's Barber Shop
Unoccupied
Lunch Room
Unnamed Store

T. Grissom Residence

Ruin Tarbet Store *(Burned)*

Moffett's Store
Holland's Store

A.L. Hughes Store

J. H. Allen & Son Store

F. L. White & Son Store

69   To Parsons

J. H. Allen Property

Cafe

H. C. Morris Store
Parker's Apothecary

69

To Savannah   Filling Station

Post Office

J. S. Holland Store

To Ferry Landing

Saltillo
Businesses
~ 1931 ~

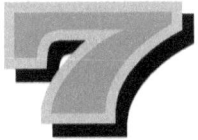

STEPPING OFF THE PORCH

On my grandfather's final day in Saltillo, the weather was foul, the temperature never rising much above freezing and a wind that cut to the bone.[1] In the sweltering summertime, the Tennessee River brought cooling breezes ashore, but in the heart of winter the wind became a wall of frigid air moving along the river's path. At Saltillo, sitting in the bend, cold blasts spilled into town. Overnight, the mercury dropped to sixteen degrees.[2] At dawn, the ground was covered by snow, and a crust of ice rimmed the perimeters of farm ponds. Milk cows huddled in barns against the cold, their exhalations a glowing vapor in the morning light.

I don't know if Boss appreciated snow's ability to change a familiar scene by cloaking everything in sight.

But I do.

On a snowy day, I spend hours looking out the span of windows at the rear of my house. From my kitchen and living room, the view is of a field that ends with a line of oaks and other hardwoods flanking the Harpeth River, which wends its way past the neighborhood. Years ago, this was all pasture. Then the owner turned it into a private air strip. When Nashville's population began to explode beyond the city limits in the 1990s, this acreage became an ideal housing tract in the suburbs. I have plenty of neighbors, but we still see wildlife—songbirds, turkeys, and deer, particularly—and after snowfalls they are more easily spotted, having lost the ability to camouflage themselves in the tree and brush line. Snow seems to shrink the world, to make you take notice of the familiar in a new way: the crown of a particular tree, undulating hills in the distance, my own home coated with a new roof of blinding white.

I wondered if Boss looked out that fateful morning in 1931 and was enchanted by the view. Did he call his daughters, still in their sleeping gowns, to the window to see the winter wonderland? Did he cradle my father in his arms, holding him up to a window so the two-year-old could take in the view? Did my grandmother observe the beauty of the snowy scene, wishing the moment to last forever?

Of course, the frustrating answer is, I don't know.

Despite the frigid weather, stores on Saltillo's unpaved Main Street, which ran in an east to west direction, came alive.[3] J. E. Holland, whose mercantile store was nearest the river on the east side of town, opened his business that he had operated for twenty-three years. On the north side of Main, Tom Grissom waited for the first customer of the day at his garage. On such an unpleasant morning, few customers were expected to be out and about, but if they did come to town, the merchants of Saltillo were there to serve.

Down at the ferry landing, Jess Lowery was at the pilot's wheel of the town ferry, waiting on a customer needing passage across the river. The ferry consisted of a pushing boat, about thirty feet in length from bow to stern, powered by an engine that belched black smoke as it pushed a barge across the channel. The ferry was a necessity because the river, about a quarter-mile wide, bisected Hardin County from south to north. There was only one bridge, newly opened in 1930, that spanned the water, and it was near Savannah, twelve miles upstream.

On the west end of Main Street, Carl W. Thompson, owner of the Saltillo Telephone Exchange and a good friend of my grandfather's, arrived to open for the day. Phones were readily adopted by residents of the town, even if the service was less than reliable and customers had to share lines with their neighbors. The phone company, on the south side of the street, was in a brick building that also housed the Hardin County Bank.

Dr. Luther A. Parker made the short trip from his two-story home on the western edge of town to his combination apothecary and doctor's office, sandwiched between a grocery and a gas station. The first order of business on such a cold morning was to fire up pot-bellied stoves with wood or to light gas heaters. Soon enough, flues funneled streams of gray smoke into the winter air.

Viewing Saltillo's Main Street from the river that morning, nothing indicated the upheaval soon to disrupt this tableau of small-town life.

My grandfather, positioned at the center of the coming disruption, had not been to the bank that week because he was ill, confined to bed much of the time.[4]

On Monday, January 12, he summoned Dr. Parker, the family's longtime physician, for a home visit.

I don't know when my grandfather was diagnosed with tuberculosis, nor do I know the circumstances of his diagnosis. The protocol for determining TB in the mid to late 1920s, when my grandfather likely contracted the illness, was nothing more than checking off symptoms: coughing, night sweats, fever, and coughing up blood.[5] An x-ray of the lungs was used in city hospitals as a diagnostic tool, but Dr. Parker didn't have an x-ray machine. In fact, the Tennessee Department of Health did not acquire a mobile x-ray unit for use in rural areas until the spring of 1930.[6] The skin test now used for tuberculosis screening, in conjunction with an x-ray image, was not invented until 1931 and not used widely for several more years.

In the 1920s, tuberculosis was a problem in Tennessee with more than 3,000 new cases diagnosed each year.[7] The death rate per 100,000 in the state was double that of the United States during the decade.[8]

Active TB is communicable, but no attempts were made to separate my grandfather from the public. Two adjoining states—Virginia and Arkansas—opened sanatoriums in the early 1900s for consumptive patients, but Boss never sought treatment other than visits from Dr. Parker. It is clear the disease did not incapacitate him. He worked his shift at the bank and spent hours on the farm doing manual labor, tasks that he couldn't have performed if TB had kept him chronically bedridden, as it did many sufferers. A possible explanation is that he was in remission, with occasional flareups.

His illness leading up to the day he disappeared may have been one of these flareups, but Dr. Parker's patient log for January 12, 1931, doesn't state this. In fact, Boss's TB status wasn't mentioned in the doctor's logs, where the physician kept general notes about his patients' ailments, the medicines he prescribed and the charges he billed.

The physician summed up his visit to the Bingham house that winter's day with only three words—"visit per Boss"—meaning Boss phoned him to arrange a house call. The physician noted that he offered a liquid tonic for pain, but the medicine wasn't identified. The $3.50 house call fee was charged to the family's account.

After the doctor departed, my grandfather continued to complain of pain in his side, and my grandmother fashioned a poultice—a homemade paste made of herbs, meal, and bread—which was warmed, wrapped in a cloth, and applied to the body. The hope was the poultice would ease the pain.[9]

Although Boss was at home feeling poorly, the Hardin County Bank remained open that Monday, Tuesday, and Wednesday.[10] His brother, Howard, the unofficial assistant head cashier, unlocked the door in the mornings and closed in the evenings. Howard took in deposits, cashed checks, and collected the mail.

After closing for the day, he delivered the collected paperwork to Boss's home, where my grandfather, ostensibly, brought the bank ledgers up to date based on that day's transactions. Howard spent the night at his brother's home instead of returning to his parents' home. That made more sense, especially in the winter.

Nine days before leaving Saltillo, Boss moderated the annual business meeting of the bank's directors, who were led by their president, Dr. Parker. The board was surely pleased to hear my grandfather report the bank had $11,500 in cash on deposit, held county warrants worth an additional $3,500 and the bank's capital stock had earned eleven and a half percent interest.[11]

Considering what was happening at other Tennessee banks, this was an excellent report. Twelve banks in the state had already gone under in 1930, including banks operated by one of the largest financial firms, Caldwell and Company in Nashville.[12] The Caldwell failure rippled through the South, causing runs on banks in Nashville and Knoxville, as well as Little Rock and Asheville, but not in Saltillo, where Dr. Parker and other board members tamped down doubts about the bank's viability. My grandfather's report justified the board's assurances.

Situated near the center of the town's business district, Dr. Parker's apothecary was a gathering place. A few tables and chairs allowed shoppers to sit and talk while prescriptions were filled. The place attracted friends of Parker's, too, who often took a seat for conversation.

At midday, Sinclair S. Dickey, one of the bank directors, visited the drug store for the latter. He was present when the phone rang, and Parker answered.[13] Dickey could tell by the look on his friend's face that something was wrong.

"What's the trouble, Doc?"

The trouble, Parker explained, was at Hardin County Bank. The caller was William McKinnie, the vice president of First National Bank in Jackson. This was not a routine call, however. Hardin County Bank's account was overdrawn by $3,000.[14] Adjusted for inflation, that would be equal to slightly more than $62,000 in value today. The bank executive from Jackson was professional, but insistent. "What are you going to do about this?" he asked Parker.

The doctor didn't have a clue how to rectify this situation. He did not understand how the bank could be overdrawn by that amount when little more than a week earlier Boss reported there was $11,500 on deposit at First National. He left his office and walked the hundred yards to the bank. In so doing he passed stores owned and operated by families he had known for years. All of them had accounts at Hardin County Bank. When he arrived, Howard informed Parker that his brother remained ill at home. The doctor quizzed the assistant bank cashier about the overdraft, but Howard said he knew nothing of the matter.[15]

After leaving the bank, Dr. Parker called members of the board of directors to inform them of the large overdraft and to formulate a plan.[16] "Where was the money?" was likely asked many times. At a hastily called meeting, it was decided that Dr. Parker and several other directors would travel to Savannah that evening to consult with Elijah W. Ross and John Ballew, two of the most well-known and accomplished lawyers in the region.

Meanwhile, following Dr. Parker's confrontation with Howard at the bank, Howard called Boss to alert him that First National reported a large overdraft.[17] It was clear to Boss that the day of reckoning had arrived.

He must leave.

My grandfather sat down to draft a letter to Dr. Parker and the bank's board of directors. Writing longhand on a notepad from a farm implement company, Boss composed what he needed to say.[18]

Jan. 14, 1931

Dear Doctor:

Owing to the condition of everything I feel it my duty to all of you who are connected to the affairs of the bank to make a statement that no one but myself is responsible for the condition of things and no one knows but me as I have done all of my work in order to try and get straight but it seems that instead of getting out, I continued to get in deeper all the time.[19]

Now I don't know what I will do or where I will go as I have been crazy for three months knowing that the time was soon to come and if anything should happen to me all that I have is for the depositors of the bank and stockholders. I have insurance in the amount of $37,500 mostly made to estate and wife, but if anything should happen to me all of it is for the benefit of the people who have money in the bank as I do hate for anyone to lose on my account. I am just following my mind and whenever I am brought to face the deed I will have to as no one knows how I feel about this and how I regret it but that will do no one any good in a financial way.

Although I have no intention of suicide, I would be glad that my time could come, and I would know that no one would lose anything. In checking the accounts, you will find two letters with tax receipts in them that has never been charged so that will account for the C.C. Hinkle Trustee account. An audit will bring this all out and show for itself where all has gone to. I trust that you will not be caused much trouble as you are not responsible for anything as you have done the best you could, not knowing the banking business.

Hoping that all will work out so that no one loses but me, I am.

L. B. Bingham

Boss surely understood such a letter would be perceived as suspicious to the State Department of Insurance and Banking. The revelations about his considerable insurance coverage combined with the overdraft at the Jackson bank would be grounds enough to close the Saltillo bank, which would lead the district attorney to open an investigation.

My grandfather understood these consequences but wrote the note anyway.

He remained at home throughout the day. One of my aunts, Mary Lou, who was five in January 1931, recalled seeing her parents clutching each other on several occasions. Their mood was somber, tearful, but no explanations were offered.[20]

By dusk, the departure plan was settled and the letter sealing my grandfather's fate was ready for delivery.

When Howard arrived at his brother's home after closing the bank, Boss sent him back to town to fill the Chevy with gas and to "bring back the large bills," from the cash drawer at the bank.[21] Upon his return he handed over $105 to his older brother. That's when Boss informed his sibling that he was leaving Saltillo because of trouble at the bank. He placed the letter he had written to Dr. Parker and the board of directors in Howard's hand and told him to deliver it the following morning.

Before he left Saltillo, however, a final task awaited at Shady Grove Cemetery. Howard was coming along to help.

Lytle Boss Bingham stepped off the porch of his Tennessee home and drove away. Boss was leaving the land he loved, the town he loved, the wife and children he loved. When all had settled down, his family would join him in whatever dry and sunny climate he chose to recuperate from TB—Arizona, most likely.[22] That was the plan.

The day began with the sight of freshly fallen snow, a pristine cover, pure and quiet. The gray of dusk yielded a starless night, dark as coal slurry with a chilling wind whipping through the forest.

I can imagine my grandmother standing on the porch watching her husband leave, wishing to alter that which had come to pass, but powerless to change the trajectory of that night's events. She was alone, without her help mate. There was no way for her to know the depth of heartache, worry and frustration that would mark her life in the years to come, no way to know the sacrifices that would be required of her, no inkling that she would remain alone for the rest of her life.

DIRTY WORK

BOSS

Before advancing into the Shady Grove Cemetery to disturb the resting place of an innocent man, let the obvious be stated: anyone determined to accomplish a staged death would not do so without a plan. Planning, meanwhile, signified a premeditative mindset. In other words, at some point in time, my grandfather determined he must leave Saltillo. That part I understand, but he concluded that disappearing into a new identity in another state wouldn't suffice. Logic born of desperation led him to this twisted thought: if the life insurance payouts were going to balance the bank's ledgers, as Boss wished in his farewell letter, there must be a body. No body, no death benefits. And that's why men of Saltillo were in the graveyard on a mid-January night in 1931.

My grandfather's deductive process fairly boggles my mind, even after years of familiarity with the story.

Boss wrote in his note to the board of directors that he had been "almost crazy" the previous three months. There's no doubt he was anxious about when the bank's troubles would come to light and the repercussions of such information. How to make his exit credible, I believe, occupied his mind for months, driving him to do the unthinkable.

There are only two ways to acquire a body, of course: choose a victim and murder them, or find a way to procure a corpse. My grandfather chose the second option, a selection that makes the decision no less repulsive and, in many ways, more problematic.

First, there's the issue of finding a suitable corpse: dead, but not too dead. Then comes disinterring a body, without anyone noticing.

On December 18, 1930, a former Saltillo resident named Joseph C. Lucas died at the home of his daughter in Arkansas.[1] He had lived with her family for some time after his wife, Roxie, died in 1919 and was buried in Shady Grove Cemetery. Upon his death, Lucas's body was transported to Tennessee where he was interred next to his wife.

It's unclear how my grandfather learned of Lucas's burial. Maybe he drove by and saw the new grave. Perhaps a customer at the bank told him about the man's passing. I don't even know if Boss knew Lucas, but I'm guessing it would not have mattered even if he did. On January 14, 1931, knowing the bank's shortage had been detected, Boss understood auditors would soon make an accounting of every penny, nickel, and dime. He needed to leave town and he needed a corpse to make his demise legitimate so the insurance companies would pay death benefits, so that all could be made right again with Hardin County Bank.

As for the procurement of poor Mr. Lucas's body, I have three stories to share on who went to Shady Grove Cemetery with shovels on that cold night.

In 1977 my brother, Steve, interviewed our Great-Uncle Howard, sixty-nine years old at the time, at his home in Nashville. Steve, a Baptist minister who has also been interested in knowing the true story behind our grandfather's disappearance, received more answers in that sitting than he had heard before. It seems that Howard was like Boss: neither brother wanted to die harboring the secret that led to decades of separation.

Sitting at the kitchen table, Howard told his version of the story from beginning to end. Steve took careful notes and later reconstructed the conversation. I'll let my brother's words tell the story from here.

"Boss, being a very caring man, had often let outstanding loans ride beyond their due dates, as he tried to give people a little relief due to the Depression. He sometimes gave back money to people just so they could have food on the table and left it up to them to pay the bank back later when they could.

"The big thing was that Boss had given a loan to three lawyers, who were somehow connected to the bank, of some substantial amount. Before the Depression, banks loaned money to be invested in the stock market which was booming prior to 1929."

Great-Uncle Howard was clear that the loans to the attorneys were off-the-books.

"Boss had lent money to these three lawyers for this purpose—'money under the table' as Howard called it—with the plan to pay the principal back to the bank after the stock was sold. Howard said Boss was not part of this investment scheme but rather doing these lawyers a favor under their persuasion."

This arrangement worked until the fall of 1929, when the stock market crashed, Howard said. The money lent to the lawyers, having not produced a profit, could not be returned to the bank.

"When this was realized, the scheme of faking Boss's death was brought up and with his death there would be no one charged with embezzlement or illegal loans. Boss would be the guilty party and the lawyers would be clear legally."

Boss's story is infused with stock speculation. The "three lawyers" story of what led my grandfather to leave Saltillo is one explanation. There's another version that I've heard from other family members, which I'll call the "three cotton gins" version. Same stock-buying scenario, except that cotton gin owners, who were among the wealthiest and largest employers in the region, were the ones borrowing money to buy stock. The idea that Boss was marked for an early death by TB was common to both scenarios. Further, if he "died," no one would have to go to jail for banking irregularities.

Stock speculating was rampant through the 1920s, even up to the eve of that day in October 1929 when the crash occurred.[2] Brokerage houses made it relatively easy to purchase stocks on margin, requiring only a small percentage of the total purchase price and using the stock as collateral. If the stock increased, as it often did in the mid-1920s, the stock was sold for a tidy profit, or empire-building windfalls, depending on how much was ventured. However, if the stock value went down, investors were squeezed for the difference, usually the precursor of bankruptcy and ruin. That investors in tiny Saltillo were participating in the orgy of wealth-making that preoccupied the nation leading up to the Depression wasn't uncommon at all. Millions of small-town investors lined up to take their share of the piece of the pie.[3] Millions lost everything when the bubble burst, too.

Now, let's return to that cold January evening at Shady Grove Cemetery. Howard told my brother that on the night my grandfather disappeared from Saltillo, Boss did not participate in the digging at the graveyard.

From Steve's written recollection: "Howard told me that when the body of a recently buried man was placed in Boss's car to fake his death, the lawyers did the digging, placed the body in Boss's car, did the driving of the car and rolled the car down an embankment and set it on fire. Boss did not participate in any of that night's activities other than a ride in a car before he got on a bus to Memphis."

However, another family account, based on an unpublished book written by Great-Uncle Howard's son, Bill Bingham of Elkton, Kentucky, states that Boss and his brother, Howard, dug up the corpse, placed it in the car, with Boss dropping his brother off at their parents' home before heading toward Jackson.

And there's Sue recollection of interviews with her father where a doctor, a lawyer and a third person led the disinterment of Lucas.

Why am I not surprised there are three disparate stories, two based on the testimony of Great-Uncle Howard and one from my grandfather's account, about what happened that night at Shady Grove Cemetery?

This brings me to a topic I couldn't imagine myself ever contemplating: the logistics of grave robbing. That train of inquiry led to the office of Hugh Berryman, a forensic anthropologist at my alma mater, Middle Tennessee State University.

Berryman, a round-faced man with neatly combed hair streaked with gray, has been a go-to person for state and federal law enforcement for decades. In a photo of him on the university's website he peered at the camera through dark-framed glasses. His left hand supported a pipe in his mouth, while his right gripped a human skull, which was tilted so that the empty eye sockets "looked" at the viewer. The pose fit Berryman, who spent his adult life exploring the secrets of the dead. Among Berryman's areas of expertise was blunt force trauma, so he's seen many examples of man's murderous treatment, one to another. When remains were unearthed by hunters or a suspect bone was dug up by a farmer's plow, Berryman was consulted, testifying at trial on hundreds of occasions.

He was trained by the best. Berryman was a protégé of William Bass, a renowned University of Tennessee forensic anthropologist who, in 1971, created The Body Farm, a patch of hilly ground near the UT Medical Center in Knoxville where corpses are buried and dug up repeatedly by student researchers gathering data on body decomposition. While working on his doctorate, Berryman was a teaching and research assistant for Bass. The Body Farm, officially the UT Forensic Anthropology Center, played a featured role in best-selling novels by Patricia Cornwell and, also, by Bass and his writing partner, Jon Jefferson, who penned stories under the nom de plume, Jefferson Bass. Berryman, in fact, was the inspiration for a character in one of Jefferson Bass's Body Farm novels.

Hunched over his desk in his university office, Berryman considered the story of Boss Bingham and the corpse that served as my grandfather's stand-in. The wheels of his uniquely fashioned mind began spinning, curiosity evident in his expression.

"For two men to do it, it would be a pretty big job," he reasoned, but added, if time was not a factor, then, "yes, a pair of able-bodied men could meet the task."

Time was a factor in my grandfather's case, however. I know from court testimony that Boss's burning car was first noticed by a farmer about five thirty, about an hour before dawn.[4] The destroyed car was located off State Highway 5 about five miles south of Jackson. It was facing south, as if returning to Saltillo.

If Boss departed his home the previous evening about nine o'clock as my grandmother testified during the insurance trials, the disinterment would have started by ten o'clock.[5] The drive from Saltillo to where the burning car was discovered would have taken about an hour and a half on a pleasant evening, but on a wintry one such as that night, it was likely a two-hour drive, or more. That meant the exhumation would have to be completed by three-thirty at the latest for the car to be set on fire and to be noticed about two hours later.

Was five and a half hours long enough for two men, one of whom was ill, to dig up a body?

Unlikely, Berryman said.

The phrase "six feet under" is associated with modern burials, but the forensic scientist said four to four and a half feet is the norm in Middle Tennessee cemeteries. "This idea of six feet deep, it's only for the military. That's the only place you'll see that a lot. They bury extra deep in the national cemeteries because when the spouses pass away, they tend to bury them on top of the bottom coffin," Berryman said.

Even at four feet deep, a casket would be encased by hundreds of pounds of soil. "I've dug a lot of holes with a shovel, and it takes a lot of effort to dig down four and a half feet to the point," he said.

The recent rainfall and snow since Lucas was buried wouldn't have helped either. "Once you disturb the soil, water will tend to run in and it's just like a sponge and stays in that area instead of running off. And so, you've got a wet coffin down there. It's going to be hard to get it open to the point to get a body out," Berryman surmised.

When the body was retrieved, it's not going to be pleasant, he added.

"At three weeks he's probably not going to smell very well. When you are alive you have all those nice helpful microorganisms inside the gut. They're helping you digest food. When you're alive they cannot migrate across tissue boundaries. They can't get outside the gut. When you die, they can. And that's when they start to reproduce. It's party time for microorganisms, reproducing like mad. Methane gas and other gases are being produced and cause the body to bloat," Berryman offered, his hands slicing the air.

The worst aspect of this task, as far as I'm concerned, came when it was time to lift the body.

"You'll get rancid oils that come to the surface, and they will separate the epidermis from the dermis. It's called skin slippage," he said. By the rules of decomposition, this biological reality usually occurs between three to six days, but in cold weather, the process is delayed, he noted. Just as it sounds, tugging the hand of a decaying cadaver leaves you holding only the limp outer layer of skin.

The process would not be enjoyable, particularly not at night in below freezing temperature with snow and sleet a possibility, Berryman said.

"The one thing they have going for them, it's just been dug, so the dirt's loose and all the roots have been cut. God, I hate roots."

Following Berryman's train of thought, I am convinced that two men could not have done the deed in the time allowed. So that takes me back to my family's stories of what happened in the cemetery. Whether it was lawyers or cotton gin owners who did the digging, or whether it was someone else, the distasteful deed was accomplished with the help of others.

Connecting that dot gives credence to more involvement than just my grandfather, grandmother and great-uncle. Unknown accomplices also helped. It's reasonable to believe they were Saltillo men who knew my grandfather. Who else could it be? This is perhaps the best evidence, circumstantial though it is, that my grandfather's getaway was not a solo effort.

The word "conspiracy" ricochets in my mind like a pinball, bouncing from one incongruency to another, from one unfathomable idea to the next, and I feel its weight. It's the full weight of The Lie and I am left to comprehend the complexity of my grandfather's deception.

During my brother's 1977 meeting with Howard, the older man's shame about what happened after Boss disappeared was evident. Howard, who was a Baptist deacon and a lay preacher, regretted his testimony during the insurance trials of 1932.

"I lied and lied and lied," he told Steve. "What was true they disproved. What was untrue they proved," referring to the sole point of contention in the insurance trials: whether Boss was dead and buried.

As I read Howard's testimony, however, I was struck by the stark truthfulness of some of his remarks. When asked by an attorney in one of the first insurance lawsuits what Boss said to him before leaving, Howard could have said that his brother told him nothing. Instead, he told the truth: "Well, he told me he was leaving, that there was a shortage at the bank."[6]

Howard also readily testified that he returned to the bank at his brother's request to "get the big bills" and confirmed that Boss didn't write a check to cover the withdrawal. Howard also admitted that his personal account was often overdrawn and that Boss "charged my checks to him."

But then there was this question from an insurance lawyer: Have you had any communications from Boss since he left? Howard's response was "No."[7] I have no idea if the word slipped from his lips without fear or if his voice quivered ever so slightly. Replying he had not been in touch with my grandfather was a lie, an untruth he did not rectify when asked the same question in the other insurance trials.

Howard told Steve that if he "had known all of the grief his parents went through and all of the suffering Mary and the children would go through, he would never have gone along with the plan to fake Boss's death and the following events that took place."

Four and a half decades after that terrible winter's night in 1931, the burden of guilt was just as heavy for Howard.

I often think of something Steve, my brother, revealed as an aside. He wrote that when our father was a teenager, a local lawyer befriended him, giving him work to do on the lawyer's farm and was generous with pay. With money saved from the chores, our father bought his first bicycle.

According to Steve, when our dad graduated from high school in 1947, this same attorney offered to fund his tuition at the University of Tennessee-Martin, the lawyer's alma mater.

In his notebook about Boss, my brother wrote: "Daddy turned the offer down as he was planning on marrying my mother soon after high school. Daddy told me that he thought it very generous and strange that this lawyer would offer to pay for a college education."

Years later, after learning of rumors about the three attorneys and under-the-table loans to speculate in the stock market, my father told Steve that he questioned the lawyer's beneficence, wondering if the offer was a payment to assuage the man's guilt.

I thought of my father's question as I recalled another line Great-Uncle Howard told Steve during their memorable 1977 visit. Steve asked what became of the three lawyers. My preacher brother was surprised by the response.

"He told me that all three lawyers died 'hard' deaths," Steve wrote. The older man didn't explain what he meant by "hard," but implied that each paid a price for their participation in the bank's demise, just as my grandfather did by shedding his identity in Tennessee and taking on a new name in Texas.

INSURANCE IS FOR THE LIVING

BOSS

Aphorisms abound about troubles begetting troubles. A familiar one in the Bible Belt is this: "Be sure your sins will find you out." The saying conjures a finger-wagging God chastising his creation for chronic wrongdoing. Humans have no secrets from an omniscient deity.

But among their own kind, secrets thrive as a form of social currency and accountability.

As the winter of 1931 held Saltillo in a chilling grip, whispers of something fishy about the death of Boss Bingham floated down Main Street like fog rolling off the Tennessee River, enveloping the homes and businesses of people my grandfather knew well. As I've pulled away the layers of his story, I learned many locals suspected that Boss was alive, but their doubts were kept to themselves. Many even comforted my grandmother at the graveside service for him at Shady Grove Cemetery.

While citizens of Saltillo spoke publicly of Lytle Boss Bingham in the past tense, the companies who underwrote life insurance policies promising to pay his widow and children thousands of dollars in case of Boss's death, did not.

As the gray cold yielded to a warm spring, then a blistering summer, one by one the insurance companies refused to pay death benefits. Their cause for action was made clear in tersely worded letters my grandmother received: none believed Boss was dead.

I cannot imagine the weight of her predicament. Untenable seems a good word to describe her troubles. Of course, there was an incontrovertible reason for those troubles: Boss was alive, not dead. My grandmother knew it. Howard, my grandfather's brother, knew it. Verna, Boss's sister, also was in on the secret. I believe there were a number of my grandmother's Saltillo neighbors who knew because they played roles in this larger-than-life spectacle. Yet, in the face of that truth, they all chose silence, and their complicity allowed my Tennessee relatives to burrow themselves deeper in secrecy.

The Lie was given birth on the day and hour that my grandfather committed to deceive the world of his existence, but it did not fester into the consuming, life-altering event that conflicted generations of my family until those closest to my grandfather, including my beloved grandmother, protected him by hiding the truth.

By the end of summer 1931, it was clear to my grandmother that the path forward, away from scandal, jail, and impoverishment depended on Boss remaining dead. Otherwise, none of the insurance companies would pay death benefits.

On this matter let me note that it was also quite clear that my grandfather believed in life insurance.[1] For a man with a growing family, it was a prudent investment. His first policy was issued in the summer of 1917, not long after he graduated from business school and married my grandmother. The issuer was Cotton States Life Insurance Co., and the policy—for $1,500—was payable to Mary Bingham "upon proof of death of the insured."

I'm sure Boss purchased the policy for the same reason I bought life insurance: to avoid economic hardship on surviving kin. In addition to working at the bank, Boss was a farmer, raising cotton on several hundred acres, as well as keeping livestock and chickens for slaughter. He also served as a sub-agent for life insurance companies, primarily scouting customers so that when the agents came to town, they had a list of possible buyers. Boss was sold on insurance to protect the small kingdom he was creating, of that there is no doubt.

In April of 1919, he purchased a second policy, this one from the Modern Woodmen of America. The benefit was $3,000, payable to Mary Bingham as beneficiary. Having two life insurance policies doesn't seem unusual. Based on his salary of seventy-five dollars a month, and earnings from the farm, I don't doubt he was able to pay the semiannual payments.

However, in 1924 my grandfather began an insurance buying spree that didn't end until just a few months before he disappeared seven years later.[2]

Two new policies were purchased in 1924, and he added another in 1926 and two more in 1928.[3] The first four of these were issued by Business Men's Assurance

Company of America and the last policy was from Shenandoah Life Insurance Company.

When he took over the bank in the late spring of 1928 after Hinkle's sudden death, Boss began buying policies in earnest. The number of policies and their dates of purchase are clues that the insurance may have been more about making things right with the bank than leaving a windfall for his family. At the end of 1928, Boss's life was insured for $17,500, nearly fifteen times his annual salary from the bank.[4]

That wasn't enough, apparently. During the bank's final two years of operation, my grandfather took out six additional life insurance policies.[5] In 1929, he purchased life insurance in January, September, and November (the American Bankers Commercial Life Club, Shenandoah, and the North American Accident Insurance Company). In 1930, policies were issued in his name in July, August and September (The Massachusetts Protective Association, Banker's Credit Life and Bankers and Business Men's Group of Guaranty National Union).

What was different about this final buying spree was the amount of coverage he purchased. Two of the policies paid a death benefit of $5,000 and two others promised $10,000. The previously purchased policies each offered a payout of no more than a couple of thousand dollars. These six new policies, alone, provided $35,000 in coverage.[6] They were purchased at a time when the bank was quickly heading toward insolvency. In his letter to Dr. Parker and the bank board, Boss was clear on why he had taken out so much life insurance: ". . . if anything should happen to me all of it is for the benefit of the people who have money in the bank as I do hate for anyone to lose on my account."

Discovering the buying spree that took place after his promotion to head cashier persuaded me to believe he knew the bank would soon fail and the added insurance was his way of taking care of the matter. Of course, he didn't have enough savings to pay the semiannual premiums so he wrote checks that in any other circumstance would have been returned for insufficient funds, but because he was the head cashier these worthless checks were absorbed by depositors' accounts.

When the bank was audited following his departure, Boss's checking account was overdrawn by more than $9,000. That and his letter to the board was enough reason for the insurance companies' refusal to pay.

My grandmother, a thirty-one-year-old mother of three, soon enough felt the weight of the world on her shoulders. Her husband was gone, leaving her to run the farm and household without his monthly salary from the bank, but worse, she was a single woman in a patriarchal era contemplating a David versus Goliath stand against large life insurance companies. She was resolute, however. They would not honor their contracts, so she retained counsel and sued.

Her litigious action, by itself, made me pause. My grandmother was not illiterate, but her formal education ended at high school. I would not judge her to be a recluse, just isolated from the procedures of judicial process, as many rural folks were. I wouldn't be surprised if she had never been to the Hardin County Courthouse in Savannah, the county seat. She certainly had never filed a lawsuit nor was subjected to cross-examination. I wouldn't be surprised, either, if the number of lawyers she had met could be counted on the fingers of one hand. So, the question looms large in my mind: how did she secure counsel? Her lead attorney was from Memphis, some 117 miles west, which in 1931 was a full day's journey, large portions on dirt roads. There is no doubt someone helped her navigate the process. It's likely that Verna, Boss's sister who lived in Memphis, contacted the attorney there, but I don't know for sure.

My grandmother was joined in the legal fray by Howard and Verna. In a few of the policies, my father and his sisters were named beneficiaries, with Verna listed as their guardian. Howard was included because he and my grandmother were co-executors of my grandfather's estate.

Their actions mystified me. My grandmother and the others adhered to legal action that depended solely upon my grandfather remaining among the dead. They knew that Boss was living and breathing in a small West Texas town. The chain was only as strong as each person's determination to remain true to the deception, but what happened if Howard or Verna or my grandmother yielded to the temptation to tell all they knew?

I've pondered this many times as I've labored to uncover the truth. If found guilty of insurance fraud, all three could have gone to jail for years.

They filed suit, I believe, because they came to accept there was no choice but to sue. If they didn't, the bank would claim all the insurance proceeds. If my grandfather's directive—using the insurance proceeds to make the bank whole—was to be followed, none of the funds would go to Boss's family. After the audit was completed, Dr. Parker told a Jackson reporter on March 1, 1931, that "the bank would go to court in the April session of chancery court at Savannah and attempt to win the insurance to offset the bank's shortage."[7]

The lawsuits were evidence my grandmother, Howard and Verna believed that would be unfair. In the months leading up to filing the first suit in August 1931, the trio decided to fight for a portion. I am not privy to their deliberations. I don't know if one or more of them had to be convinced, or if they were of one accord from the beginning, but the result was to retain counsel.

Let me at this point deal with a worrisome Boss question: was my grandfather a cowardly thief? When all that I had come to know was ingested, sifted, and sorted, two choices emerged.

First, I had to acknowledge, distasteful as it was to me, that my grandfather could be the embezzler some said he was. At this point in my research, all the unsavory epithets hurled at him could be true. It was possible Boss was a crook.

The second scenario did not make him a hero, but much less of a pariah than the first. This line of reasoning suggests the bank failed because of poor management, not only by my grandfather, but by the late Robert Hinkle, the former head cashier. On this front I did have some evidence. Correspondence between Dr. Parker and D. D. Robertson, superintendent of the State Department of Insurance and Banking lends credence to this possibility.

In the fall of 1930, the bank received notice that a large bank in Memphis no longer accepted checks from Hardin County Bank accounts. The reason given was that Boss was slow to send remittances to the Memphis bank. After receiving a phone call alerting him to the matter, Dr. Parker confronted Boss to resolve the issue. In a letter dated October 27, 1930, Dr. Parker apologized to Robertson for Boss's failures, stating "some of his apparent lax business methods are due to the former cashier."[8] Parker noted Hinkle did not properly train Boss and "some of his (Hinkle's) banking methods had proven not very good at all, though he was a very fine man."

So, was it simply a matter of my grandfather being in over his head because he took over a bank that was destined to fail? Perhaps, but I wasn't convinced about this line of thought either.

But both sets of what-ifs lead me to the same conclusion. If my grandfather's confessional to the board of directors was to be believed, then life insurance was his method to recoup the bank's losses. Such a plan was a foolhardy gambit. He must have known that the discovery of so many insurance policies issued in such a short period of time would clearly raise questions if he were to die within a few months or even a few years of the issue dates. Not to mention dying within twenty-four hours of writing the letter to the bank board.

There's the real rub, isn't it? For the insurance plan to succeed, my grandfather had to die. Not just disappear into the thickly forested hills of Hardin County or launch a johnboat downriver and drift to the Mississippi. He had to make the authorities believe he was dead and buried in Shady Grove Cemetery to have any chance of any insurance money trickling down to the bank.

Likewise, for my grandmother and her children to receive any of the proceeds, Boss had to remain dead . . . and mouths zipped for fear the truth was revealed.

Combing for what seemed the thousandth time through the expanse of correspondence between the lawyers involved in the May 1932 insurance trials, I spotted a reference to a Memphis case from 1926 that went unnoticed before.[9] That litigation involved proceeds from life insurance policies issued to a bank cashier who embezzled a large sum from his employer. Curious, I researched the lawsuit, looking for relevance to my grandfather's situation and was intrigued by the findings.

Clarence Henochsberg was an assistant cashier at American Savings Bank Trust Company. His life began unraveling on December 2, 1926, when auditors discovered a shortage in the ledger handled by another employee of the bank, a bookkeeper named Rush Parke.[10] As soon as the shortage was known, Parke fled town. He was later captured and tried.

Bank examiners ordered a thorough audit of the bank's books, a move that Henochsberg opposed. He explained to his wife, Jeannette, that the bank would not survive the loss brought on by the bookkeeper and Henochsberg would be "ruined."

The audit was to begin on Monday, December 7.[11] The night before, a distraught Henochsberg confessed to his wife that he had embezzled $300,000, much more than Parke. According to his wife's testimony at trial, the cashier planned to commit suicide so his wife and children "could live on the income from his life insurance."[12] The next morning at 5 a.m., Henochsberg telephoned a member of the bank board and confessed.[13] He tried to negotiate a private settlement, hoping the shortage would be covered, allowing Henochsberg to avoid arrest and trial, but the board member said only the full board could make that decision. Henochsberg declined to wait for an answer. At 8 a.m., when the bank opened, the troubled cashier was at home. He held a pistol to his head and pulled the trigger.[14]

Henochsberg left a note to bank officials on the back of an envelope. Under the heading "all the accounts I can remember," he listed the customers he had shorted for his own gain.[15] His method was to mark a depositor's passbook, then place deposit slips in a private drawer, preventing them from being logged in the bank's ledger. He pocketed the customer's money.

At the time of his death, Henochsberg's life insurance coverage promised $110,000 in death benefits, even if he committed suicide. As with my grandfather's policies, the bank and the State Department of Insurance and Banking sought a stake in the insurance proceeds.

Obviously, there are differences in the Memphis and Hardin County cases. Henochsberg admitted his sole motive was to steal and, when caught, he killed himself.[16] There is no question that he's buried in Temple Israel Cemetery in Memphis beneath a headstone that bears his name.[17]

But it occurred to me that the Henochsberg case may have guided Boss and those who assisted in his extrication from Hardin County. I think it's reasonable that Boss had read of the Memphis case. Bad news in a profession usually spreads widely even in 1926. Memphis newspapers, which reported on the assistant cashier's suicide and the subsequent chancery court trial, circulated in Saltillo, although delivery occurred several days after the day of publication. Could Boss have been inspired by Henochsberg's dilemma to come up with an insurance protection plan? If so, that would explain the policy-buying spree between 1926 and Boss's disappearance in 1931. Did he decide to leave like Parke but "die" like Henochsberg?

Before word of my grandfather's automobile accident reached Saltillo, Dr. Parker was approached by Earl Bingham, first cousin of Boss and his brother.[18] Earl handed over the letter that my grandfather had composed to Parker. Earl told the physician that Howard had instructed him to deliver the letter only to him.

After reading Boss's note, the alarmed Parker and other members of the board tried to find him, but without success. Only when my great-grandfather, Boss's father, came into the apothecary to purchase medicine did they learn that the cashier had departed the previous evening.[19]

A short time later, Parker and the whole town learned that Boss had been burned alive in a single-car accident outside of Jackson. A graveside service was held Friday, January 16, at Shady Grove Cemetery.

That same day, the region's largest newspaper, *The Tennessean*, published two stories about my grandfather.[20] Both were found on page five under the headline "Hardin Cashier Burns to Death as Car Overturns." The first carried the dateline of Jackson and focused on the coroner's ruling of accidental death.

The second story, with a Saltillo dateline, focused on the impending arrival of a bank examiner at Hardin County Bank who would conduct an audit following the death of L. B. Bingham.

If my grandmother, Howard, or Verna believed a body in the ground would be the most daunting of obstacles in securing the insurance payoffs, they were mistaken. The companies united, refusing to honor the policies. They drew a figurative line in the dark loam of the bottomland: Boss was alive, the insurance firms insisted, and were confident proof was forthcoming.

Proof in the form of Lytle Boss Bingham, himself.

My grandmother was unfazed. Her lawyers prepared for the trials to come.

The Hardin County Bank in Saltillo never reopened. It was one of scores of Tennessee banks deemed insolvent between 1929 and 1934.[21] As 1931 ended, the Depression held fast. A crop cycle had come and gone, not that it mattered. Boll weevils and low sale prices broke the spirits of many a farmer, including my grandmother who struggled to avoid foreclosure. She was a hard worker, but my grandfather's absence of nearly a year no doubt weighed heavily on her mind and body. Her children missed their dad, asked about him often, but my grandmother never told her daughters or son that their father was alive and there was hope of reunifying one day.

There was too much at stake to utter the truth.

The Lie's grip was tightening.

THE CHARRED CORPSE

On the morning of January 15, 1931, Ulrich A. Watlington, a forty-five-year-old farmer who lived a few miles south of Jackson, Tennessee, rose before dawn, as was his custom. Overnight, snow had fallen, covering the fields surrounding his frame house with a thin white blanket, just enough snow to cover grass and collect on tree limbs. The view from his kitchen window offered a pretty scene, one that occurred once or twice a winter in this part of Tennessee. Pulling on his shoes, Watlington went outside to fetch a load of firewood. The large farmhouse would soon be bustling with activity as children prepared for school. He and his wife, Jennie, had eleven, whose ages ranged from twenty-one to two.

While approaching the wood pile, Watlington's attention was diverted to the western horizon where the sky was lit up on State Highway 5, a two-lane, north–south highway that ran from Jackson to the Mississippi border.[1] The road was 200 to 300 yards west of his home.

Initially, Watlington didn't consider the source of the bright light to be something that should concern him on a frigid winter morning. He knew there was no house in that vicinity. He figured someone, a hobo, or hunters, built a campfire while camping in the woods across the highway, but he learned otherwise when his teenaged son, Sam, returned shortly after seven o'clock from checking rabbit traps the boy had set near the main road.

"A car is on fire," the son, out of breath from rushing back to the house, told his father.[2]

After helping to get his kids off to school, the elder Watlington decided to go see for himself. He arrived at the scene about eight o'clock and made his way down to the smoldering car, his footprints marking the fresh snow. The burned Chevrolet had come to rest about ten feet off the southbound shoulder at the bottom of an embankment, positioned somewhat perpendicular to the highway, with the car straddling a drainage ditch.[3]

The farmer peered into the blackened interior of the Chevrolet two-door sedan and immediately wished he hadn't. Inside was the horrible sight of a human form badly burned. He quickly scampered to the road, flagged down the first vehicle and told the driver to call the Madison County Sheriff's Department.[4]

The message of "a man burned up in a car" was delivered to deputies who relayed the message to Ewing Griffin, a local undertaker who also served as county coroner.[5] Within a half hour, the charred car on the side of the road was swarming with people. Even in the bitter temperature, drivers heading to work in Jackson stopped to gawk. More than a few passersby ventured closer, stomping through the snow. They, too, no doubt, wished they hadn't after observing the condition of the car's sole occupant.

Soon, the car was surrounded by dozens of footprints, obliterating evidence left by anyone who had been on the scene before Watlington noticed the blaze.

When Griffin arrived in the funeral parlor's hearse, which also doubled as an ambulance, deputies shooed the curious away and kept traffic moving while the undertaker began his examination of the car in preparation for removing the body. At forty, with graying hair combed back and a round face, the undertaker had been in the funeral business for going on twenty-five years. He earned an embalming license at the age of eighteen, making him at the time the youngest undertaker in Tennessee.[6] In his career, he had prepared hundreds of bodies for burial. Most were the elderly who had grown gray and withered until succumbing to organ failure or stroke. Young people and children died, too, of course, from disease or accidents, primarily car crashes and drownings. Griffin had also seen his share of homicides, victims knifed or gunned or choked to death. In these Prohibition days, moonshine, the consumption of it or the risky business of peddling homemade hooch, was sometimes a common denominator.

However, what he saw looking through the melted glass of the driver's window on Highway 5 was not customary. He had handled burned corpses before, but the remains of this man (or woman, he couldn't tell at first look), was burned as badly as he had ever witnessed.[7]

The body was lying across the front passenger's seat, which was folded down.

The padding and covering had burned away, leaving the iron frame exposed. The victim was lying face up, the body splayed diagonally across the seat, head pointed toward the right rear quarter of the car, legs pointed to the accelerator pedal.

Griffin drew closer, trying as best he could to ignore the stench of burned flesh that flared his nostrils. He looked the body over from head to foot and quickly concluded the fire that had engulfed the car had been a very hot one.[8] In fact, flames continued to lick at the body more than two hours after the fire was first noticed and the vehicle's steel chassis remained too hot to be touched without gloves. Curiously, the fire was contained to the inside compartment, Griffin observed. Neither the engine nor the rear exterior appeared to be damaged.[9]

But the interior had been obliterated by an inferno, and the body had taken the brunt.

The victim's feet were missing, burned away between the foot and the knee.[10] The arms were burned away, too. No fingers or wrists, only short nubs leading to blackened elbows. The torso was intact but thoroughly ravaged. Flames erased all signatures of a face, leaving only charred bones of the cheek, jaw and forehead showing.[11] A small section of the skull where the victim's head rested against the sidewall behind the passenger's seat had been untouched by the flames. The skin was light-colored, so Griffin knew the deceased was white.[12]

Extricating a thoroughly burned body from the narrow confines of an automobile is not an easy task. If the corpse hadn't been burned, the job would have been accomplished by opening the passenger door, grabbing underneath the arms, and pulling the body outside the vehicle onto a waiting gurney.

But the situation before Griffin required more delicate handling. For one thing, the corpse offered no give.[13] The bend in the torso couldn't be straightened, the result of a phenomenon called "boxer's pose." When a body is badly burned, there's an automatic flexing as muscle is destroyed. The knees bend and the hands fold toward the body, taking on the defensive stance of a boxer. The stubs of the legs remained tucked and the arms, what was left of them, were also locked in position.

Griffin called out to a man who worked for him at the funeral home and the employee pulled out a gurney from the back of the hearse. Together, the men pulled the corpse backward to align the body with the open door. Their grip on the remains had to apply just enough pressure to get the job done. If they were too rough, there was a risk a piece of charred human anatomy would crumble to ashes. Carefully, the smoldering body was maneuvered through the door. In the open air, flames reappeared from beneath the armpits as what remained of the corpse's shirt and jacket caught fire. Griffin was forced to pat out the flames with a free hand, a gruesome vision that witnesses didn't soon forget.[14] The smoking body was placed on a gurney, covered by a sheet, and slid into the rear of the hearse.

Afterward, the undertaker returned to the car for an inspection. Identifying the body was paramount. Somewhere, someone was waiting for word of a loved one who did not return home on a snowy evening. The car was heading southbound so perhaps this individual lived in one of a dozen small towns to the south.

In the back seat, Griffin found a single-barrel shotgun. The wooden stock was significantly damaged by fire and the intense heat caused the steel barrel to warp. He took another look around the car, his gaze eventually landing on a shiny object positioned on a ledge of the door frame, just forward of the front passenger's seat. He recognized it as a key and when he picked it up, saw it was connected to a shoe buttoner. Griffin slid the items into his pocket.[15]

He continued his examination by turning to the exterior, finding the right rear tire was flat. He didn't have a clue if a blowout caused the car to leave the roadway or if the tire was damaged by the fire.

Walking to the front of the Chevrolet, the undertaker noticed a blanket was covering the radiator, something many people did in cold weather to prevent the water from freezing up. When he slipped off the covering, Griffin found a Masonic medallion attached near the top of the radiator.[16] Another clue to the identity of the charred corpse now awaiting transport in his hearse.

But the best clue was the car's rectangular license plate attached to the bumper. Griffin made note of the numbers and returned to the funeral home. By that time, it was nearly nine o'clock, about three hours since the blaze was noticed. As he departed the scene, the burned car was still attracting curious passersby, the snow around the vehicle now a muddy slush.

Back at the funeral home Griffin called the county court clerk's office in Jackson and was informed the Chevy's auto tag was issued in Hardin County. A second call, this one to the clerk's office in Savannah, reported the car was registered to L. B. Bingham of Saltillo.

That information prompted a call to the telephone exchange in Saltillo. And that's how my grandmother, Howard, the bank's board of directors and the rest of the townspeople in Saltillo officially learned that Boss Bingham had burned alive in a single-car crash while traveling home from Jackson on a snowy night in January.

Carl W. Thompson, a good friend of my grandfather who was also the justice of the peace, answered the call from Griffin because he owned the telephone exchange. Thompson took in the news that Boss's car had been found wrecked and burned with a body inside and immediately went next door to the bank to inform Jiggs.[17]

The two of them set out in Thompson's vehicle for Jackson within a half hour. The news traveled quickly. James E. Holland of Holland and Son Mercantile just down and across the street heard the news from a customer. He made his way to Grissom's Garage where Tom Grissom was filling up James Wiley's car with enough fuel to get to Jackson and back. Wiley's son, Jess, and Grissom were going, too. Holland asked if there was room for four and jumped in when the answer was yes. Less than an hour of hearing that Boss's fire-destroyed Chevy had been found south of Jackson, two cars carrying men who had known the head cashier most of their lives were hurtling north.[18]

In the meantime, Griffin's younger brother, Vanden, who was employed at the funeral home, visited the car at his brother's request to retrieve the burned ignition key.[19] Vanden Griffin didn't mind because he was curious about the accident. Taking note of the cabin, he saw that a section of the floorboard had burned through and through, and a tire jack and other tools had fallen onto the ground.

When the automobiles from Saltillo arrived at the blackened hulk of the burned car, the men stopped to make sure it was Boss's. They noted the familiar blanket over the radiator and the Masonic emblem. There was no doubt to any of them that this was their friend's automobile.[20]

They moved on to the funeral home, where Ewing Griffin had moved the body into the embalming room. All but Howard asked to see the remains for identification purposes. Howard testified in the trials that he did not want to see his brother's mutilated body.[21] Griffin did not question the men's motives and ushered them to the back room.

At this point, let me halt the narrative I've constructed about the day that Lytle Boss Bingham was pronounced dead to make a few observations, raise a few questions and, generally express my disbelief that January 15, 1931, ended as it did.

I have known the basic truth about my grandfather—that he did not die in 1931 but lived to create another existence for himself in Texas—since I was in college. In my adult life, not many months have passed without him coming to mind. In the past decade, as my need for answers about Boss became an obsession, few were the days I did not ponder his situation and its repercussions. I retraced his steps from Tennessee to Texas. I read and re-read more than a thousand pages of court documents. I became an amateur sleuth of census records in my quest to find the grandchildren, and sometimes, great-grandchildren, of Saltillo residents from long ago to ask if their ancestors told stories about a man named Boss.

All has led me to the embalming room of Griffin Funeral Home. I am convinced beyond doubt that what transpired there was key to The Lie's viability. This juncture is crucial to its believability. What was said at the funeral home by the men of Saltillo who rushed to Jackson for the sole purpose of viewing the remains of a charred corpse, set a precedent for other Saltillo residents. These men's voices counted for something.

Forensic science is not an interest of mine, but I've watched enough true crime television to know that identification of a burned body is not accomplished by a visual examination alone. Today, teeth would be compared to dental records, tissue collected for DNA examination and no doubt, evidence would be tested for presence of an accelerant.

But in 1931 there was no testing lab and no genetic analysis. There were only men who had known Boss Bingham most, if not, all, of their lives. Five of them looked at the burnt and blackened form of a man and confirmed that it was their friend.

I am imagining this scene in my mind, asking how did they know it was Boss?

Boss was five foot six. The legs on the body laid out before them were missing, totally burned away. In their minds did they compute how tall this corpse would be if the limbs had not been missing? Mr. Lucas, the man who's grave was robbed so that a stand-in corpse could be made available, was seventy. My grandfather was thirty-five. Was such an age difference not evident even to an untrained eye?

I have questions for the coroner. The corpse had no feet, but no remains of his shoes were found on the floorboard. Wouldn't there have been remnants, a mound of melted rubber sole or strips of crispy patent leather? Did Griffin think it odd that a man might be out on a winter's night without shoes?

The coroner's assessment that the fire had been a hot one, was indeed correct. But did it occur to him how the small interior of the 1920s model Chevrolet could be so thoroughly ravaged by flames, yet the engine of the car and the rear, including the gas tank, be unaffected? How did a fire of such intensity begin and, more importantly, how was it sustained long enough to consume flesh and bone?

In a crematorium, where bodies are intentionally reduced to ashes in a controlled setting, it takes several hours at a temperature between 1,400 and 1,800 degrees Fahrenheit.[22] But what about the compartment of a car? Was there sufficient flammable material available around the body to burn long enough to reduce bones to ash?

No, not based on Griffin's testimony in the insurance trials. That leads to consideration of an accelerant. Gasoline, which burns at more than 1,700 degrees Fahrenheit, would have worked, but the fire would have to be sustained for a considerable amount of time, perhaps more than an hour, for the legs, hands, and face to disappear.

I began this journey wanting to know the truth about my grandfather and without warning found myself contemplating burn rates of flesh and bone and how the human body flexes in reaction to fire. I was reluctant to connect dots when I didn't have the evidence but learning what I know about the condition of the corpse, I came away understanding a hard truth about my grandfather's burned car: someone, on a freezing winter's night, set the stand-in body on fire and continued to pour fuel on the corpse until the job was done. The image that came to mind was not pretty, but it was the only plausible explanation based on the science.

Back to the funeral home, the charred corpse, and the men from Saltillo. How were all these questions I have raised not problematic for the undertaker? Why did he take the word of the Saltillo men as to the identity of the corpse that was burned beyond recognition? Why did Griffin testify at the insurance trials that he believed the corpse to be "fresh," that is, alive until the flames consumed the body? Wasn't there evidence of advanced decay?

I don't have the foggiest notion. Maybe Griffin truly believed the men's earnestness, their care for a fallen friend. Or it may be as simple an explanation as those days were simpler. Questions that couldn't be answered just weren't asked.

If Griffin had suspected anything was awry, he surely would have alerted the authorities. Only two questions would have been asked: if this poor, burned soul was not Boss Bingham, then who was it? And where was Boss? That last question would expose my grandfather's getaway. Authorities would ask questions of more and more people, including Howard, my grandmother, and others, until a clearer picture emerged. A manhunt for my grandfather would begin. Buses would be stopped while Tennessee Highway Patrol officers walked down the aisle looking for him. Hitchhikers would be questioned. Boss's photo would be splashed on the pages of newspapers across the South. Indictments would surely be handed down, trials conducted, and lives interrupted by the slamming of prison doors. In this scenario, The Lie of the Bingham family would never be given form and function.

But none of that happened.

Together, these pillars of Saltillo agreed that the grotesque figure presented to them—legless, armless, with a face melted away to bone—was the one and only Lytle Boss Bingham, their banker, Sunday school director, fellow Mason, and friend.

And the Madison County coroner believed them. As to the manner of death, Griffin summed the situation in five words on the death certificate: "burned to death in car."[23]

Within six hours of a Tennessee farmer noticing a fire on the horizon, my grandfather received a break that allowed him sufficient time to get the hell out of Dodge, or Tennessee, as was the case.

WAITING FOR NEWS

Sayre, Oklahoma, is known for two icons of American life. The first is its county courthouse, an architecturally impressive building, three stories tall and featuring pairs of Tuscan columns flanking two entrances. Built in 1911, the impressive edifice acquired lasting fame when it was prominently featured in the 1940 film classic *The Grapes of Wrath*.[1]

Sayre is also a Route 66 town. The fabled stretch of asphalt, which was among the first long-distance American highways, bisects the city. The road was made famous by a 1946 recording by Nat King Cole, which features a double-time recitation of towns the highway connects. Sayre didn't get a mention in the lyrics. Nevertheless, over the decades the small town benefited from tourists that Route 66 brought its way. In the 1950s and 1960s the blacktop from Chicago to Los Angeles beckoned millions of Americans in love with the open road.

In the 1930s, however, the highway was a major thoroughfare for down-on-their-luck families seeking a new life out West after being chased from their homes and farms by either the Depression or the Dust Bowl, or both. When my grandfather went on the run in 1931 to avoid legal problems in Tennessee and to improve his health in a sunny clime, he couldn't have chosen a better town to hole up for a spell.

Gas and oil deposits were discovered in Beckham County, of which Sayre is the county seat, in 1920.[2] By the time Boss made his stop there a decade and a year later, the town's population had nearly doubled due to the oil boom, rising to 3,200. Single men abounded. There were those who worked in the oil fields and, as the Depression took hold, there were men who showed up in Sayre, located halfway between Oklahoma City and Amarillo, as they hitchhiked or hopped westbound freight cars. My ailing grandfather's arrival in Sayre in late January or February apparently drew no undue attention. Taking a room in an inexpensive boarding house, he hunkered down and waited to see what would happen.[3]

In other words, to learn if L. B. Bingham was dead and buried, or if the law was on his trail.

Following his departure from his Saltillo farm on that cold January night, Boss arrived in Jackson. Then he headed West. That's known for sure.

From the Tennessee side of the story, my grandfather caught an early-morning bus from Jackson to Memphis. The timetable from 1931 shows a Smith Motor Coach bus departing Jackson at 5:15 a.m. and arriving in Memphis about three hours later.[4] There was also a 7 a.m. bus, as well as four other scheduled trips to the city throughout the day. In the Tennessee version of his journey, he was met in Memphis by Verna, his younger sister, but he didn't stay long because he feared that sheriffs were looking for him. He soon boarded another westbound bus and was gone.

My Texas aunts, Sue and Bobbie, however, said my grandfather told them of hitchhiking from Jackson to Memphis, across Arkansas and all the way to Sayre on the far western side of Oklahoma.[5] "He got right out there and hitchhiked," Sue said.

The amount of time it took him to travel from his burned car on the side of State Route 5 to the rooming house in Sayre is pertinent because Boss's handwritten last will and testament was heard in probate court on February 6, 1931, three weeks and one day after he said goodbye to my grandmother.[6] That's important because it's a date set in stone.

The will was dated September 20, 1930, about seventeen weeks before my grandfather faked his death, but there is circumstantial evidence the will was written after the "fatal" fiery wreck and backdated to September. Of course, that was illegal, another infraction that would have been added to the charges had Boss's faked death backfired.

When the Tennessee and Texas families connected after Boss/Brooks died in 1973, the half siblings began sharing information. Each side was eager to know what the other knew about their father's exit from Saltillo and the 1930 will was a document of interest to both.

In a 1985 letter to her Tennessee relatives, Aunt Sue wrote: "He (Boss) was told that a will was needed . . . he waited for (Verna) to bring him a will to sign, and she also brought him some money."

But during my 2015 face-to-face interviews with Bobbie and Sue the women were sure their father wrote the will in Oklahoma and mailed it to Tennessee, most likely to Verna in Memphis. Meanwhile, Mary Lou Tirpak, my Tennessee aunt, informed her Texas half siblings in a 1985 letter that Uncle Jiggs found a will several days after Boss's 1931 funeral, but Mary Lou said nothing about how Jiggs came to possess it.

My grandfather's signature on the will matched his signature from insurance applications so it's obvious he signed the document. The question of when he signed, before the accident that led to his "death," or after, is another question I cannot answer with certainty. If the will was backdated, however, posting it in the mail seems the likeliest answer.

Officially, the last will and testament was found "among his valuable papers, lodged at his home . . ." That was the explanation given in the "Order of Probate" issued on that February day in court.

Probate records indicated my grandmother, Howard, and Verna, appeared in court with their attorneys Warren H. Sloan and Perry Harbert. Under Tennessee law, an unwitnessed holographic will was allowed, but at least two individuals were required to attest that the handwriting was Boss's. My grandmother, Howard, Sloan and two other men, J. C. Johnson and Raymond Smith, testified upon oath that the will was written in my grandfather's handwriting. Sloan and the two other men were described as "disinterested in the matter and not related to any of the parties." I don't know who Johnson and Smith were. They may have been depositors at the bank but records aren't clear. No matter, their assessment of Boss's handwriting was accepted by the judge.

After a week or two of dealing with the unreconciled provenance of the will, it occurred to me I was asking the wrong question. What I should have asked was why a will was so important to my grandfather? That's what I needed to know. I turned my attention to the document for a line-by-line examination.

Here's the text:

Sept. 20, 1930
Will of L. B. Bingham
Realizing the uncertainty of life and the certainty of death, I do hereby make and declare this my only and last will. I hereby bequeath to my wife, Mary L. Bingham all personal property consisting of livestock, bank stock, gin stock and Tennessee Mortgage and Loan stock, all notes and accounts and all lands held by me at my death and all insurance made payable to her and my estate and she is to pay all my debts out of said property and insurance.

I bequeath to my children Margaret Lois, Mary Lou and Lytle Brooks Bingham all life insurance made payable to them. Said insurance to be collected by a guardian later mentioned in this will and said payments to be turned over to Mary Bingham to be used as she sees fit in caring for said children and said guardian is to accept a receipt from Mary L. Bingham as a satisfactory settlement for said money as she may demand of her for the care of said children.

I do hereby constitute and appoint Mary L. Bingham and Howard Bingham executor of this will without bond. And Verna Bingham, guardian of all my children, without bond. She, having the right to release all responsibility of the insurance companies upon receipt of payments accepted by her from said insurance companies. This is done to avoid the necessity of her making bond for said insurance to said companies that they may be protected as they should in their payments to the said Verna Bingham, guardian.

This Sept. 20, 1930

L. B. Bingham

Reading the will with fresh eyes, I realized Boss may have assumed that having a will cemented his family's claim on the insurance policies. If so, this was wrong. The state could still file a claim for a portion of the payouts, which is exactly what happened.

Another point I had not pondered was why my grandfather found it necessary to name a guardian for his children when their mother was still alive? The answer was found in how the law viewed minors who received money, whether it be from inheritance or an insurance settlement. Parents are natural guardians of their offspring, but when a child came into money, a separate guardianship was required and that person accounted to the court for expenditures. The minor's assets were protected this way.

And that's why my grandfather needed a will, I believe. He wanted someone he trusted to make sure his children received what was due to them from the life insurance policies. This, of course, contradicts his departure letter to the board, where Boss wrote: "if anything should happen to me all of it (the insurance payout) is for the benefit of the people who have money in the bank." Could it be that once my grandfather put a few hundred miles between himself and Saltillo he thought better of leaving his children without support and wrote the will as a precaution?

It's possible, as is apparently anything in the Boss/Brooks story, but his last will and testament did not facilitate a quick payout. The death benefits were not readily distributed because the companies didn't believe he was dead.

Before leaving Sayre, my grandfather ordered back issues of newspapers, presumably from Memphis, Jackson, and Nashville, to determine if he was in the headlines.[7] It would be risky to order the papers under his given name. He was a fugitive, after all, and if a clerk in the newspaper circulation departments matched his name with the "L.B. Bingham" on the front pages, this information would point authorities to Sayre. My guess is somewhere in Oklahoma Boss erased his given name, replacing it with Marvin Lester Brooks.

Boss out.

Brooks in.

When the newspapers arrived, Boss Bingham was not mentioned in any of them. He was in the clear, it seemed.

By the end of February or first week of March, Brooks was again on his way to the sunny West. Looking at a road map from that period, a reasonable hitch-hiking route would have taken him to Amarillo, then across the balance of the crown of Texas to New Mexico. From there he would have been one state away from Arizona, where he supposedly was heading all along.

For whatever reason, my grandfather didn't follow that route. Perhaps he got spooked by lawmen. Perhaps he just changed his mind. Instead of west, he turned south, most likely at Amarillo, and made his way 652 miles to Corpus Christi.

There, according to the narratives of my Texas aunts, he found temporary work at a "big cow show."[8] A search of the local newspaper led me to news of the fifty-fifth annual meeting of the Texas and Southwestern Cattle Raisers' Association, a confab that occupied the front pages of the *Corpus Christi Times* during its three-day run from March 17 through 19. A favorite attraction were hundreds of purebred cattle shipped in from the famous King Ranch, along with a bathing girl revue and a parade. It's reasonable to assume my grandfather talked himself into a low-level job feeding cattle or moving cows from pen to pen.

Why Brooks detoured to Corpus Christi instead of continuing to Arizona isn't clear, but a friend he made at the cattle show became a pivotal connection, one that led him to the West Texas county where he lived and worked for the remainder of his life.

John Toliver Rutledge, known as "Tol" to his friends, was seventy-four when he met Brooks at the cattlemen's meeting.[9] I'm not sure what the older man saw in Brooks that he liked, but over the three days of the cattle exhibition the two became friends. Brooks told him his health required a semiarid locale, and Rutledge encouraged the younger man to consider moving to Sherwood, Texas, in Irion County. Rutledge claimed the climate was dry and the air was pure, just the place for a man to mend. Rutledge even promised a job on his ranch if Brooks moved there.

When the cattlemen's convention ended, Rutledge departed for home. No one knows how long Brooks remained in Corpus Christi. Perhaps he picked up odd jobs to save a bit of traveling money before hitchhiking north. According to Bobbie, Brooks told of covering the 351 miles between Corpus Christi and San Angelo in just two rides. How long he walked between the two rides isn't clear, but based on interviews with my Texas aunts, my grandfather arrived in Irion County in late April 1931, plus or minus two weeks.

Weary from his journey and weakened by his poor health, Brooks appeared at the town's general store and inquired of Rutledge, but the older man wasn't around.[10] A Sherwood rancher, Frank Emerick, was in the store that day and was so affected by the stranger's story of seeking a place to heal his body that he offered him a camping spot on Spring Creek, which ran through his ranch. Emerick provided a canvas tent, helped him with a few supplies and gave him chores when Brooks felt up to a day's work.

Brooks and Emerick remained fast friends until their passing.

There's a rich vein of irony here that even Brooks didn't recognize at first.[11] Among the first Texans my grandfather got to know was Rutledge, who had twice been sheriff of Irion County in 1897 and 1905 and Emerick, who served as the county's top lawman from 1918 until 1923. As Boss he feared being trapped by officers from Tennessee, but as Brooks he became friends with two former Texas sheriffs.

I must hand it to him, my grandfather's new persona knew how to pick friends.

TIMELINE TROUBLE

Bobbie Ann Brooks Williams, the youngest of my grandfather's daughters, born in 1942, has blue-green eyes framed by narrow oval glasses and ginger hair gathered neatly into a bun. When she spoke, Bobbie was precise with her words, no doubt a trait that served her well during her decades-long career in the office of a national oil company. Her specialty was production accounting, keeping tabs on how many barrels of oil were extracted from hundreds of wells across Texas. It was a job for a detail-oriented person and that's Bobbie.

As I planned my Texas trip, she had been an enthusiastic accomplice, helping with logistics on her end. Now we were face-to-face, my notepad in hand, and I sensed our time together was an occasion she had anticipated.

I wasn't surprised that her interview proved to be the most in-depth. Since learning when she was a girl that her father had another family in Tennessee, Bobbie remained curious about his past.

We started with an easy question: What was family life like in the Brooks household?

"It was very simple. We never went hungry, but we never had very much extra. We played outside and made our own fun. And we had friends that gave us hand-me-downs which we thought were great, because it was good-looking clothes," she said matter-of-factly.

"Of course, we didn't have indoor plumbing until I got out of high school. We had an old two-holer, with spiders and wasps and everything that came with it.

"We helped on the farm. We all picked cotton and hoed cotton for weeds. We gathered watermelons and gathered the eggs. I milked some but I didn't have to milk as much as the other two," she said, referring to her older siblings, Sue and Freddie.

Hog slaughtering time was important on the farm because pork was a large part of the family's diet, Bobbie said. After the first freeze in the fall, the family made a day of butchering hogs fattened up for the occasion. First, the animal was killed and bled, followed by a baptism of the carcass in scalding water, which loosened the pig's wiry hair for scraping off.

"Any time there was a hog kill we helped with the scraping."

Similar duty was required when chicken was on the menu. Bobbie said her mother was the executioner of the hens, but the kids were given feather-picking duty. It was the same when her dad or Freddie was successful at turkey hunting.

Venison was another matter. "We didn't have much to do on deer. I don't know where they got them processed, but we didn't have much deer meat. Mostly, we had pork at our meal."

Bobbie said her parents made a good pair. In hard times they made do with what they had. They found joy in simple things, watching sunsets, playing ball with the kids, playing card games.

Her parents met in September 1935, not quite five years after my grandfather left Tennessee, Bobbie said. Elizabeth (Hootsie) Freeman was a "cook and bottle washer" on a neighboring ranch. Brooks, still living in a tent on the bank of Spring Creek, had recuperated enough from TB to put in a day's work and, apparently, to become a suitor.

Hootsie hailed from Stephens County, northwest of Abilene, where she was the ninth of ten children, a brood of six boys and four girls, all born in a fifteen-year span between 1902 and 1917.[1] Her father, a rancher, had the unusual given name of Nofflette, but he was known, as many men were, by his initials, N. F. Her mother, Carrie, died in October 1918, a month before the youngest baby, a daughter named Nora Lee, turned one-year-old. Hootsie was three when her mother died. She had an older sister, Ethel, who was six. Because of their mother's death when they were quite young, the three youngest girls formed a tight bond growing up and they lived their lives within a two-hour drive of one another. Hootsie lived in Irion County, while Ethel lived in San Angelo in adjacent Tom Green County. Nora Lee moved farther west to Pecos County after she married.

Hootsie received her nickname at the ranch where she worked, but no one knew the origin story. "She had a bubbly personality so maybe that had something to do with it. We don't know," Bobbie said.

The courtship began with an introduction by a mutual friend, Bill Miller, who also had a girlfriend and, more importantly, an automobile.[2] On weekend nights the two couples often double-dated, with Brooks pitching in gas money. Love blossomed quickly between the lean, quiet man from Tennessee and Hootsie, a round-faced, wide-smiling woman who turned twenty-one just before Brooks proposed marriage in early 1936. If friends or family thought the divide of fourteen years in their ages was too far, there's no record of their objections. It would be more than three and a half decades later before Hootsie learned her husband was almost twenty years older than her. Of course, she would learn much about her husband that she did not know.

A justice of the peace married them on May 30, 1936, and the newlyweds moved into the hotel in Sherwood for several months until Brooks, who was still working on the Emerick Ranch, installed a floor in the creek side tent and made improvements to a one-room structure built next to the tent.[3] That was their start in wedded life.

Reminiscing about her dad always brought a certain image to mind, Bobbie said. Inevitably, he's wearing his Texas rancher's uniform: khaki pants and a long-sleeved shirt, with a pair of scuffed brogans on his size six-and-a-half feet, except for when he was working around the muddy livestock pens. At such times he wore high-top rubber boots.

"I don't think I saw my dad in a suit but twice, well, three times. There's three weddings," Bobbie said, referencing the marriages of Sue, Freddie and herself.

"He would give me a nickel to wash his stinky feet. I don't know how old I was, four or five. He let me shave him with a straight razor. He was brave," she said.

All the Brooks children learned the rudiments of driving on the family's 1948 Farmall Model B tractor. After mastering the tractor, they advanced to the Chevy pickup. Bobbie hadn't forgotten the first-time thrill of driving the truck by herself, sitting on the edge of the seat so her foot could reach the gas and brake pedals. On one occasion Sue, Freddie and her mother were out of town for a few days. "Daddy and I were the only ones at home. So, I was going up to the post office and getting the mail every day in the pickup by myself. Mama got home and I said, 'Daddy can I go get the mail?' Mama looked at me and said, 'What are you talking about?' Hootsie listened with a mixture of disbelief and horror that Brooks had allowed a ten-year-old girl to get behind the wheel. "She liked to have died," Bobbie said.

"She's a good driver," was her father's retort.

Bobbie said her father's personality was more serious than Hootsie's, which she described as "outgoing."

"I wouldn't call him an affectionate father. He was a quiet person around me, but he was always there. And you could always depend on him. He had many very close friends. I don't know if he confided in them or not, but they would do anything for him, and he would do anything for them. His handshake was as good as gold. Very few things were done with a written document. It was a handshake."

His reputation, she remembered, was tested once when he mistakenly signed his last name as "Bingham" on a check he wrote at a San Angelo store. "After he left, he realized he had signed the wrong name and he went to the bank. I can't remember the names of the bank presidents and vice presidents, but he went to one of them and said, 'I wrote a check and it's going to have the wrong name on it, would you cash it, run it through.' They said sure. As far as I know, they never asked him why." Bobbie was not surprised at the bank's reaction. "It was still West Texas and I think there was probably a lot of people in town might have had a life they had put behind them."

As for her father's past, Bobbie learned the truth in 1972 after Brooks suffered a stroke. His decision to leave Saltillo was somewhat of a committee-like decision, Bobbie explained. The getaway was planned by five men, including a doctor and "someone connected to the bank," but she couldn't remember their names. Howard was there, as was her father. There were two other men, but she didn't remember anything her father said about them.

"He said he was going to die because he had that tuberculosis and they felt it would be better if he moved West to try to survive. Well, he was going to die anyway, so he thought, let's do this. In my mind, it was presented to him, and he didn't see any reason not to because of the condition of the bank and his health."

"He said they had gotten up the replacement body and said who the name was, but he didn't say who dug it up. To me he didn't," Bobbie said.

"What was your reaction?" I asked.

"It would be like shock," she said.

"He hated that he had to do what he did, and he hated that we didn't ever know anything. He wanted to make amends, but what can you do? After he told his side of the story this is the only thing that could have been done. I didn't consider any of it illegal but then I found out some of it was."

Regarding Bobbie's bedside conversation with my grandfather in the hospital, two aspects were of great interest to me. One was also very disturbing.

My grandfather told her that over the years he wanted to return to Tennessee. "Oh yes, he would have loved to have seen his family, but he knew the risk he would take and the lives that would be turned upside down if he tried it. I don't think he dared go back," she said.

Brooks told his daughter that he kept up with events in Tennessee through his sister, Verna, who lived in Memphis. Their correspondence didn't survive, for obvious reasons. "As far as I know he destroyed (the letters), burned them, whatever. I never saw evidence of any contact. I do know he had a box number in San Angelo that he would check every time he'd come (there) and that's how people would contact him."

Once again, I was pleased to hear of my grandfather's interest in his Tennessee family. I wondered if he ever came close to getting on a Greyhound bus in San Angelo headed east, if only to see his Tennessee family from a distance.

My grandfather, however, did have face-to-face contact with his brother, Howard, on one occasion, Bobbie insisted. Based on interviews with Tennessee relatives, I had also heard of this secret meeting between the siblings.

"After their dad died and supposedly things were settled, he brought him some money. I never knew the exact amount, but I heard it was like four hundred dollars," Bobbie said. The money, I assumed, would have represented proceeds of land sold following my Great-Grandfather James Morgan Bingham's death in 1940.

Bobbie noted that during this visit, Howard brought a letter from my grandmother. "Yes, that's when he brought a letter that Mary had written to say that, you know, we're just going to have to start new lives," Bobbie said. Sue told me the same story in her interview, but something about this 1940 meeting seemed off-kilter, but I couldn't reason why in the moment.

Later, checking the "Boss chronology" I had assembled over the past decade, I understood why Bobbie's story was disconcerting.

The narrative told on the Bingham side regarding the dissolution of my grandparents' marriage is very different. After living about a year in Texas, my grandfather asked my grandmother to join him. Mary replied she couldn't leave because private detectives working for the insurance companies were tracking her every move. In return, she begged him to return to Tennessee, even if it meant facing criminal charges. By 1932, a year after her husband headed West, my grandmother "was tired of living a lie." This information is based on what Howard told my brother, Steve, in 1977.

My grandfather was not interested in returning to Saltillo, Howard added. Boss/Brooks feared he would bring ruin and shame not only to the Bingham family, but to many of their friends. Howard said his older brother wrote that it was better if the suffering was limited to one family than a host of others. According to Bingham oral history, my grandmother's 1932 reply to her absent husband was a letter declaring each of them was free to begin new lives apart from each other.

But if the date of that homemade divorce decree was 1940, as my Texas aunts described, this presents a serious timeline problem.

By 1940 my grandfather had been married to Hootsie for four years and was the father of one child (Sue) and had a son (Freddie) on the way. Had my grandfather been so indifferent to the plight of my grandmother and his Tennessee daughters and son that he could blithely start a new family in Texas without sending word to Saltillo?

It goes without saying that if someone on either side of the family had saved correspondence between my grandparents, I wouldn't find myself in the unwanted position of once again sorting another contentious point in my family's story.

I'll be frank. Even though I don't have definitive proof (i.e., her divorce letter) of when my grandmother gave up on her marriage, I support the 1932 version if for no other reason than Howard knew my grandmother well. If he heard her say she was "tired of living a lie," then he was certain that reconciling the marriage was a nonstarter. All that I knew of my grandmother's sensibilities told me the same.

I understood why these letters were surreptitiously delivered, and destroyed, but can't a twenty-first century granddaughter solving her family's ninety-four-year-old mystery catch a break? Apparently not.

My interview with Bobbie came to a close as she illuminated interesting details about Brooks, the grandfather I never knew. For instance, his mathematical prowess was impressive. He could add a column of five-digit numbers in his head.

Brooks sometimes sipped a beer, but only if a friend stopped by with a six-pack.

He lost his county commission seat in 1960 due to alleged voter fraud by another candidate who had been a good friend.

Finally, TB symptoms plagued him past middle age.

"When we were kids, he would get to coughing and he would get up on his hands and knees like a baby, and he would cough and cough and cough," she said.

I was very interested in Bobbie's information, particularly about the night at the hospital when she listened to her father talk about his transition from Boss to Brooks. The details of his life, his habits, were also helpful, giving form to this man I had traveled so far to know.

But the question raised about the letter of divorce bothered me. I wanted definitive answers, but feared I was on a fool's errand because I couldn't corroborate information. Should I even be on this journey, I asked myself. Why did I care about this man who abandoned my grandmother, who wasn't around to see his namesake, my father, grow up to be a great dad to my brother and me, a loving grandfather to our children?

In my mind I momentarily left Boss, Brooks, whoever he was, on his knees, head bent to the floor, coughing uncontrollably, questioning if I would ever understand this man who left Tennessee for Texas back in that god-awful year of 1931.

Lytle Boss Bingham poses for a photo at Hardin County Bank, circa 1929.

This photo is believed to have been taken in 1918 when Boss was completing his studies in Kentucky.

Boss gathers his children in his lap. Margaret Lois is on the left, Mary Lou is on the right and Lytle, the youngest, is in the middle, circa the summer of 1930.

Boss holds Margaret Lois, his first born. They are standing next to the family's car, a Chevy, circa 1924.

This remarkably sweet moment was captured around 1915, while Boss and Mary Louise were still dating.

Mary Louise Bingham strikes a pose outside her home, circa mid-1930s.

Hardin County Courthouse, site of the insurance trials of 1932. This photo was taken in the 1930s. The building later burned and was replaced with a new building. Photo courtesy of the Hardin County Historical Society.

The 1931 death certificate for L. B. Bingham was issued after friends identified the burned body.

STATE OF TEXAS 226-01-2 118-00	CERTIFICATE OF DEATH	15613

1. PLACE OF DEATH		2. USUAL RESIDENCE (Where deceased lived, If Institution residence before admission)
a. COUNTY Tom Green		a. STATE Texas b. COUNTY Irion
b. CITY OR TOWN (If outside city limits, give precinct no.) San Angelo	c. LENGTH OF STAY in 1 b. 1 week	c. CITY OR TOWN (If outside city limits, give precinct no.) Sherwood
d. NAME OF HOSPITAL OR INSTITUTION St. Johns Hospital		d. STREET ADDRESS (If rural, give location)
e. IS PLACE OF DEATH INSIDE CITY LIMITS? YES ☒ NO ☐		e. IS RESIDENCE INSIDE CITY LIMITS? YES ☒ NO ☐ f. IS RESIDENCE ON A FARM? YES ☐ NO ☒
3. NAME OF DECEASED (Type or print) (a) First MARVIN	(b) Middle LESTER	(c) Last BROOKS 4. DATE OF DEATH February 12, 1973
5. SEX Male	6. COLOR OR RACE White	7. Married ☒ Never Married ☐ Widowed ☐ Divorced ☐	8. DATE OF BIRTH September 14, 1900	9. AGE (In years last birthday) 72	If UNDER 1 YEAR Months Days	If UNDER 24 HRS Hours Minutes
10a. USUAL OCCUPATION (Give kind of work done during most of working life, even if retired) Stock Farmer	10b. KIND OF BUSINESS OR INDUSTRY Agricultural	11. BIRTHPLACE (State or foreign country) Tennessee	12. CITIZEN OF WHAT COUNTRY? U.S.A.
13. FATHER'S NAME Unknown		14. MOTHER'S MAIDEN NAME Unknown
15. WAS DECEASED EVER IN U.S. ARMED FORCES? (Yes, no, or unknown) (If yes, give war or dates of service) No	16. SOCIAL SECURITY NO. 466-50-1220	17. INFORMANT Mrs. M.L. Brooks

TEXAS DEPARTMENT OF HEALTH

RECD. MAR 5 1973

BUREAU OF VITAL STATISTICS

			INTERVAL BETWEEN ONSET AND DEATH
18. CAUSE OF DEATH	IMMEDIATE CAUSE (a) Cerebral vascular accident with		
	which gave rise to DUE TO (b) right hemiplegia		7 days
above cause (a). DUE TO (c)			
PART II. OTHER SIGNIFICANT CONDITIONS CONTRIBUTING TO DEATH BUT NOT RELATED TO THE TERMINAL DISEASE CONDITION GIVEN IN PART I(a)			19. WAS AUTOPSY PERFORMED? YES ☐ NO ☒
Mild right hemiplegia (5-3-69)			

20a. ACCIDENT ☐ SUICIDE ☐ HOMICIDE ☐	20b. DESCRIBE HOW INJURY OCCURRED, (Enter nature of injury in Part I or Part II of Item 18.)				
20c. TIME OF INJURY	Hour a.m. p.m.	Month	Day	Year	
20d. INJURY OCCURRED WHILE AT WORK ☐ NOT WHILE AT WORK ☐	20e. PLACE OF INJURY (e.g., in or about home, farm, factory, street, office building, etc.)	20f. CITY, TOWN, OR LOCATION San Angelo	COUNTY Tom Green	STATE Texas
21. I hereby certify that I attended the deceased from 9-14-61 19 to 2-12-73 19 and last saw the deceased alive on 2-11-73 19 Death occurred at 4:30 A.m. on the date stated above, and to the best of my knowledge, from the causes stated.					
22a. SIGNATURE (signature)	22b. Degree or title M.D.	22b. ADDRESS 14 S. Jefferson, SanAngelo, Tex			22c. DATE SIGNED 2-21-73
23a. BURIAL, CREMATION, REMOVAL (Specify) Burial	23b. DATE February 13, 1973	23c. NAME OF CEMETERY OR CREMATORY Sherwood Cemetery			
23d. LOCATION (City, town, or county)		24. FUNERAL DIRECTOR'S SIGNATURE			

The 1973 death certificate for Marvin Lester Brooks was issued
after he died from a stroke.

Mary Louise Brooks Bingham in a photo taken a few years before she died in 1971.

Brooks and Hootsie pose for a photo at their Texas home, circa 1962.

Author Kathy Bingham Turner (far left) poses with her Texas relatives. Next to her, from left are Linda Brooks (wife of Freddie), Sue Crow, Freddie Brooks, and Bobbie Williams. Photo by Leon Alligood.

Sonny pulls in his sisters for a photo during a family gathering in Girvin, where he's lived for many years. Photograph by Leon Alligood.

Bobbie Williams and Kathy Bingham Turner pause to look at Spring Creek. Photo by Leon Alligood.

Kathy follows her aunts into a field on their way to find the location of Brooks' creek side camping spot. Photo by Leon Alligood.

Looking toward Spring Creek from the location of where Brooks camped out for several years after his arrival in Texas. Photo by Leon Alligood.

At the Sherwood Cemetery in Texas, Bobbie and Sue point out graves of family and friends. Photo by Leon Alligood.

The final resting place for Marvin Lester Brooks and his wife, Elizabeth (Hootsie). Photo by Roger Gant.

This photo of Marvin Lester Brooks is on his tombstone in Sherwood, Texas. Photo by Roger Gant.

This simple headstone at Shady Grove Cemetery in Saltillo is only a memorial to the man who left Tennessee in 1931. Photo by Leon Alligood.

Mary Louise Bingham chose to bury her daughter, Margaret Lois, in a different section of the cemetery than near her father's false grave. When Mary died, she chose to be buried next to her daughter.

Verna was her brother's confidant and protector when he fled Saltillo for Texas. Here she's seen in a circa 1930s photo.

After high school, Mary Lou moved to Nashville to attend a business school. She's posing in front of The Parthenon, circa 1946.

A view of Saltillo's Main Street in 1931, looking west from the Tennessee
River to downtown. Hardin County Bank is in the distance on the left.
Photo courtesy of the Hardin County Historical Society.

SIFTING THROUGH NUMBERS

Eustace Atherton Jackson appreciated the abstract beauty of numbers. The Memphis native enjoyed sifting through them, totaling columns of figures, reconciling one sum to another. After high school, he tried a few jobs, but none suited him until he was hired as a clerk at Memphis Trust Co., not the biggest bank in the city, but a good place to begin a career.[1]

However, the day-to-day routine of the banking business—cashing checks, accepting deposits, and greeting customers—grew tiresome. Jackson apparently wanted to swim in numbers, not wet his toes. So, he became an auditor for the state. Banks were required to have their books examined on a routine basis. Jackson became the man who was given access to the annual, monthly, and weekly reports showing how much money was taken in, how much was loaned out, how much cash was on hand and how much was deposited in other banks to earn interest. And he was given access to the holy grail of banking, the ledgers, the day-to-day accounting of additions and subtractions to individual customers' accounts. By the end of his stay, Jackson prepared his report, a grade, if you will, of the bank's viability, of whether the institution was doing right by its customers. Exceptions to best practices earned a reprimand that was accompanied by orders such as to change accounting procedures or reduce loan volumes or do a better job of collecting on bad debts.

Banking in the 1930s was very much a paper-centric business. There were no computers, and creating a spread sheet, although that term didn't come to the dictionary until the 1950s, was a labor-intensive affair that might take more than a day to compile. Jackson enjoyed the work that many would call tedious, even if the banks under his scrutiny probably didn't appreciate his attention to detail. When his duties moved from banks that were "going concerns" to "closed banks," whose doors had been shuttered due to mismanagement or malfeasance, Jackson found his talents for sifting through numbers appreciated and in demand.

By the time he was summoned in mid-January 1931 to examine the remains of Hardin County Bank, Jackson, forty-six, had performed forensic examinations of ten failed Tennessee banks.[2] One had been a large Memphis bank. The others were small-town concerns.

My grandfather left Saltillo on Wednesday night, January 14. His burned car was found the next morning and a funeral was held on Friday. Jackson was on his way to Hardin County from his Memphis home as the graveside service for my grandfather was conducted.

Judging by the size of the bank in Saltillo, the experienced auditor surmised the job would take five days to sort through the books. Perhaps less. Before leaving home, he probably told his wife that he would return in a week. However, Jackson was not prepared for the condition in which he found Hardin County Bank.[3]

On Saturday morning the sun barely made an appearance in the overcast sky above the Tennessee River and the temperature at dawn hovered near twenty degrees.[4] Winter's grip held firm. The sun stayed hidden for much of the day and the thermometer rose slowly into the low forties, but with an ever-present wind coming off the river, the air felt much colder.

Saltillo's mercantile owners opened their stores for what was usually the busiest shopping day of the week. Folks who lived in the country often came to town only on Saturdays. Hardin County Bank would often be on the list of stops to be made, yet the bank door was locked. The bank had not been open since Wednesday morning when Boss's death was announced, and the board of directors received my grandfather's letter in which he took the blame for the bank's woes. Speculation was rampant. Everyone asked if their money was safe? Jackson would be the one to say. He had faced questions like this from anxious depositors in other locations, but the auditor wouldn't have quick answers for the folks in Saltillo. His examination of the Hardin County Bank records would be unlike any other inspection assigned to him.

This became obvious upon entering the interior of the forty foot by thirty foot brick building. Papers—official bank correspondence, loan documents, news-papers—were piled without order on a wooden table, on the floor, on Boss's oak desk, stacked a foot and a half high in some places. The place was dirty. Every object in the bank, from the wooden teller's station that stretched across the front of the room, to the cantankerous Burroughs ledger printing machine that set to the left of Boss's desk, to the plastered walls on which dozens of various notices had been tacked, was coated with dust and grime.[5] Of all the backwater banks Jackson had audited, this one was certainly unique. Taking in the view, two conclusions were apparent to the auditor: this bank had not been properly run for some time . . . and he wasn't returning to Memphis any time soon.

Indeed, Hardin County Bank was a mess.[6] As Jackson began to gather and sort papers collected from every corner of the room, even the simplest of tasks proved problematic. For instance, practically all the ledger sheets he found did not mark the year for which the transactions covered, leaving him to deduce the chronological order based on clues found in the purchases. For instance, a payment to a fertilizer merchant indicated spring. Nor were the ledger sheets confined to one binder but were scattered about the bank with no apparent reason to explain why they weren't bound together.

The bank vault was in a rear corner of the office.[7] The door, manufactured by Steel National Co., was about a yard wide and about six feet tall. It was six inches thick and framed by steel panels on each side. The door opened to a small room containing a Mosler safe, forty inches tall, forty inches wide, with an interior that was a little more than two feet deep. Empty of documents, the safe weighed an estimated 800 pounds and was so heavy that it was positioned first and then the vault door with its steel-reinforced frame was installed.

Jackson found the vault also cluttered and dirty. Scattered about were all manner of official bank papers treated as if they were awaiting a janitor to bag them up for the trash. Each piece required examination to reconstruct the data.

At the end of the first week, an exhausted Jackson paused to take stock of what the heck had happened at Hardin County Bank. This was not like other banks he had audited, such as American Savings Bank in Memphis where a cashier (Henochsberg, mentioned in Chapter 9) shorted accounts of wealthy customers over a period of years. Sorting that one was easy, primarily because the cashier called a bank director and admitted the defalcation. Shortly after hanging up the phone, the embezzler killed himself. When Jackson began his work at American Savings, the dead cashier's confession served to inform the auditor where to look for evidence of misappropriated funds. After confirmation, his next task was double-checking to make sure fraud did not extend to other accounts. That investigation was a matter of following the evidence.

On the other hand, the apparent negligence of recordkeeping he found at the Saltillo bank made no sense.[8] The typical client was a boom-or-bust farmer, not a wealthy business owner and the bank was capitalized at a lowly $15,000. It was true that Boss Bingham, before his death, composed a letter taking responsibility for the bank's insolvency, but he didn't admit to pilfering accounts per se. He admitted only to attempting repair of the bank's losses, without success, and, of course, buying insurance policies whose death benefits, he hoped, would be enough to make amends. So, what was Jackson searching for in this sea of disorganization? One week in, he didn't know.

All he knew was that Hardin County Bank had been mismanaged for months.[9] No transactions from the previous four to five weeks had been posted. No deposits, no withdrawals, no loan payments. For a bank to go that long without reconciling accounts was derelict; it was like a pusher boat captain of modern times trying to thread a tow of barges through heavy fog on the Tennessee River without using sonar to keep the vessel in deep water. Eventually, luck faded and consequences began. Two weeks after my grandfather disappeared, Jackson was rib-deep in the consequences of a bank that seemingly did not give a tinker's damn for numbers.

A little more than a month earlier, the board met for their annual meeting and Boss informed them the bank had cash reserves of $11,000 and stock capital had earned 11 percent growth. They accepted the report. These were the most successful men in Saltillo, but all had been duped. Jackson thought it very odd they didn't detect anything awry.

Among the transgressions was a significant shortage in the Hardin County Trustee's account. In that era, the county trustee sent tax notices to the bank, and Boss was supposed to withdraw the taxes from individual accounts and transfer the funds to the county's account.

Instead, a number of these notices, or receipts, as they were called, were not charged at all to dozens of taxpayers even though the county's account was credited, on paper, with nearly $5,000 in payments.[10] Jackson discovered the misdirected tax receipts in two envelopes among the mountain of accumulated papers in my grandfather's office.

Depositors' records were equally confounding.[11] Bank customers presented the auditor with their pass books as proof of their debits and deposits. The passbooks were palm-size notebooks on which transactions were recorded. The balance in an individual's passbook was supposed to match what the bank ledger had on record for that account. However, as Jackson immersed himself in the jumbled records of Hardin County Bank, he learned a great many accounts were wildly out of whack. A Saltillo woman claimed her account should have more than $6,000. The audit, however, revealed a balance of only $500, the loss blamed on my grandfather. Those kinds of discrepancies were easier to assign blame to than cases like that of a widow named Mary Smith. After notification that her account was overdrawn by nearly $300, Smith vehemently denied the allegation. She told Jackson her overdraft was limited to $4.09, and she had deposited into Boss's hands an equal amount to settle the matter. Smith told the auditor she moved her money to a bank in Savannah soon thereafter.

Sure enough, just as the widow Smith claimed, Jackson found her small overdraft had been settled and her account was closed, yet the remainder of the ledger sheet bearing her name contained dozens of transactions. After a half-day of digging, Jackson discovered that transactions for a man named R. C. Smith had mistakenly been entered on the woman's ledger sheet. So, there was an overdraft, just the wrong Smith was responsible.

In another example, accounts for two different families with the last name of Watson were frequently mixed up.[12] Checks written by one family were debited on the other family's account and vice versa. It was the same for deposits. The Watson families, understandably, were quite surprised when Jackson unearthed the discrepancies.

Part of the problem was the most modern piece of equipment in the bank: the Burroughs ledger posting machine.[13] Less than five years old, the machine was often used by small and large banks. It was a workhorse, bringing order to ledgers, getting rid of problems caused by poor penmanship. That was true, however, only when the printing ribbon was changed as needed. Hardin County Bank's ledger printer had needed a new ribbon for some time, maybe even for more than a year. The printing was dim and uneven. The numeral "eight" often couldn't be distinguished from a "three." More than once, Jackson fumed about the printer, but all he could do was to hold a magnifying glass close and make a guess.

But the ledger printer had nothing to do with problems in some accounts.[14] For example, Carl W. Thompson, owner of the Saltillo Telephone Exchange, initially claimed his business didn't have an account at the bank, but Jackson found plenty of cleared checks for the phone company. Thompson later "found" a passbook showing a balance of several hundred dollars instead of an overdraft of nearly a thousand. Jackson got nowhere in sorting out the account to Thompson's satisfaction and told him he'd have his day in court.

The auditor found dozens and dozens of inaccuracies among depositors' records. Customers' checks were undercharged, that is, a check would be written for twenty dollars, but only ten dollars was debited from the account. Other accounts were overcharged: someone wrote a check for ten dollars, but twenty dollars was deducted from their account. These issues were not an obvious indication of fraud so much as they were an indictment of slipshod accounting, Jackson fumed.[15]

Bank customers frequently interrupted the auditor in his work to make inquiries and, to his credit, the Memphian took the time to see what his search had revealed.[16] After a few customers learned their account balances had decreased, rumors circulated that Jackson was altering balances, which led to contentious meetings with unhappy account holders. In some cases, the customers came to agree with the auditor's figures; other customers decided to take their chances in court.

As Jackson brought order to the Hardin County Bank records, he found a disturbing pattern in my grandfather's personal account.[17] Discovering the situation, Jackson was unsure if he was correctly interpreting the numbers, so he sought a second opinion. He turned to Thomas Stanphill. A former cashier at a Mississippi bank, Stanphill, 38, tall and mustachioed, had been appointed liquidating agent by the state banking office about a week after Jackson was named auditor. The liquidating agent's job was to officially close the bank's books, identifying those with overdrafts, initiating the foreclosure of properties and, generally, trying to decrease the losses and increase payments to depositors. Stanphill, by all accounts, was a pleasant man who had the ability to execute a most unpleasant duty with compassion, but in accordance with the law. He got along with local folks well enough that when the job ended in 1933, he and his family continued to live in the area.

Stanphill perused the ledger entries of L. B. Bingham that Jackson held out for inspection, and he agreed the numbers did not lie.[18] My grandfather was cooking the books for sure, but certainly not in a clever way. When a ledger sheet became full, the balance from the bottom of the full sheet was supposed to be transferred to the top of the next ledger sheet. On his personal account, Boss ignored the balance from the full sheet and on the top of the new sheet entered a positive balance.

For example, in late 1930, the final entry on his account's ledger sheet indicated a negative balance of $5,740.09, which should be noted, was a small fortune in the Depression.[19] The next ledger sheet inexplicably began with a balance of $117.59. This was not a one-time mistake. Another full sheet showed an overdraft of $2,797 but the balance carried forward to the next sheet detailed a balance of thirty dollars even. In fact, Boss's account had positive balances at the top of ledger sheets only to have the column of numbers turn negative at the bottom numerous times in 1930. By the time my grandfather departed Saltillo, his personal account was overdrawn by more than $9,000.

The audit of Hardin County Bank took five and a half weeks, the longest time it had ever taken Jackson to reconcile a bank's records, a fact the Memphian no doubt spoke of for the remainder of his life.[20] His inventory to the State Department of Insurance and Banking presented the findings in thirty-one typed pages. Named were 108 individuals who still owed loans cumulatively valued at slightly more than $21,000. A total of 124 accounts were found to be overdrawn, the smallest in error by two cents and the largest, my grandfather's, by $9,756.71. Boss's overdraft accounted for nearly one-half of all the overdrafts uncovered by the audit.

The largest category of errors, however, was one called "irregularities and omissions," which totaled $36,087.85.[21] This was a catch-all category, where Jackson, for instance, enumerated discrepancies between depositors' passbooks and the ledgers, aberrations he was unable to reconcile. The biggest depositors, naturally, resisted any attempt to discount what they believed was owed to them by the bank. They were left to deal with Stanphill, the liquidating agent, long after Jackson had moved on to the next failed bank in need of reconciliation. Stanphill took his job seriously. Consequently, there were numerous trials which pitted Jackson's carefully crafted columns of figures against depositors who claimed they had more cash in the bank than records showed. Stanphill always testified to the veracity of Jackson's numbers.

Most of the liquidating agent's time, however, was spent dealing with foreclosures, and it's this part of his job that gives me pause. Whether my grandfather was an embezzler or an inept bookkeeper, the consequences of what happened at Hardin County Bank from 1928 to 1931 ruined many families.

After the bank closed, the majority of the bank's customers were visited by process servers or received mailed notices informing them that their debts to Hardin County Bank were due. Saltillo residents scrambled to come up with cash.

Dozens of pleas from desperate customers facing foreclosure were received by the bank's attorney, E. W. Ross. Reading them left me blinking away tears.

A Methodist minister, W. C. Baker, who owed $78.81, wrote that he couldn't pay because he hadn't made a living wage in three years, was recovering from a major operation and he "was on the very brink of having a nervous breakdown."[22]

Adrienne Irwin reached out to Ross on behalf of her sister, Kate Dudley, who was delinquent on a loan. Irwin told Ross that the woman "hasn't a dollar in the world, no income and it will be impossible for her to pay this note."[23]

Eleven friends of E. O. Edwards, a farmer, sought mercy on his behalf. The petitioners asked that Ross "consider the times, the Depression and hardships before selling Mr. Edward's property."[24]

Ross was understanding but firm. "We have no discretion in the matter of these collections. The bank matter must be settled," was his standard reply.

A farmer named Arch White, who lived several miles out of Saltillo, owed $158.06. In a court-ordered agreement he pledged to pay off the debt by selling "two horse mules, one a dark bay, about nine years old . . . and the other, a light bay about nine years old . . . and being the only mules I own."[25] In addition, White was letting go of his Weber log wagon.

The farmer displayed a measure of moxie, however, negotiating to delay the auction of his animals and wagon, which was manufactured in Chicago and advertised in its day as the "King of all farm wagons." His debt would not be due until the fall of 1933 after harvesting one last crop of cotton on five acres of river bottomland he rented from a relative.

How bittersweet and frustrating that job must have been for White, working in the searing heat of a Tennessee summer, fighting boll weevils, worrying about the price of cotton and knowing, all the while, that every bead of sweat on his brow would not yield money in his pocket. Instead, the proceeds of the harvest and the auction of his beloved mules and wagon, would be applied to the debt at the bank.

If he were lucky, the debt would be paid, and he could start over.

I am left to wonder if White thought of my grandfather while tending those five acres of cotton. Was Boss his friend or foe?

For the board of directors, Jackson's inventory of the assets and liabilities of Hardin County Bank offered a victory, of sorts. When he took the job as head cashier, the bank took out a performance bond on my grandfather, paying a premium of about fifty dollars every year. This was an insurance policy that promised to pay $10,000 as a hedge against irresponsible and illegal action by Boss. The company, the United States Fidelity and Guaranty Co., stalled in paying at first, but after Jackson issued his report, the company dropped its resistance, and a check was promptly issued. $10,000 didn't make up the losses, but it was a start.

More than a year after his work in Saltillo was done, Jackson returned to Hardin County to give a deposition in the insurance trials. He was asked: "In the number of banks, large and small, audited by you, how did the condition of this bank and the way its books and records were kept, compare?"

The auditor from Memphis did not hesitate in his reply: "No doubt the worst I have ever seen, I will say."[26]

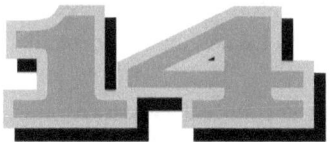

THE VANISHING LETTER

MAY 7, 2015: BROOKS

Several nights a month, Freddie Brooks gathered with friends for a round of poker. They've played for years. Nothing serious about the betting but he enjoyed the challenge, Freddie said. Some nights he won the pot and sometimes he folded.

Although my uncle didn't inherit his father's lean face, Freddie's bluish eyes offered the same studied look of concentration seen in the photo of Boss seated at his desk in the bank. At the poker table, I'm guessing that look, combined with the firm-set jaw of the war-tested Marine that he was, served Freddie well. No one knew his hand until he laid out his cards.

As I interviewed him, I often saw this serious look. Seated in a straight-backed chair, comfortably unperturbed, Freddie sometimes paused after a question, fixed his eyes on a point outside the window and then spoke. There was no doubt he possessed the faculty for telling a story. He stayed on topic, resisting the urge to chase details that were not germane to the narrative he was crafting. I wondered if this was how my grandfather told stories.

He wore a short-sleeved, blue-checkered shirt tucked neatly over his rounded stomach into a pair of khaki pants. His hair, cropped short and parted on the right, was the white of eggshells and his chubby cheeks were slightly ruddy. If his voice had offered an Irish lilt, one could easily believe Freddie was from County

Cork, but his drawl quickly identified him as Texan, through and through. He peered at the world through large round glasses and his dark eyebrows sat like two thin dashes below a wide brow.

Freddie retired after four decades of selling International Harvester trucks at a dealership in San Angelo. He doesn't like to travel and acknowledged he's left Texas very few times. The notable exception was 1966 when he was drafted into the Marines at the age of twenty-six, much older than most of the other inductees, who were eighteen and nineteen.

Freddie, the second oldest of my grandfather's Texas children, surprised me with his answer to the first question.

"Would you state your name, age and where you live?"

His reply began: "My name is Freddie Lester Brooks . . . "

With this utterance I learned that Brooks passed along the middle name of his new identity to his oldest son. After my grandfather left Saltillo in the winter of 1931, headed West, he changed his name to Marvin Lester Brooks. Lester was the name of my grandmother's brother and Brooks was her maiden name. So, there were two Lester Brooks in the world, each with a connection to my grandfather . . . and to me.

Freddie had more surprises in store.

He was born in September of 1940, sharing the same birth month of his father. His sister, Sue, was two when he was born and his parents had been married for four years. Freddie understood as a teen that his family came from less than modest means, but Freddie said he never felt deprived in any respect. Besides, many in Sherwood lived their lives clinging to the necessities of shelter, food, and work, he noted.

"We had no television, no running water. Daddy and Mama played softball with us, and volleyball, cards, a lot of dominoes. We had to do a lot of family entertaining together," he said. Every Saturday evening the family gathered by the radio to hear the Grand Ole Opry broadcast.

"We played a lot of baseball. He told me he and Jiggs used to play so much baseball growing up."

Freddie said he couldn't call his father a "real loving dad." He wasn't the hugging type, nor quick to praise. For his part, Freddie admitted being an unruly child.

"Everybody will tell you I was ornery as the dickens. If Mama didn't spank me every day, I wouldn't think she loved me, but after she spanked me for three weeks straight, she'd say, OK, the next one is gonna be from your dad, and he wore my butt out when he did the job. I guess I was so derned ornery that he stayed on my hiney so much that we didn't have a real loving deal."

Not that Freddie considered himself unloved by his father. As he prepared to leave for Vietnam in the autumn of 1966, Freddie knew his father was very concerned about him. Brooks understood Freddie would not be the type to avoid battle. On this point, the father's anxiety was well-founded. Lance Cpl. Brooks served in Third Battalion, Fourth Marine Regiment, which was posted near the demilitarized zone. He frequently saw action on patrol. In fact, he was in harm's way nearly every day of his deployment because of his proximity to the front line.

"We actually lived in the jungle. We dug a different foxhole every night when I was in Vietnam. My whole tour was within ten miles of North Vietnam. We protected the DMZ from the Tonkin Gulf to the Laos border. That's about all we done, go over it back and forth," Freddie said.

Leaders of "M" Company learned the Texan made a good point man. On one patrol it became clear that officers had gotten the unit hopelessly lost in the jungle, making the soldiers an easy target. Freddie took charge. "I wasn't lost," he said. "I took them back to where we needed to go."

In May of 1967, the Marines were pushing hard against enemy forces very close to the North Vietnam border. On May 27, his unit received word they would be part of an offensive push the next day against advancing North Vietnamese Army troops. Freddie assumed he would be the point man but was told by a lieutenant that someone else would take the lead.

"So, in about 15 or 20 minutes my name was called to go up to the headquarters, which was just a tent on top of the hill we were staying on. The captain had been from Waco, Texas. He said to come in. He looked at me and said, 'What do you think I've got you called up here for?' I said I have a pretty good idea. I think you're fixing to give me orders to take us to (North) Vietnam and be the point man. He said, 'No you're wrong. We're going to ask you if you would do it?' I said, well I will do it under one condition. He said, 'What's that?' That I have a radioman with me at all time."

Usually, Freddie explained, when he was on point, he was separated from his company by as much as 300 yards. If he spotted an enemy position, he'd backtrack to the company commander and ask for a squad to join him. Having a radio man with him would save valuable time, he told the officer.

"So, the captain pointed to one of his radiomen and said, that man will be with you. You go straight to (the radio) for anything that you need. I said OK. I thought that radioman of his was going to pass out," he said with a chuckle.

That mission, officially known as Operation Prairie IV but unofficially as the assault on Hill 174, proved to be the most dangerous of his tour.[1] While on point, he was wounded by fire from a machine gun nest. Two Marines behind him were killed. Even though he was wounded, Freddie returned fire and ventured close enough to toss a grenade into the nest, which neutralized the enemy.

Before he was sent to a hospital ship for treatment, Freddie was told he'd be receiving the Bronze Star for his actions on Hill 174. Congressman O. C. Fisher, who represented the West Texas district that included Irion County, wanted to hear Freddie's narrative about the fighting so the Marine from Sherwood was interviewed via phone by the Irion County Selective Service chairman, who supplied a transcript of the interview to the congressman.

"Keep this to yourself," Freddie requested of Fisher. "The main reason is my folks. Dad told me not to try to be a hero."[2] The Marine didn't want Brooks and Hootsie to know that he stayed in position while wounded to direct the men in his platoon, most of whom had never seen combat before.

"I felt that someone with combat experience should stay there to direct our new men. I felt that since I knew the situation on the Hill that I should stay, so I did."

Four months later, however, he was more than willing to tell his father what was happening to him in Vietnam. His tour of duty was supposed to end in early October. Other members of his unit received their orders, but Freddie's never arrived. He was told he'd have to wait another month. Freddie suspected the wait was a ploy to convince him to re-enlist for another term of service, but he wasn't interested.

My grandfather insisted that his son's time in Vietnam not be extended.[3] Brooks first called the local Selective Service Board to complain and then contacted Congressman Fisher, whom he knew from his time as a county commissioner. A string of letters between Brooks and the congressmen indicated how determined my grandfather was to see his son home from war.

He was successful. Pressure from Fisher got Freddie a flight back to the states in late October. Meanwhile, in Vietnam, officers from his unit were left wondering how a lance corporal from Sherwood, Texas, got a US congressman to intervene on his behalf.

The answer was my grandfather, the stoic man of few words, except when his son was being kept in a war zone longer than required. Learning of his action made me proud, and I felt good knowing that Freddie appreciated the helping hand.

Freddie said he had known since he was twelve or thirteen that his father had another family in Tennessee. "At that time, I didn't know his identity had been changed. He told me his health was so bad he had to leave Tennessee, or he could have died." As Freddie matured, the father came to view the son as a confidant and told him more about his Tennessee days, but Brooks insisted on confidentiality.

"A time or two I'd bring it up and he'd say, 'it's best to leave a dead dog lie.' That's what he wanted so I didn't pester him about anything, about tell me where you were raised and what you did, what the kids' names were and all that. I never did question him about that. I respected his privacy when it came to that."

Freddie then riveted my attention with this nugget: "That might be the reason he wrote me the obituary, wrote about his life and gave it to me to seal."

When Freddie was sixteen, his father handed him an envelope containing a handwritten letter of several pages, which Brooks described to his son as the story of him leaving Tennessee and coming to Texas. His instructions were clear: the envelope was to be opened only upon the father's death.

"I took the letter and put it away. I didn't read it," Freddie said.

My mind was whirring, trying to pinpoint this event on the chronology of my grandfather's life. Freddie turned sixteen in September of 1956, so sometime in that next year, about sixteen years before Brooks died from a stroke, the father pulled his son aside and placed this supposedly tell-all letter in his possession.

My first thought was this: here's *another* handwritten letter from my grandfather. This time, the Texas version. The words of the first letter, which he left for bank officials to read in 1931 after he exited Saltillo, reverberated through my Tennessee family for generations producing a fault line that never closed. Now, I learned, there's another missive from my grandfather, a letter to be read only upon his passing. And this one hinted at the promise of explaining everything.

Freddie played his role, keeping his father's words in a safe place through high school, college, his tour of Vietnam and his job selling farm equipment. Following Brooks' funeral in 1973, the family gathered at Freddie's house in San Angelo for a meal. That's when he retrieved the letter from a box on the top shelf of a hall closet.

What did it say?

Freddie had no idea. He handed it, perhaps, to his mother, and did not recall reading the letter. Neither did his siblings. Bobbie said she saw the envelope. Sue said she never saw it at all. In dealing with their mother's grief, as well as their own feelings of loss, the letter didn't seem important at the time. It was something to be explored later. Goodbyes were said. Hugs were shared. Sue and Bobbie returned with their families to their homes elsewhere in the state. Sonny and Hootsie returned to Irion County.

When mention was made of the letter many months later, no one could find it. The envelope that Freddie secreted among his belongings for more than a decade had vanished. Freddie and his siblings offered two theories. In one scenario the letter was accidentally discarded or misplaced during a sprucing up of Hootsie's home in the weeks after my grandfather's passing. Another view is that Hootsie purposely hid or destroyed the letter to protect her late husband's reputation.

Both may be moot because a fire destroyed the homeplace several months after Brooks died. The blaze, which started from an electrical short caused by a roof leak, destroyed Sue's wedding photos, five of Freddie's guns and a set of china dishware that Bobbie gave her mother. The envelope containing the pages of my grandfather's story, told in his own handwriting, could have been consumed in the fire, too.

Freddie was indifferent to the loss of the letter. The son kept his father's confidence and obeyed the order given to him when he was a teen. That was most important to Freddie. Sue and Bobbie expressed a greater interest in reading the letter, but neither were confident it would reveal new facts.

I understood my uncle's and aunts' points of view. By the time Brooks died, they knew details of his secret past that he had personally disclosed to them. They heard his words, directly from his mouth. His words connected them to half siblings and other relatives from Tennessee. My grandfather's dying request was to link his children, his two families, and he succeeded. Consequently, the missing letter became superfluous.

But not to me. If my grandfather's intent with this final letter was to clear the air, for good, perhaps he answered some of the questions that have proven unanswerable to me during my research, starting with how his getaway on January 14, 1931, was planned. Maybe in this missing letter he detailed the mistakes he made as a bank manager or identified who dug up the body of Mr. Lucas, the stand-in cadaver burned in my grandfather's Chevy. Maybe he offered a heartfelt message to his children he left behind in Tennessee.

For my part, I found it reasonable to assume that this letter, penned when Brooks was a healthy late middle-aged man, might have offered a more thorough telling of his life as compared to the story he told his children in 1971 when he was frail, recovering from a stroke. The written narrative may have provided more nuance and details. Not that I'm ungrateful for what my aunts and uncle told me. I just yearned to hear my grandfather's story in his own words.

Perhaps, my grandfather's letter would have excised the thick veil of mystery, explaining not only what was happening in his life at the time of his departure, but also the lives of his Saltillo relatives and friends. I felt cheated of being able to position this letter at the apex of my grandfather's story, to let it explain why he did what he did.

But the letter vanished as if it had never been written.

About a year before his first stroke, Brooks spent a week at Freddie's fish camp on the Rio Grande. "I had vacation time to use, and Dad and I went down there. I had a comfortable trailer house down there. We went out on a Saturday and didn't come back till the following Sunday," he said. The way Freddie talked about that time I could tell he had fond memories of the trip.

An extended father-son fishing trip seemed like the proper venue for telling untold stories, but Freddie said that wasn't the case.

"I don't think there was ever a word talked about his past. Probably it was as much my fault as it was his. I didn't question him about it. His favorite word—let a dead dog lie—so I never brought it up again."

SCRUTINY

The work week beginning Monday, May 2, 1932, was an unusually busy one at the Hardin County Courthouse in Savannah. During most weeks, business was limited to county offices such as the property assessor or the trustee. Court sessions were only held once every three months in the stately two-story brick building, which featured a columned portico on the second floor overlooking the main stretch of downtown. The week of May 2nd, however, brought a flurry of trials unlike anything seen in the county before that time. Seven chancery court lawsuits involving four insurance companies would be heard and judged in five days, all with the same complainant.

That would be my grandmother.

One by one, the insurance companies rejected Boss's death certificate as proof he was no more among the living. When they balked at paying the claims, my grandmother took them to court, filing the first suit in August of 1931 against Modern Woodmen of America. Other suits against other insurers followed.

Meanwhile, the Hardin County Bank's board of directors filed a lawsuit against her. The bank declared it was due a share of any insurance proceeds should my grandmother's claim be successful. As an added legal complication, one month later, in September of 1931, the Tennessee Department of Insurance and Banking joined the case just to make sure that any proceeds were funneled equitably to depositors of the failed bank.[1] From this legal wrangling, the parties formed an unusual alliance: my grandmother, the Hardin County Bank's board of directors and Tennessee Superintendent of Banks D. D. Robertson.

By agreement of the three parties, insurance proceeds received would be deposited into an account administered by the county clerk and master. After the lawsuits were adjudicated, there would be a thrashing out among attorneys representing my grandmother, the bank and the state as to how much she and the children would receive and how much would be allocated to refund the defunct bank's depositors.

The cases would be closely watched in the county, that was certain. Some Saltillo families lost meager amounts in the bank fiasco because they had already lost most of their money to the Depression. Other families saw small fortunes—thousands of dollars saved across generations through cotton farming—disappear like smoke rising to the draft of a well-made chimney. The money was there; then it wasn't.

Neither was Boss. But due to his tell-all missive that quickly became the talk of the town, everyone knew my grandfather was a heavily insured man. It would truly be a soul who had not read the papers or minded the gossip on Saltillo's Main Street for the past year who did not comprehend the mathematics of these court proceedings. If the widow Bingham and the bank triumphed, a large portion of the insurance proceeds would eventually trickle down to broke depositors. The payoff would likely be dimes on the dollar, but in this economically fractured time, something was better than nothing.

On May 2, 1932, however, no one dared predict how this thorny mess would end. Indeed, the process leading to this week of court proceedings had been a year-long grind of legal maneuvering. Although two insurance companies paid the death benefit rather than go to trial, the others refused.

On March 18, 1931, Solon T. Gilmore, general counsel of Business Men's Assurance Co., headquartered in Kansas City, wanted his client's position made clear. "I may say, so that you may understand the company's position entirely, that it has been suggested to them that there is a serious question whether or not Bingham is dead," Gilmore wrote to Elijah W. Ross, who represented Hardin County Bank.[2]

On March 30, 1931, George G. Perrin, counselor for Modern Woodmen of America in Rock Island, Illinois, expressed disbelief, too. "The difficulty with respect to the proofs of death as filed is that there seems to be no satisfactory identification of Lytle Bingham as the dead person," Perrin wrote, also in a letter to Ross.[3]

The cases were first set for trial in October 1931, but insurance company lawyers complained that the complexity of the legal issues required more time to prepare. Counsel for my grandmother objected to a delay, but Chancellor Tom C. Rye gave the insurance companies plenty of leeway.

Of course, this was nothing but a delaying tactic. The insurers hoped that someone would talk, or Boss would come out from his hiding place. Several of the companies believed he was concealed in a safe house somewhere in the thick forests of Hardin County or perhaps in a cave.

A new trial date was set for January 26, 1932, but on the opening day, Business Men's Assurance Co., dropped a bombshell. Gilmore, the company's general counsel, insisted the firm had proof Boss was alive and requested a continuance.[4] Gilmore informed Chancellor Rye: "In a short time, Lytle Bingham will be found alive and (we) will be able to show this fact." The lawyer offered no proof in open court to back this claim. In an affidavit filed with the company's request for a continuance, Gilmore said the situation demanded that his company not disclose particulars.

"That should the defendant be required to state with certainty and definiteness the facts expected to be proven by the witnesses and the names of the witnesses at this time, then Lytle Bingham could be notified of these facts and seek another and different hiding place," the affidavit stated. In conclusion, Business Men's Assurance argued "that to compel this defendant to go to trial at this time or to disclose all the facts in connection with its application for a continuance would sacrifice and prejudice its rights."

Attorneys for my grandmother, the bank and the state resisted another change of trial date, but the chancellor agreed with Gilmore. The trial transcript offers no explanation why Rye delayed the trials until the first week of May of 1932. Perhaps the chancellor believed it possible that Boss would soon be brought into his courtroom.

If my grandmother or her lawyers, or counsel for the bank and state, took Gilmore's declaration seriously, they talked about it only among themselves. There's no written evidence found in the mountain of court papers to indicate they believed anything other than Boss was dead and buried at Shady Grove Cemetery.

As to what the insurance companies were up to, the lawyers' files and my grandmother's experience show just how desperate the insurance providers were to prove my grandfather was alive.

For several months following his disappearance, at least two private investigators showed up in Saltillo, asking questions and observing my grandmother's movements on the farm, hoping to catch her in a secret rendezvous with my grandfather. One of these private detectives, identified in court documents as William Harrison Cody, went so far as to check my grandmother's mailbox for letters from her husband and to confront her face-to-face, once while she was picking cotton in the fall of 1931.

"A certain man came to my house, and really came to the field where I was at work, said my husband was seen alive," she testified in a deposition.

"Mr. Cody, said he was."[5]

I can't imagine that the hired gumshoes, out-of-towners, blended in well with Saltillo residents, but that didn't keep them from asking questions or accusing people of conspiring with the former bank manager. Nor did Cody hesitate to cast his net widely, hoping to find someone who would talk.

The case of R. Neely Jernigan, of Haleyville, Alabama, comes to mind. Jernigan was an insurance sales representative for the Shenandoah Insurance Company, with a sales territory that included northern Alabama and a large chunk of central and western Tennessee, which he shared with his brother, Richard P. Jernigan of Jackson. That's how the brothers came to employ Boss as sub-agent for Shenandoah. As a side job to banking, my grandfather drummed up business for the Jernigans and collected a fee for each policy they sold.

Every few months, Neely Jernigan or his brother, or both, met with Boss to discuss potential clients. Additionally, my grandfather was a Shenandoah customer. In May and September of 1928, he took out two life insurance policies with death benefits totaling $5,500. When Boss was declared dead three years later, the Roanoke-based company opted to pay the death benefits rather than take on the expense of a lawsuit. (The funds were held by the Hardin County Court Clerk's office until the trials were over.)

Perhaps, it was Shenandoah's acceptance of Boss's demise that prompted Cody to explore a link between Neely Jernigan and Boss Bingham. Cody's allegiance, after all, was to the insurance companies who were willing to dispute Boss's death and slug it out in Hardin County Chancery Court. Shenandoah's payment of the death claim may have led to Cody's curiosity about the agent who sold Boss the insurance policies, hoping to find something the private detective could use as leverage.

I know of this because Jernigan informed his superiors at Shenandoah about a series of meetings with Cody and an attorney, R. P. Hobson, who was employed by Inter-Southern, another of the insurance companies. The first of these meetings occurred on March 30, 1932, about five weeks before the trials started in Savannah.

"They asked me about my acquaintance with Bingham and the work I did with him from time to time, and about his death or disappearance. They asked me what I thought about it, and I said from what I had learned in discussing it with various individuals it seemed very mysterious. They asked where I was on the night he disappeared or burned to death, whichever it was, and I told them at the Colonial Hotel in Waverly, Tennessee," Jernigan wrote Shenandoah executives.[6]

"Then they asked me what I would say if they brought me face-to-face with a person who saw me at the scene of the burning of the car that morning about 5 o'clock and saw Bingham get out of his car and get in mine. I told them I would say the fellow was lying. They said, 'Well, you might say that, but we can prove by three parties who know you, that it is a fact.'"[7]

The private investigators were adamant Bingham was alive and that Jernigan was "in constant communication with him," but offered no proof. According to the Alabama insurance agent, the men told him, "You're in a bad spot, Jernigan. If you cooperate with us, we can help you. If you don't then it's just too bad for you."[8]

The more he thought about the visitors' accusations, the more Jernigan was rattled. "I did not think so much about this for a couple days, then got to thinking about it one night and figured out that there was a lot of money at stake and that there was no telling what they might do at my expense to try to carry a point," he stated in the letter.[9]

The Alabama man also understood the ramifications to his life and livelihood if these accusations were to be made public. He needed advice, of the legal kind, so he reached out to an acquaintance, Homer Ballew of Savannah, who happened to be the law partner of Elijah W. Ross, and they were both representing the defunct Hardin County Bank in the lawsuits against the insurance companies.

Jernigan shared all he knew about Cody with Ballew, as well as copies of Jernigan's correspondence with Shenandoah's headquarters.[10] Ballew advised the shaken man to "not let them bluff you out with a lot of charges which are false upon their face, and which they cannot and would not attempt to prove in court or anywhere else."[11]

In early April of 1932, a month before the trials opened, Jernigan wrote to his bosses that Cody contacted him again. Jernigan said the private investigator said there was a man who could identify him as the man who picked up Boss Bingham on State Route 5 before dawn on January 15, 1931, and this witness was coming to Haleyville, Alabama, where Jernigan's office was located.[12]

Wanting to put this business to rest, the insurance agent agreed to a meeting, but Cody called a short time later to say the man was injured in a car crash in Russellville, about twenty-five miles north of Haleyville. Cody suggested putting off the meeting until another day. Jernigan told his Shenandoah bosses that he insisted on the meeting.

"I told him I wanted to get it off my mind, and I would drive him up there to see this fellow. I did that and found a man who says he knows me very well, but I don't think I ever saw him more than twice or three times up until a few weeks ago and he at that time wanted me to get him some liquor, which I declined to do," Jernigan wrote.[13]

"His name was Teuton. He had gotten drunk on his way to identify me and had turned his car over and was lying there, in bed, bloody as a hog, when (we) arrived. Cody went in and after taking an hour or more getting him in presentable shape . . . he called me in and Teuton said, yes, he would have to say it was true that he saw me that morning about five o'clock. I said, 'Teuton, what kind of car was I driving?' He said, 'The very Nash two-door sedan you are driving now.' When I said I didn't buy it until last July he seemed to change that part of his story and said he might be mistaken about that."

At that point, the ruse was essentially over. Jernigan wrote to his boss that Cody approached him once more in early April, offering another opportunity to confess. The investigator asked: "If we could promise that no harm would come to you, would you then tell the truth?" But Jernigan understood he was being manipulated by the fast-talking Cody, who was crumbling under intense pressure to produce a living, breathing Boss Bingham.

The insurance companies wanted to make a spectacle of routing him from his hiding place and, of course, avoid paying thousands of dollars in death claims. It became clear that Cody's year of snooping had assembled rumors but no substantive leads. By bringing Jernigan into the situation, Cody appeared to be grasping at the flimsiest of straws. Recruiting this fellow, Teuton, as an eyewitness was apparently the private eye's last chance. Based on the timeline of events outlined in Jernigan's letter to the home office of Shenandoah Life, it's more than coincidental that the insurance companies asked for a continuance in January. Shortly before is when Jernigan said Cody began "trailing him."

The private investigator convinced himself that the Alabama insurance agent was involved in my grandfather's disappearance, but Cody chose poorly by bringing in Teuton, who was identified only by last name, with no information supplied as to his hometown, age or profession. By Jernigan's description in his letters, Teuton was a man who could be tempted to say anything you wanted him to say if a bottle of whiskey was procured in those waning days of Prohibition.[14]

I am not privy to Cody's explanations to his employers, but I assume the news was glumly received. His failure to roust Boss from a hiding place meant Mary L. Bingham et al. v. Business Men's Assurance and the trials involving the other companies would commence as scheduled. There would be no more continuances.

Had Cody succeeded, the insurance trials would have been moot. Instead, my grandfather would have faced a series of criminal charges, as prosecutors had ample evidence to seek indictments for embezzlement and fraud. Others would likely have faced prosecution, including my grandmother, for aiding and abetting.

Cody never came close to finding my grandfather, I'm certain. If he had known Boss had drifted to Texas, Cody would have headed there. There were people in

Saltillo, I believe, who could have offered clues, but they didn't. My grandmother and Great-Uncle Howard could have directed him to Texas but didn't. A year and a half after Boss departed, The Lie had thoroughly saturated the fabric of the Bingham narrative.

A long week of trials was a certainty. Whereas the coroner who signed Boss's death certificate had asked few questions, the attorneys for the insurance companies would not be as easily satisfied.

They couldn't produce Boss in the flesh. Instead, they took aim at those who knew him best: his friends, his brother and his wife, my grandmother.

Especially my grandmother.

THE TRIALS BEGIN

"Call your first witness."

The five days of court trials that placed the Binghams front and center began with those four words, uttered by Chancellor Rye on the morning of May 2, 1932.

"We call Mary Bingham," replied Grover McCormick, one of my grandmother's three lawyers.

The trim figure of my grandmother rose and walked to the witness stand.

A trial transcript is an informative document, offering answers to questions as opposing solicitors seek the undisputed truth. But the information is always one-dimensional. What a transcript leaves out is the humanity of the situation, a description of the emotions displayed by witnesses under questioning. Oftentimes, it's left to journalists with eyes for detail and ears for inflection to weave an account that offers interpretive cues.

That didn't happen in the Hardin County trials. There's nothing in newspaper accounts to indicate my grandmother's appearance or demeanor. Did she wear her best dress? Did she wear a hat? She never owned diamond bracelets, but she was fond of rhinestone brooches. When she attended church or posed for a formal photograph, one was always part of her wardrobe. Was a brooch pinned to her dress when she approached the witness stand? All I have are her words, typed by a court reporter more than ninety years ago, but I longed to read her face as she sat in the witness box. If time travel was possible, I would enjoy observing her from the gallery. I wondered if I would discern disquietude in her voice and mannerisms. Or would she be collected, composed? She was thirty-three then. Would I have recognized her? Could the ordeal of the past year be seen on her face?

How miserable the preceding months must have been for my grandmother. The winter of 1931–32 was a wet slog beginning in December with nearly eleven inches of rain and followed in January with almost a foot of rainfall.[1] Creeks flooded and the Tennessee River near Saltillo spilled into bottomland fields. County-maintained dirt roads remained a muddy mess for weeks at a time. Sometimes they were impassable, leaving rural residents like my grandmother homebound until the weather cleared. Unfortunately, February and March were also wet months, which kept the ground saturated and the tributaries running swift.

I saw her in my mind. She's at the farm, which was not quite two miles from Saltillo, sitting by a window in her home, watching drops of rain effortlessly slide down the glass panes. Three years earlier, her family had grown to five with the birth of a boy, Lytle, my father. Now, there were four, just her and the children. She missed her husband terribly; the older girls asked about him often. However, for my father, who was two when Boss disappeared, the memory of his dad was quickly fading. Watching the gloomy weather that winter, my grandmother couldn't help but carry a burdensome weight that seemed heavier and heavier with each passing gray day.

Finally, precipitation returned to normal in April and farmers prepared fields and vegetable gardens for planting. The latter was needed more than ever due to the Depression, which made subsistence farming a necessity, not a choice. Spring 1932 came as a welcome relief for Hardin County, if not for my grandmother, whose private life was about to be thoroughly examined in the most public way: testifying in a court of law.

She never spoke of the insurance trials to me. I'm uncertain if she ever talked about that time of her life with anyone. Perhaps she talked with Great-Uncle Howard on occasion, but looking back, I sense she felt the less said, the better. If ever I wished for a time when my grandmother kept a diary, it would have been during those five days in May 1932, when she stood before God and man, her left hand on a Bible and her right palm upright, pledging to tell the truth and nothing but the truth.

A chancery court trial is similar to a criminal court proceeding. Chancery court, often called equity court, was used to settle disputes of a non-criminal nature, such as an alleged breach of contract or a property line disagreement between neighbors. The chancery court judge was addressed as "chancellor," a throwback to its origins in England, when an appointed chancellor acted as the "king's conscience."

In a chancery trial, the complainant's side presents its case first, with each witness subject to cross-examination by attorneys for the defense (the insurance companies). When the complainant rested, the defense called witnesses, who were subject to cross-examination by opposing counsel. Decisions could be made by a jury of twelve or the judge could act both as judge and jury and issue a verdict from the bench.

There were four insurance companies involved in the seven trials that week: Banker's Credit Life, Business Men's Assurance Co., Inter-Southern Life Insurance Co., and Modern Woodmen of America. It was Business Men's Assurance that had the most to lose because it had issued four policies to Boss. The death benefits, which on one policy included double indemnity for death caused by an accident, totaled $10,500. Each of the other three companies had single policies covering my grandfather.[2]

I don't know how many spectators sat through the trials, but the proceedings attracted a bevy of lawyers. Although corporate lawyers came to Savannah for the preliminary sessions, they did not return for the trials. Instead, they hired the best Tennessee lawyers they could find within a hundred miles of Savannah to represent their interests.

Business Men's Assurance Co. had three attorneys on the payroll: William K. Abernathy and Millard Lee of Selmer, and John A. Shelton of Adamsville.

Of the three, Abernathy's name carried weight.[3] At fifty-two, he was a well-connected state senator, former district attorney general and former mayor of his hometown, as well as the owner and publisher of the weekly newspaper in Selmer. His appearance in the insurance litigation came at the height of his political power and influence. Eighteen months earlier, Abernathy had directed the successful re-election of Gov. Henry Horton who had been expected to lose.

Lee and Shelton, ages fifty-two and fifty-three, respectively, did not have the same level of name recognition as Abernathy, but brought considerable trial experience.[4]

Banker's Credit Life Insurance Co., and Inter-Southern Life Insurance Co. were represented by Clarence E. Pigford and W. Neely Key, partners in a venerable Jackson law firm with considerable trial experience in insurance disputes.

Pigford, fifty-eight, was a man of means and influence in West Tennessee.[5] After graduating from the Cumberland School of Law in Lebanon, Tennessee, he returned to Jackson to begin his successful practice. Pigford was the owner and publisher of the *Jackson Sun* newspaper, served on the board of directors of two banks and served on the Tennessee Historical Commission and the Tennessee Planning Commission.

Neely Key, fifty-two, wasn't in the public sphere as much as his law partner, but Key had the reputation as a counselor whose nimble mind was always prepared for trial.[6]

Modern Woodmen of America hired the Henderson firm of Galbraith and Mitchell. Jere I. Galbraith, fifty-two, and David E. Mitchell, forty-two, were both raised in Henderson. In two decades, they became the go-to defense lawyers in the region, even though they hailed from a small town far off the beaten path.[7] In addition, Galbraith had served as mayor of Henderson for two terms and was well-known in West Tennessee political and social circles.

The Hardin County Bank was represented by the Savannah firm of Ross and Ballew. Elijah W. Ross and Joseph Homer Ballew were well-established lawyers. Ross, sixty, had done well in business dealings and as an attorney was deemed fearless. Even in 1932 he was still remembered for a murder case sixteen years earlier when he defended a local Black man, Lennie Kendall, who was charged with the murder of a white man. Eyewitnesses said Kendall acted in self-defense. Ross was successful in moving the trial to another county and in having the charges reduced.[8]

Ballew, forty-five, fought in World War I, entering as a captain in the infantry but coming home as a major.[9] He earned his law degree at Union University in Jackson, his hometown, and afterward joined Ross in Savannah. By the time my grandmother's insurance trials came into view, their legal partnership had stretched to thirteen years.

My grandmother's team included Memphis-based attorney Grover McCormick, and two Savannah attorneys, Warren H. Sloan and Perry M. Harbert. Of the three, McCormick was the leader, without a doubt.

McCormick turned forty-six during the year of the insurance trials. In 1908 he began law school at Cumberland School of Law and after graduation moved to Memphis to begin his practice. As a young attorney he made an impression and was elected to the state House of Representatives where he served for two terms.[10]

Perry Harbert, fifty-four, was born and raised in Hardin County. After law school he returned to Savannah to open a practice, representing numerous businesses.[11] At thirty-five, Sloan was the junior member of my grandmother's team and was the youngest of any of the lawyers associated with the insurance litigation.[12] He continued to represent my grandmother long after the trials ended.

Finally, there was Chancellor Rye. In 1932, Rye was in his fourteenth year as a chancery jurist, serving the twentieth judicial district, which covered a broad swath of West Tennessee counties stretching from the Kentucky border to the Mississippi state line. At the age of sixty-nine, Rye was nearing the end of a long career of public service, including two two-year terms as governor from 1915 to 1919.[13]

When I began reading the transcripts of the insurance trials, I imagined an army of big city lawyers parachuting into Savannah to take on my grandmother, but that's not how it played out at all. The attorneys, all men, knew one another. Most of them had seen each other work in other courtrooms and jurisdictions. Six of them were graduates of Cumberland School of Law. There were political connections, as well. Several of the lawyers were still serving in the legislature or had served at one time. For instance, during McCormick's stint as a legislator in 1915, he was among the first to endorse Rye for governor.

If my grandmother felt beleaguered or perturbed by her proximity during the trials to so many hard-charging educated men, she kept her concerns to herself. But I'm sure she felt out of place and to be the center of attention was uncomfortable.

Each of the trials began with my grandmother settling into the witness box as the first to testify. There was another commonality. In each trial, she was repeatedly asked to speak louder because her voice didn't carry well in the high-ceilinged room.

The first lawsuit to be heard involved one of the Business Men's Assurance Co. policies. My grandmother's attorney, Grover McCormick, moved to the heart of the matter very quickly.

McCormick: "Where is Mr. Bingham now?"[14]

Mrs. Bingham: "Dead."

McCormick: "I didn't hear you."

Mrs. Bingham: "He is dead."

And with that admission, under oath, found on page three of the trial transcript, my grandmother crossed a line from which she could not retreat. By stating her husband was dead when she knew he was alive, The Lie became her lifelong companion, always a reminder of her untruthful testimony. During the week of the trials, my grandmother was asked whether her husband was dead or alive, in various ways, nearly four dozen times. Each time she replied that Boss was buried.[15]

McCormick then asked my grandmother if she had provided proof to Business Men's Assurance that Boss had died.

Counsel for the insurance company, Millard Lee, objected that McCormick was unnecessarily drawing out the proceedings by raising a point the insurance company had already conceded, or thought they had. Yes, Mrs. Bingham had provided proof of death, Lee acknowledged.[16] This caught McCormick off guard.

McCormick: "Then you make no question about that?"

Lee: "No sir, we haven't made an issue of that at all."

McCormick: "The only issue is whether or not he is dead?"

Lee: "That is right."

This was the first of many times that my grandmother's attorneys would remind the juries and the judge that the only point of contention in the litigation held that week in May 1932 was whether Lytle Boss Bingham was alive or dead.

Her lawyers used my grandmother's time on the stand to review and display evidence that Boss was indeed buried at Shady Grove. She was asked to identify a key, scarred by fire, that was attached to a shoe buttoner. It was the key that opened the front door of Hardin County Bank. Other keys were shown to her for identification. One was the switch key to her husband's vehicle. Another was a small key to a lock box where Boss kept the insurance policies and other personal papers. Both keys, which she readily identified, also bore marks of having survived a fire.

Asked about her husband's car, she noted there was a Masonic emblem on the radiator and a rug positioned over the radiator to keep it from freezing up in winter. She also identified a badly scorched shotgun recovered from the back seat of the burned sedan as belonging to her husband.

Finally, questions turned to the body.[17]

McCormick: "When did you next see the remains of your husband, if you did see the remains?"

Mrs. Bingham: "I didn't see the remains."

McCormick: "Why?"

Mrs. Bingham: "Because there was nothing much to see."

McCormick: "I didn't hear you."

Mrs. Bingham: "I didn't wish to see what was left."

The insurance companies, unable to produce the absent bank cashier in the flesh as predicted several months earlier, had no choice but to strike hard during cross-examination. Attorney Jere Galbraith, representing Modern Woodmen, inquired of Boss's state of mind on that cold day in January 1931 when he was last seen in Saltillo. He was trying to lay the foundation for Boss's mental breakdown.[18]

Galbraith: "Did you notice anything about him, Mrs. Bingham, that would indicate he was having, or laboring, under any mental trouble of any kind?"

Mrs. Bingham: "No, I didn't notice. He was up part of the time and in bed part of the time and talking over the telephone part of the time."

Galbraith: "Did he have any fever?"

Mrs. Bingham: "Well, we had the doctor out there and he said he didn't have a fever at that time."

Galbraith: "Mrs. Bingham, didn't you tell Dr. Parker the day he was there, didn't you state to him, Dr. Parker that 'my husband is nervous and can't sleep?'"

Mrs. Bingham: "Well, he had been suffering until he couldn't sleep."

Galbraith: "Was it suffering kept him awake or was it a nervous feeling?"

Mrs. Bingham: "I suppose he suffered because he spoke of pain in his side. I made him a poultice."

Galbraith: "And he didn't seem to be nervous?"

Mrs. Bingham: "No, because he wasn't a nervous man."

Galbraith: "And you didn't state to Dr. Parker on the twelfth of January 1931, your husband was nervous, couldn't sleep?"

Mrs. Bingham: "I told him I thought he was in a run-down condition."

Apparently satisfied with those answers, the Modern Woodmen counsel moved to another line of questioning.[19]

Galbraith: "Mrs. Bingham, did you know anything about the condition of affairs at the Hardin County Bank?"

Mrs. Bingham: "No, sir."

Galbraith: "Did your husband confide those things in you, about his business affairs, discuss them with you?"

Mrs. Bingham: "None at all."

Galbraith: "That (the bank's failure) was a surprise to you?"

Mrs. Bingham: "It certainly was."

Many of my grandmother's responses were answered this way: to the point, employing an economy of words. Other insurance company attorneys also tried to get her to acknowledge conversations where Boss may have told her about his role in the dismal condition of the bank. She stuck to her story, that she didn't know the bank's troubles. She insisted her husband's departure to attend to bank business in Jackson on a winter's evening wasn't concerning in the least. Galbraith was especially skeptical.[20]

Galbraith: "Mrs. Bingham, wasn't it kind of a surprise to you that your husband would leave, go away from home just at eight or nine o'clock at night?"

Mrs. Bingham: "Well, no, I wasn't surprised."

Galbraith: "Well, he had been going to Jackson, but hadn't he been going in the daytime to transact business?"

Mrs. Bingham: "Sometimes he would, but sometimes he would go late in the afternoon."

Galbraith: "Did you know what kind of business he was going to transact in Jackson?"

Mrs. Bingham: "I suppose it was the bank. The bank there was the corresponding bank, and that is all I knew about that."

Galbraith: "The banks in Jackson didn't stay open at night?"

Mrs. Bingham: "I don't know."

Galbraith: "You couldn't say about that?"

Mrs. Bingham: "No."

Reading the transcript, it's easy to sense Galbraith's growing frustration with my grandmother's resoluteness. She didn't give him anything on which he could pounce. But he pounced anyway.

Galbraith: "You had no intimation at all that there was any trouble as far as the Hardin County Bank was concerned, and he left home at eight or nine o'clock at night to drive something like fifty miles and that didn't excite your suspicion at all?"[21]

Mrs. Bingham: "No sir."

As counterpoint to this line of questioning, my grandmother testified during direct examination by her lead attorney, McCormick, that Boss frequently went to Jackson on business.[22]

McCormick: "Did he say he was going to be spending the night in Jackson?"

Mrs. Bingham: "Yes sir."

McCormick: "What did he say about returning home?"

Mrs. Bingham: "Well, practically nothing, but I didn't think anything about it because he had been going to Jackson and spending the night occasionally. I asked him about coming back and he said it would be too cold."

My grandmother noted that night was "the coldest of the year." Again, I am left only with her words and am not privy to her facial expressions and tone of her voice, which might have hinted at an underlying emphasis.

Defense attorneys, particularly Lee, representing Business Men's Assurance, attempted to pick apart my grandmother's testimony. Lee's strategy was disingenuous to be sure. He asked my grandmother repeatedly if Boss was alive or if she had been in communication with him. In one trial, Lee asked her the question four times on one page of the transcript. When she replied each time that her husband was dead and she had not communicated with him, Lee took logic on a twisted ride, implying that because she hadn't talked with Boss then she couldn't be sure if he was alive or dead.[23]

Lee: "Then you don't know, as a matter of fact, whether your husband is dead or living?"

Mrs. Bingham: "I am sure he isn't living."

Lee: "And the only reason you say that is because you have been told these things, and you don't know of your own knowledge whether he is dead or alive?"

Mrs. Bingham: "I haven't a thing in the world to tell me that he is alive, not a thing."

Lee: "And you don't have anything to tell you he is dead."

Mary Bingham: "The proof seems to be stronger that he is dead. You can always tell in your heart, you know."

Lee: "And that is all you can tell, he is gone, and the only thing you know is, he left home and hasn't returned."

Mrs. Bingham: "Why sure."

Lee: "All right."

Mrs. Bingham: "That is all I know."

Of course, it wasn't all she knew.

SPRING CREEK

Once again, the smell of frying bacon was my wakeup call. That and the spirited conversations of my aunts drinking coffee in the kitchen with my uncle, who occasionally chimed in, no doubt standing by the stove, fork in hand, ready to turn the bacon. Once again, I was forced to triangulate my position on earth. I was at Freddie's house in San Angelo, Texas. Freddie was my uncle. This was another day in the land of my grandfather, and today I'm visiting Sherwood and Spring Creek, places whose names I knew well, but not much beyond that.

After this nugget was telegraphed through the synapses of my foggy brain, I was wide awake, knowing how much I needed to accomplish before returning to Tennessee.

Upon my arrival in San Angelo, I didn't know how willing Sue, Bobbie and Freddie would be in sharing not only their father's story but also their stories of coping with their dad's duality. There was no need to worry. Stories flowed all the time, during meals, while driving and especially sitting around the kitchen table sifting through photo albums late into the night.

I learned my grandfather was a creature of habit, eating eggs with bacon or ham for breakfast each day. He had a routine. Eggs were eaten first, but he'd reserve the last bite until after he downed a spoonful of white Karo syrup. "When he got through with that, he'd eat that last piece (of egg) to take the sweet out of his mouth, then he would drink his coffee," Bobbie told me. "I do the same thing. I need something to clean my palate," she added.

When Sue, Bobbie and Freddie were in high school, they all played basketball. Freddie even played at the college level at Angelo State for a few seasons. My Texas aunts and uncle said Brooks and Hootsie always attended the games, even during tournament time when games were played at different schools an hour apart from one another.

Bobbie and Freddie remembered how their father suffered pain and discomfort from a hernia for years but refused to see a doctor. The reason? A good friend went in for hernia surgery but "when they cut him open, he was eat up from cancer down there," Freddie noted. "He was afraid that would happen to him, too." Only after Brooks cut off the tip of a finger on his right hand while sawing wood, did he agree to his doctor's plea to have the operation.

I also learned how my grandfather officially established his identity in Texas. According to my aunts, Marvin Lester Brooks registered to vote in Irion County not too many months after arriving in Sherwood. No proof of identity was required. The official in charge of voter registration was apparently the friendly sort. Bobbie said the man took a glance at her father and said, "You gotta be 'bout thirty." Brooks readily agreed, she noted.

"That's how five years got dropped off his age," Bobbie noted.

One-on-one interviews also produced several hours of uninterrupted stories that explored the depths of the Boss-Brooks story in ways I would not fully appreciate for months. I had answers to some questions but, as usual, plenty more questions were raised.

The weather was gorgeous for an outing: a cobalt-blue sky and a welcomed breeze. Our first destination on this May morning was a twenty-seven-mile drive to Sherwood, the small town where Brooks arrived in the spring of 1931, roughly four months after departing Saltillo. Sherwood is positioned on the eastern side of Irion County between a line of low hills and Spring Creek, the placid waterway my grandfather camped beside during his convalescence from tuberculosis.

From my view, sitting in the rear of Bobbie's ruby-colored Cadillac, I took in the Texas landscape, generally flat, punctuated by juniper and mesquite trees. Stretches of land were green, while others offered the varying shades of khaki and brown that I had noted on my arrival flight. Once we were out of Tom Green County, where San Angelo is the county seat, the houses in rural Irion County were often isolated from one another by a half mile or more, but occasionally there were clusters of homes. Even then, I could tell these were positioned on multi-acre lots. Everyone out here likes their elbow room, I surmised.

We drove in a southwesterly direction on US Highway 67 out of San Angelo for about twenty-two miles before turning south onto a series of county roads a few miles from Sherwood. On one of the final turns, we descended a small rise and out my window an imposing structure came into view, a sight so unexpected, towering as it did above the surrounding landscape, that I issued a gasp.

"What is that?" I said with some incredulity, still not believing that a mirage wasn't fooling me.

"That's the old courthouse," Bobbie said from the driver's seat. "It's on the National Register."[1]

The Irion County Courthouse, a square, two-story building completed in 1901 of quarry-faced ashlar limestone is an architectural wonder. The rock, weathered to a yellowish patina by the decades, was quarried locally, each block cut and laid with a precision that even my untrained eye appreciated. Entry to the first floor was through arched entrances on each of the four sides. Punctuating the arches on two sides were owls carved by hand. The building's metal roof tapered to form a square clock tower, and the Roman numerals of a clock face were visible on all four sides. But the clock is a painted facade, with the hour hand roughly pointing to the seven and the minute hand aimed toward the twenty minutes past the hour mark. Local lore holds that the architects, two gentlemen remembered only by their last names, Martin and Moodie, chose the setting. It's said to be a nod to 7:22 a.m., the time of death of Abraham Lincoln some thirty-six years before the courthouse construction was finished.

The grand building's usefulness was relatively short-lived. "Death by railroad" is how Texas historians describe it. In 1910, the Kansas City, Orient and Mexico Railroad opened rail lines not through Sherwood, but through a new town named Mertzon, a mile or so southwest of Sherwood.[2] From that point, Mertzon steadily grew in population while Sherwood's growth yielded to inertia. In 1936, the year my grandfather married his Texas wife, the county electorate voted to move the county seat to Mertzon, and the grand courthouse was abandoned by Irion's government and used only as a venue for community gatherings.[3]

But in the spring of 1931, when my grandfather ambled into town after hitch-hiking from Corpus Christi, Sherwood was still the place to conduct county business. I tried to imagine him entering this majestic courthouse to register to vote, making his transformation from Boss to Brooks official. Was he afraid his cover was about to be blown as he climbed those steps under the watchful gaze of those carved owls?

Being in Sherwood and Irion County, the town and county where my grandfather made his new home for the second half of his life, was exciting. I sensed my breath quickening, my heartbeat rising, my emotions wheeling at the recognition that I was walking on soil where my grandfather's boots had trod. I had done the same in Saltillo, walking down Main Street, but it was different in Texas. Here, through the memories of his children, he felt three dimensional, fully formed. It was a feeling that accompanied me all day long but was particularly intense at the next stop on the itinerary Bobbie planned for us: my grandfather's creek side camp site.

Spring Creek is an anomaly in this semiarid region, a stream where water flows year-round.[4] It's one of three creeks in the county created by springs from a subterranean aquifer far below the dry and dusty surface. An early settler, Fayette Tankersley, recalled a trip when he was a boy to the headwaters of Spring Creek in the late 1860s with his father.[5]

"I had never seen such cold nor crystal clear water nor springs that bubbled up ... The whole creek was clear and looked to be full of all kinds of fish," Tankersley wrote in a hand-written memoir he penned for his family in his later years.

My grandfather made the bank of Spring Creek his home for more than two years, living in a tent through the stifling summer and the bitterness of winter. He did so with the permission of a local rancher named Frank Emerick. The two men met in Sherwood the day Brooks arrived, and a fast friendship formed, one that lasted until Emerick died of a heart condition in 1945.

Emerick must have sized up the lean newcomer and found him trustworthy. Otherwise, he wouldn't have offered employment or given him supplies to make camp on the creek. That's another attribute of my grandfather I noted. In Texas, he was, as Sue described him, "a man of his word."

Separated by twenty-two years of age, Emerick took on the role of employer, mentor and, over the years, confidant, to my grandfather. Bobbie and Sue believe their father likely told the rancher of the reason for his departure from Tennessee. If so, Emerick, the former lawman, never betrayed his younger friend's confidence.

Bobbie drove the car out of Sherwood on a dusty unpaved road, headed for Spring Creek, which I'd heard so much about. In the wake of the Caddie, an opaque curtain of dust floated lazily in the air.

"We're here," Sue announced.

"Here" was a closed farm gate in front of a dirt lane that meandered onto someone's property that was clearly marked "NO TRESPASSING." Although the Emericks no longer owned the land, Sue and Bobbie "thought" they knew the new owner and, regardless, insisted no one would mind if we moseyed across the fence for a look-see.

"If anyone asks, we'll just explain what we're doing," Bobbie said with confidence. That would have been an interesting conversation, telling the convoluted Boss/Brooks story to a landowner who may or may not be peeved that a trio of women didn't heed the posted warning against trespassing.

With Bobbie navigating, we crossed a field of scrubby grass whose tops bent to the whim of the ever-present breeze. Songbirds seemed to follow us, flitting from tree to tree, trilling all the while. We passed a patch of blooming prickly pear, a type of cactus flat as an outstretched hand and well-armed with pointy spines. At the point was a bright yellow flower. Our arrival coincided with the peak of blooming season. While pretty, ranchers consider "pear," as it's called, a nuisance. In the Depression, local men, including Brooks, were hired by the government to "grub pear," hoeing the plants down to their roots as a form of eradication, but the effort was a failure.[6]

Bobbie wore jeans, an orange knit shirt and a red ball cap, her ginger hair streaming out the back. She walked briskly, with Sue, wearing a knit shirt and khaki shorts and sneakers, following behind. I was in last place, wishing I had reconsidered my attire for the day, particularly shoes that were more sensible for a walk through a pasture. But I managed to catch up.

My worries about being charged with trespassing or choosing the wrong shoes faded with the sound of water.

Spring Creek came into view. The division between land and water was elegantly defined, with the lip of the land positioned ever so slightly above the sheet of moving water. The creek, about eighty feet in width, flowed dark and steadily, gurgling as it moved past pecan trees, their canopies reflected in the water.

This waterway, an oasis in this dry region, has provided for man long before my grandfather came to Texas.[7] Native Americans fished the creek for centuries. US Cavalry troops in the 1840s brought their horses to drink here. For westbound pioneers, the creek was one of the last places to enjoy fresh water. From Irion County, the creek flows north and east to join the Concho River, about twenty miles away, and from there the Concho turns southeast to empty into the Colorado River, which flows through Austin on its way to Matagorda Bay in the Gulf of Mexico, several hundred miles farther to the east.

Sue walked along the streambank away from me, obviously looking for something. A moment later she pointed to the water.

"See that rock, that kind of an island out there? I believe he said it'd be right by those trees over there."

My grandfather's campsite had been overtaken by a stand of saplings. I walked over to view the stream from that vantage, formulating in my mind the world of my young grandfather as he camped. The jutting rock was in his stream view. Behind him was the grassy field through which we had tromped. I imagined him roasting a rabbit over orange embers from a wood fire, swimming in the creek, reeling in a fish for supper, bringing a dogie lamb into the tent with him to keep it safe. When his coughing spasms overtook him, I imagined him huddling in his tent, fending for himself as best as he could.

My mind raised questions. On mild nights, did he pull his sleeping pallet from the musty tent and sleep beneath an ocean of stars? Did he stare into the creek, losing himself in memories of another waterway, the Tennessee River? Did he write letters to my grandmother, or read her letters to him, by oil lamp? Did he fall asleep thinking of his children? Did he ever think of the bank's customers? Was he aware of the auditor's biting report?

I longed for one photo from his time by the creek, one view of my grandfather's lean face looking directly into the camera so that I might compare it to the photograph taken of him three years earlier when he was beginning his tenure as head cashier at Hardin County Bank. Would a streamside picture reveal a man free of worry or a man with unspoken woes? Which one did I prefer? I didn't know.

Bobbie, Sue, and I stood still watching the cool water pass us by. I suddenly realized that this grassy spot was as important to the sisters as it was to me. Here was where their daddy survived the elements, as well as the ghosts of Tennessee, to make a life for himself, for them. Here was the place where he fell in love with their mother. For Bobbie and Sue, this was a beginning place.

For me, I could easily say this was an ending place, where my grandfather severed ties to his Tennessee roots. From this creekbank, from the very plot of ground where I stood, he cemented his decision to forfeit a life with my father and his sisters in Saltillo. From here he decided Boss Bingham should stay in the past.

I also realized Bobbie, Sue and I found ourselves at this verdant spot for the same reason. Each yearned to see beyond the campsite. The Brooks sisters wanted to know about their father's life in Tennessee; I wanted to learn of my grandfather's life in Texas. Here we were at the place where Brooks diverged from Boss, staring at the smooth water my grandfather also studied long before we were born. We held our positions there for some time, lost in our separate thoughts about this man of mystery in our lives, long dead and buried, but who still possessed the power to summon and connect us.

By the time we arrived at my grandfather's final resting place about a mile north of town off a county road, Bobbie's Cadillac carried a thick coating of dust from our day's journey. She parked near the entrance marked by two sixteen-foot-tall iron posts. Arching between the posts, S-H-E-R-W-O-O-D C-E-M-E-T-E-R-Y was spelled out in letters about two feet high. The side of the large graveyard that faced the road was lined by sections of black iron fence positioned between white columns. It wasn't Shady Grove Cemetery, guarded by century-old trees on a lawn of green, but the Texas cemetery displayed a beauty in the late afternoon light that I wouldn't have seen in the glare of midday sun. The landscape, now saturated in an artist's pallete of colors, stretched beyond the ornate fence in all directions for miles and miles.

Pausing to get her bearings, Sue took the lead this time. With her hands clasped behind her back, she led us down a lane of bleached white gravel into the cemetery, then ventured into rows of tombstones. She didn't stop until she was standing in front of her father's and mother's graves where a wide slab of marble offered their names, birth dates and dates of death, along with photos.

At last, I was standing before the grave, the real grave, of my lost grandfather. I knelt, reaching out to touch the smooth stone with my fingers. My eyes swelled with tears. I wanted to say something but couldn't find the words. I felt a hand on each shoulder, Sue and Bobbie comforting me.

When I was a little girl, I believed what I was told by my grandmother, that my grandfather was buried at Shady Grove beneath a simple stone that bore only his name and year of birth and death, nothing more.

I know that was a lie. Years ago, I began searching for my grandfather, and now I was kneeling by the grave where his Bingham bones rested undisturbed a few feet beneath the rocky soil. My heart ached with the understanding that I would know him only through story, but I was grateful for that, grateful to have Sue and Bobbie as my guides.

On internet grave-searching sites, the names L. B. Bingham and Marvin L. Brooks offer the same photo on each entry, but there's no explanation of how these two men were connected.[8] Again, my family's story is not one to be told in a few words.

I snapped pictures of the grave, but it was not until I returned to Tennessee that I saw something special about my grandfather's photograph on the tombstone. The photo was likely taken in his sixties. His hair was graying, with a few streaks of white. I'm uncertain of the occasion, but he wore a coat and tie. The tie appeared to be silk and was neatly knotted. He was looking at the camera, head turned slightly to the right, just as he posed for the bank photo.

But it wasn't my grandfather's clothes that captured my attention. It was his teeth. An eye tooth on the right side was longer than the left, forcing his lips slightly apart on the side of the longer tooth. My father inherited this cuspid peculiarity. I did, too.

In this photograph, because of that tooth, my grandfather offered to the camera the barest of smiles, but it was a smile just the same.

THE SETTLEMENT

Regarding the week of trials in May 1932, my grandmother prevailed, winning judgments in every case against the insurance companies. The total of the death benefits to be paid was nearly $27,000, a colossal sum for those hard times, but it was less than the amount of coverage reported after my grandfather disappeared.

When my grandmother first sued, the payoff amounted to $37,500, but upon closer inspection, Boss was behind in payments and beyond the grace period on three policies so those were not in force at the time of his disappearance.[1] A fourth policy was issued by a company unlicensed to sell insurance in Tennessee, which nullified coverage.

In three cases, juries awarded the decisions; in four other trials, Chancellor Rye issued a bench ruling in favor of the joint complainants: my grandmother, Mary Louise Bingham, Hardin County Bank, and the State Department of Insurance and Banking.

For five days the witness list remained, with few exceptions, the same in every trial. Chief among them were my grandmother, Howard (Boss's brother), and Dr. Parker, the bank board president. They were followed in various order by the Jackson, Tennessee, father and son who found Boss's burning car, the Saltillo men who identified the body at the funeral home in Jackson, the funeral director-cum-county coroner who signed Boss's death certificate, the funeral director's brother, the bank auditor and the liquidating agent. In some trials, one or two of the board of directors and a few of the bank's customers were subpoenaed. The insurance company lawyers whose cases began late in the week took notes on testimony in the early cases hoping to question even the most minor change to a witness's story.

The cadre of attorneys who represented the insurers were far from incompetent, but a rocky field is difficult to plow. They did their best to paint my grandfather in many ways, as an absconding scoundrel one day and a bumbling accountant the next. The defense sought a wedge of sufficient width to convince a jury or Chancellor Rye that Boss was alive and, consequently, that death benefits were not due. This was a ploy born of desperation. They knew it. Reading the transcripts as many times as I have, their frustration was substantial, as the deliberations moved swiftly under the chancellor's guiding dictum in his charge to the jury: was L. B. Bingham dead and buried in Shady Grove Cemetery? This was the sole matter of contention.

The Savannah Courier summed up the week of trials in a 181-word article under the headline "Insurance Cases."[2] No witness testimony was recounted, nor did the newspaper quote any of the multitude of lawyers who had participated in the litigation. The short piece was positioned on the lower left of the front page surrounded by twelve other stories. The big story of the week was about the importance of trading with local merchants and hiring homefolks from Hardin County. However, the weekly, noting my grandfather died just before a shortage was discovered at the bank, stated in stilted prose that the insurance companies went to trial "on the theory that said Bingham is not dead."

Indeed, that was the crux of the matter. Without producing my grandfather in the flesh, the insurance companies had nothing.

Here's another point in time where I wish my grandmother had expressed her thoughts in a journal. Was she pleased that jurors of her peers and the chancellor, a former Tennessee governor, believed her? Was she ashamed for repeatedly lying on the stand? Did she believe this nightmare was over and life could return to normal? Again, I fall back to the phrase that has bedeviled me every step of my journey to unravel The Lie: I don't know. I did not embark on this path to raise more questions than answers, but that's apparently what I do best.

So, I returned to what I have, which are court documents. Thank God for court reporters.

My grandmother would have been naïve to entertain any ideas that her affiliation with attorneys and the judicial process had come to an end. In many ways, the fight had just begun. There was now a motherlode of cash to be divided, but first there would be appeals. Initially, all but one of the insurance companies indicated they were going to appeal the chancery court decisions, but only two, Business Men's Assurance Company and Modern Woodmen of America, did so.

I understand Business Men's decision. They were on the hook for $15,000 in death benefits, the most of any of the companies. Two of their policies paid double indemnity for accidental death.

However, Modern Woodmen's payout was $3,000. I'm unsure why the Illinois-based firm wanted to appeal, except perhaps to make a point. Modern Woodmen was organized in 1883 as a fraternal nonprofit, an organization that espoused ideals of community betterment, compassion for others and thrift.[3] Modern Woodmen offered financial security and camaraderie through its "camps" in thousands of small communities like Saltillo. My grandfather had been active in the organization's activities.

Of all the insurance companies, Modern Woodmen's vitriol against Boss was the harshest. "This was no accident but was the plan and executed scheme of Lytle B. Bingham to escape the consequences of his wrongful act," Modern Woodmen attorney Jere Galbraith wrote in response to a motion filed by my grandmother's attorneys.[4]

Galbraith also lashed out at the bank's board of directors. "The officials of the Hardin County Bank at first viewed the disappearance of Lytle B. Bingham with alarm. After it was found that he had . . . insurance, they pointed to his disappearance with pride," the lawyer argued.[5]

It could be that Modern Woodmen's leaders felt my grandfather violated the sanctity of the company's ideals. The company chose to stand on principle, a position I understand and one, ironically, that my grandfather and his Saltillo friends would have appreciated, too.

The insurance companies not contesting the chancery court decision paid the death benefits, with the funds deposited in an account in Savannah controlled by the county clerk and master. Not a cent was dispersed, just yet. This goes counter to the talk in Saltillo at the time, when people assumed that since the cases went her way, my grandmother was flush with cash. In fact, many years after her husband left Saltillo, my grandmother struggled mightily to manage her farm along with other duties.

The Business Men's Assurance and Modern Woodmen of America cases were heard in the West Tennessee section of the State Court of Appeals in late 1932 and moved on to the Tennessee Supreme Court in early 1933. That saying about repeating the same action, hoping for a different reaction, could be applied to both insurance companies. They trusted that circumstantial evidence raising questions about Boss's death would yield a better reaction from black-robed judges and justices in the higher courts. Their faith was misplaced. The tone of each decision implied umbrage that the question was even being raised.

The Court of Appeals stated: "We think the conclusion reached by Judge and jury was not only supported by material evidence but was the only reasonable conclusion to be drawn from the proven circumstances."[6]

The Supreme Court's rebuke was even stronger. The justice's noted a protracted investigation into Boss's death "had been prosecuted continuously and diligently . . . yet not a syllable of proof was produced by (the) appellant to show any fact or circumstance indicating that Bingham was alive, or that he had not died at the time, at the place, and in the manner alleged by complainants."[7]

With that unanimous decree from the state's highest court, the insurance companies had no choice about paying the death benefits, but settlement wasn't simply a matter of checks being mailed. There were complications. Many of the life policies my grandfather purchased in the two years before he disappeared were purchased with checks written on his account, which the audit found to be more than $9,000 overdrawn at the time the bank closed. That was among the reasons the bank and the State Department of Insurance and Banking sought to join my grandmother's suits. Soon after the high court's decision was published, the next round of litigation began. This time it was my grandmother and my grandfather's estate being sued by Hardin County Bank and the Tennessee Department of Insurance and Banking.

Elijah W. Ross, who continued to represent Hardin County Bank, received a letter of encouragement in this endeavor from D. D. Robertson, state superintendent of banks. "I believe you will be equally as successful in recovering that portion of the insurance that justly belongs to the bank," Robertson wrote.[8]

Defining how much of the thousands in death benefits "justly" belonged to the bank and its customers became a source of contention. In as much as lawyers representing my grandmother and the bank got along when they were on the same side seeking the insurance funds, when the dividing lines were redrawn, the lawyers were not as amicable.

Through the dry month of June of 1933 when crops parched under twenty days of temperatures above ninety degrees, including four days when the mercury reached one hundred degrees, the lawyers held conferences, but failed to reach an agreement.[9] The talks stretched into autumn, as West Tennessee farmers harvested 19 percent fewer acres of cotton than the previous year due to economic hardships and a lack of rain. For the first time in five years, cotton production in the state slipped below one million acres harvested.[10]

A major step toward agreement came in October of 1933 when both parties set the date of March 22, 1929, as the earliest date my grandfather's bank account was overdrawn. Premiums paid prior to that date would be considered funded solely by Boss. Premiums paid after that date would be considered funded by the bank, via my grandfather's overdrawn account. Where evidence showed there was a mixture of funds used, a pro rata formula was to be applied to divide the money. The two sides returned to their corners to mull over the ramifications of this agreement as the first frost of fall covered the river bottomlands, the time of year for slaughtering hogs. Fat hams and slabs of pork belly were salted and put away to cure in smokehouses as the lawyers argued how the insurance proceeds would be divided.

Meanwhile, by the fall of 1933, my grandfather had not been addressed as "Boss" for nearly two years. He had settled into Texas life where he was known simply as Brooks. Home was still a floorless pole tent pitched on the bank of Spring Creek but his health improved. Dr. Parker was right, the drier climate eased the TB symptoms. On the ranch Brooks was a general cowpoke. Occasionally, he'd raise dogie lambs to maturity, feeding them with a bottle until they were of weaning age. He had the husbandry touch, the ability to nurture a foundling whose mother had died. My stoic grandfather had a soft heart for an animal in need.

Brooks wrote infrequently and discreetly to my grandmother.[11] His sister, Verna, and brother, Howard, served as go-betweens. The correspondence was destroyed to avoid detection by the private investigators hired by the insurance companies but I can't help wondering what he wrote.

Maybe he described the differences between the khaki-colored soil of West Texas and southwest Tennessee's darker loam. Perhaps he compared sunrises and sunsets in Sherwood to what he remembered from Saltillo. Or perch fishing in Spring Creek compared to hooking catfish on the Tennessee River. Surely, he inquired of his children, asking how tall the girls had grown and how rambunctious his namesake, my father, had become. I like to imagine he wrote long letters expressing his love, reassuring my grandmother that their absence from each other was not permanent.

By the time settlement talks had begun, however, my grandmother knew reconciliation was going to be impossible and that's when, I believe, she wrote a letter to her husband, giving him permission to start a new life without her.

While the letters between husband and wife, separated by 853 miles, did not survive the decades, what I do have is evidence of my grandmother's resolve to see the insurance settlement through . . . alone. As the documents that would bring an end to the litigation were being prepared, my grandmother's sole purpose became survival, finding a way to keep her children fed, clothed, and educated through the despair of the Depression.

I am left to ponder her will and to respect her fortitude. I believe sheer grit fueled her through the trials of 1932 and the seemingly never-ending settlement talks that followed. I do not fully understand why she participated in the coverup of her husband's fake demise, but I do understand why she perpetuated insurance fraud. To her, Boss really was dead. If ruin was to be avoided, the heavy lifting of saving herself, her daughters and son would be a duty performed by her as a single mother.

In November 1933, the two sides settled on terms. My grandmother's lawyers proposed to distribute funds based on whether premiums were paid before or after my grandfather's checking account became overdrawn.[12] Following this formula my grandmother would have received a little more than $17,000 and the bank a little more than $9,000.

The offer included language that refuted the auditor's report. "While we do not admit as a fact that there was any shortage or overdraft of his account on that date . . . this contention of (the) complainant is used as a basis for the settlement herein offered," my grandmother's attorneys noted.

However, the State Department of Insurance and Banking did not accept the offer.[13] In fact, state banking authorities were willing to put the matter to a jury.

In mid-April 1934, with less than two weeks to go before trial, the bank countered with a simple settlement. If my grandmother paid the bank $10,000 from the insurance payouts, the bank would make no other claims to the proceeds of the policies.

"I think the proposition that I have made is exceedingly fair to the widow and the minors," Ross wrote to Grover McCormick, my grandmother's lead counsel.[14]

Ross's letter ended with a personal statement indicating his exasperation with the process: "I am anxious to wind up the case and get the matter entirely disposed of." Indeed, the Bingham case thoroughly tested the attorney's resolve to see the case through to settlement. In a December 1933 letter to a lawyer for one of the insurance companies, Ross acknowledged he was "ready to get this Bingham decree settled, finally, absolutely, for good, eternally, forever, and, at last, and no one will be more delighted than I at the conclusion . . . "[15]

Although my grandmother's lawyers may have shared Ross's frustration, they were not in a mood to capitulate. Three days later, Warren H. Sloan, another of my grandmother's attorneys, countered with the less round figure of $8,708.04.[16] Sloan said if the offer was unacceptable then "we may proceed to go to trial on this next week."

Apparently, there's nothing like a pending trial to bring opposing counsel to the settlement table and that's what happened. On May 3, 1934, Chancellor Rye agreed to give each side a few more days to reach a compromise. Within a week, the matter was decided, two years after the 1932 trials ended.[17]

In exchange for transferring $9,500 from the insurance proceeds to Robertson, acting as receiver for the bank, the state banking agency would "take no other or further interest in any policy or policies of insurance issued on the life of L. B. Bingham, deceased."[18]

In other words, the remainder of the funds, a little more than $16,000, belonged to my grandmother and her children.[19] But they received much less because of other complications. First National Bank in Jackson won a judgment in 1931 to collect on a loan that Boss defaulted on. With interest and court costs added, that took $2,000 off the top of their proceeds.[20]

Another large chunk went to my grandmother's trio of lawyers, who finally received a payday.[21] From the payouts on policies where she was named sole beneficiary, McCormick, Sloan and Harbert took one-third, giving them $4,666.13. However, Chancellor Rye took exception to awarding the lawyers one-third of the proceeds due the minor children. He ordered the clerk and master to negotiate compensation for their work representing my father and his older sisters. The lawyers settled for $2,700, equal to about one-fourth of the amount the children received.[22]

After the post-litigation accounting was done, my grandmother and her children received $6,869. Again, a single check wasn't mailed. About half of the proceeds belonged to my father and his older sisters because they were the sole beneficiaries of several policies. Consequently, their funds, as well as a portion of the proceeds due to my grandmother, stayed under the control of the Hardin County clerk and master. When cash was needed, my grandmother, through an attorney, petitioned Rye for an allotment, usually every other month or so. This was a way to ensure the assets were properly distributed to my aunts and father.

My grandmother, as it turns out, was equally determined that her kids receive what was due them.

Court records, yellowed with age, tell the story of her return several times a year over the next twelve-plus years to the same Hardin County Courthouse where, in 1932, she repeatedly proclaimed under oath her husband was dead.[23] Through her longtime attorney W. H. Sloan, she petitioned the court for funds to reimburse her for purchases of school supplies, clothing, grocery items and medicine. The process required keeping thorough records and all receipts.

There was a peculiarity about this arrangement.[24] Rye authorized the clerk and master, C. S. Welch, to loan a large portion of the insurance proceeds to county citizens. On several occasions, more than one-half was loaned out on interest to farmers and businessmen, some of whom were from Saltillo. Ironically, the money Boss "bequeathed" to his children via insurance payoffs was loaned as if the clerk and master was a banker. Over the years the arrangement guaranteed more money for the Bingham siblings because they collected hundreds of dollars in interest payments from these loans. Apparently, the loans were safe, too. There is no mention of defaults in any of the monthly reports.

In 1939, my grandmother asked for payment of several hundred dollars as reimbursement for expenditures from 1937 and 1938.[25] During that time, she handed over the receipts to her attorney, for safekeeping, but Sloan lost them. Consequently, her April 1939 request was a five-page missive detailing what she had bought, dates of the purchases and with whom she had done business.

The request isn't noteworthy for what she purchased but for information about daily life at the farm and for the undeniable truth that my grandmother had become a woman in charge, boss of the farm. She hired her younger brother, Chester, to plow and plant a cotton crop in 1937, in exchange for boarding at her home. The result was a harvest of only seven bales of cotton, but the sale provided some much-needed cash. The following year, she entered a share-crop situation with "a man named Carter," but 1938 proved a bad year for cotton. Only four bales were collected. The yield matched expenses but produced no profits.

She reported to the judge that she bought groceries at J. H. Allen and Son's store in Saltillo and produced charge account records indicating she spent $261.57 at the store during the years of 1938 and 1939.

"In addition to the expenditures at Allen's Store, a great many items for the children have been ordered from Sears, Roebuck & Company," her request continued. "The family has ordered extensively from Sears, Roebuck & Company because the guardian of the wards, Verna Bingham, was for a great many years employed as a stenographer in the office of Sears, Roebuck & Company at Memphis."

My father went to school wearing Sears dungarees, it seems.

My grandmother took pains to document her thrift for Chancellor Rye, declaring she bartered every week with peddlers, exchanging eggs gathered from the ninety chickens in her henhouse and pounds of home-churned butter for items carried by the "traveling stores," as they were called. From a neighbor farmer, she purchased two dressed hogs, buying one with the children's funds and one with her own money. "This meat was placed in the home and was used by the entire family," she stated.

One item in the 1939 request particularly caught my eye. She sought reimbursement for two years of premiums on a life insurance policy for my father, then ten. My grandmother explained that Boss had purchased policies for his daughters and those policies carried the provision that in the event of his death, while they were minors, the girl's policies would remain in force, but no future premiums would be collected.

My grandmother wrote that perhaps she erred by seeking reimbursement for her son's insurance, but felt it was a necessary cost "for the further reason that the family is insurance minded, due to the fact that all they have, came by insurance."[26]

Was she just being unfalteringly honest or pointedly flippant? I'll never know, but her long-winded reimbursement request was granted, and Sloan, embarrassed for misplacing his client's receipts, never made that mistake again.

My grandmother's requests for funds continued year after year. New shoes for my father. New dresses for my aunts. Cash to buy the children's schoolbooks, pencils, and paper. As the kids grew older the expenses were greater. Mary Lou, the youngest of the two girls, attended business college after high school and needed money for tuition and living expenses. As my father, Lytle, approached his senior year at Saltillo High, he was appropriated $100 "to meet the extraordinary expenses of said high school."

I heard stories of my grandmother's dislike of making those trips to the court-house in Savannah each time she needed funds. The act of entering the building was a reminder of loss and shame. I'm sure she also feared what people were thinking: there's the widow Bingham coming to collect her winnings made on the back of a bank ground into insolvency by her husband.

In late 1938, however, I believe my grandmother stopped caring what others thought or was too busy to give a care. Margaret Lois, the eldest daughter, con-tracted tuberculosis at the age of fifteen, and her symptoms were much worse than her father's. The mother became the daughter's primary caregiver and ad-vocate. She requested $200 from insurance proceeds to add a room to the house where Margaret Lois could live and be treated apart from the rest of the family.[27] Chancellor Rye agreed. By the summer of 1939, Margaret Lois moved into the new room, her home for the remainder of her life. She died in 1947.

I imagine witnessing her daughter's slow decline to the same disease that weakened her husband was a horrible blow to my grandmother. She probably wondered if Boss had somehow transmitted the disease to Margaret Lois before he left Saltillo and symptoms didn't show until eight years later. Did she blame him? Or did she believe Margaret Lois's case was God's retribution? It didn't matter. In the end, I believe, my grandmother just decided that hunkering down, serving her sick daughter as best she could, was her only choice and that's what she did. If gossipers wagged their tongues about the insurance money, my grandmother gave no mind.

Lawsuits associated with the bank failure continued into the era of World War II. Customers who couldn't meet their obligations to the bank were sued, and a few customers sued the bank. Boss's parents, James M. and Josie Bingham, were among those sued for nonpayment of a mortgage loan. They contended Boss marked the loan "Paid," but the audit showed a balance owed of more than

$300. Boss's father was adamant on the stand that the note had been paid in full. Pressed by E. W. Ross, the bank's attorney, for an explanation of how this could be, my great-grandfather, sixty-seven, exploded in frustration.

"I do not know why a lot of things was done that is done. Lots of things was done that was not done by the Binghams that they were accused of," he said.[28] While his statement lacked the polish of a good speaker, his message was received clearly by me. He didn't believe his son was either a crook or a poor accountant. He didn't know what caused the bank to fail, but he knew his son, and he believed that Boss did his best to keep the bank solvent.

My great-grandfather was never privy to The Lie. He died six years later in 1940 never knowing his oldest son was alive in Texas.

The insurance payments to my grandmother, my father and my aunts continued deep into the 1940s. The payments outlasted Chancellor Rye, who retired from office in 1942 after two decades in the post. In 1946, a little more than $1,500 remained to be distributed, according to the October monthly report from that year.[29] If there were other reports filed, they have been lost or misfiled, so I don't know when my grandmother paid her final visit to the courthouse.

But I'm confident she was happy, at last, to be relieved of that duty.

DYING

I come to the telling of Marvin Lester Brooks' last days laden with emotions. Through the narratives of my Texas aunts and uncles, I developed a vicarious connection with the grandfather I never knew.[1] Their memories took me into the cotton fields where he planted orange-meated watermelons for his children to enjoy on a hot day and into high school gymnasiums as he and Hootsie cheered on their children's athletic pursuits, even if it meant dashing from one town to another.

I learned that in his later years he became a fan of "the stories." At midday, he and Hootsie watched soap operas on their small black-and-white television, with their favorite being "As the World Turns." It was a daily ritual they did not dismiss. If shopping in San Angelo, they made sure to be in the TV sales department at Sears when the show aired so as not to miss an episode.

His fascination with soap operas intrigued me. I wondered if watching the convoluted story plots unwind on daytime television gave my grandfather hope that his story could one day be made straight, too.

I know that he didn't hold grudges. His Texas daughters told the story of a rift between my grandfather and a longtime friend in the 1960s. Brooks sought reconciliation and the friendship was mended. When the friend died, my grandfather paid the gravedigger's fee to open the ground to accept the friend's coffin, just as the two men had agreed decades earlier. When Brooks died, the friend's widow paid to prepare my grandfather's grave.

I learned of his fondness for a simple life rooted in the land, of his desire to serve his community, of the layer of sentimentality beneath his stoic nature.

Now, his death—his real death—beckoned and I dreaded the telling, for this is the saddest chapter of my grandfather's story.

When the Sisters of Charity of the Incarnate Word, a congregation of nuns from San Antonio, expanded their mission work to West Texas in the early 1900s, their plan was to build schools in the relatively new hardscrabble town of San Angelo, whose early history included lawlessness, brothels, gambling halls and saloons.[2] Soon after their arrival, however, the sisters were persuaded by town leaders to expand their mission to include a hospital. The pragmatic nuns secured a plot of cheap land a few miles from town. In 1910, St. John's Sanitarium, a four-story red brick building with thirty beds, opened for business. Locals were elated, for prior to its opening the injured and ill were either treated at home or were shuttled long distances. It was the first hospital to open between El Paso and San Antonio, a gap of 550 miles. By 1971, when Brooks had his first stroke, the facility, renamed St. John's Hospital, had one year earlier completed a large expansion, including the addition of an intensive care unit with six beds.[3]

Just in time to save my grandfather's life . . . and his story.

Neither Sue, Bobbie nor Freddie was living at home when Brooks was felled by the stroke. Sue resided in Odessa. Bobbie was in El Paso and Freddie, a few years past his Marine days, was living in San Angelo. Sonny was not yet a teenager and doesn't remember details about the day his father became ill. What's important is that Brooks arrived at the hospital quickly enough to be stabilized and was discharged five days later, weak, but without paralysis or impairment to his memory and speech.

The latter is a crucial point. If the stroke had taken my grandfather's cognitive ability you would not be reading this book. I would be a retiree content with her life of hobbies, taking trips to the beach and having fun with friends. Solving the mystery of my lost grandfather would not be my life's obsession because I would have no knowledge of the mystery. Details of Boss's hurried departure from Saltillo—digging up the corpse, setting his car ablaze, holing up in western Oklahoma, arriving in Sherwood—may have never been shared with my father and my aunt. It's possible The Lie could have died with my grandmother, Jiggs and Verna.

Yes, other clues would have indicated something was amiss, particularly thousands of pages of court documents produced in my grandmother's lawsuits against the insurance companies, but I doubt I would have been intrigued by dust-laden transcripts. Further, I don't believe the doubts raised by the insurance companies about my grandfather's death would have attracted my attention, and if they had I would have likely chalked up such claims as red herrings cast into the fray by high-paid lawyers. I might have listened with interest to the speculation about my grandfather's auto accident, but it wouldn't have been a clarion call. I would not have taken time from my busy life to sort questions about a man I never met.

I'm sorry to say, I was not curious enough to unravel this tale alone. My grandfather's assistance was required. Without his survival of that stroke and his subsequent desire to peel back the hardened layers of his darkest secret, I would have never known details of his dual life. I would have become an unwitting accomplice in keeping The Lie safe because I never would have thought to ask questions.

As always with the Boss/Brooks story, this pivotal point was accompanied by a symmetry to the narrative. For what happened in Texas, there was an equal and opposite reaction in Tennessee and vice versa. Brook's admission of what happened on that night in 1931, when he was another man with another name, produced a shock wave through the Binghams and the Brooks. We were never the same, each group ambushed by Newton's third law of motion. Who knew physics applied to both the familial and the natural worlds?

The unraveling began with a request for paper and pencil.

"I have something to tell you," Brooks told Bobbie from his hospital bed.[4]

She inspected her pocketbook for a pen or pencil and a piece of paper on which to take notes. She had never seen such an earnest expression on her father's face and moved nearer to the bed to hear every word.

"You've been looking for the family, but you've been looking for the wrong name," he said.

"My name is Bingham, not Brooks."

The unspooling of my grandfather's secret began with the utterance of these six words. For more than forty years he had protected his new identity.

Brooks not Boss.

How many times in the early Texas years did he worry that he would introduce himself as a man who was dead and buried? He learned his lesson well. No one suspected he was anyone other than Marvin Lester Brooks. No police agency was ever on his trail.

His Texas daughters knew about a few Tennessee relatives—half siblings, an uncle named Jiggs and an aunt named Verna—since they were in grade school, but their father never offered details. The idea there was another family fascinated Sue and Bobbie. They studied the map of Tennessee, wondering where their lost kin could be.

"He never did tell me not to talk about it," Sue said, but it was clear her dad was not offering further information.[5] The sisters said they often opened the bureau drawer in their parents' bedroom to stare at photographs of their Bingham half siblings. Their curiosity was sustained into their young adult years.

Sue began her search for Howard shortly after she got married. If she could find the correct town, maybe luck would be on her side and someone would know of a man with the nickname of Jiggs, and he could connect her to the cast of other characters in her father's history.

"Back in those days you could get an operator on the phone. You just told who you were looking for. I looked all over the eastern United States. Daddy said last he heard Jiggs was in Chicago, so I called in that area," Sue said. "Then I narrowed it down to the lower part of the United States. I'd call and call. I'd do this when I couldn't sleep at night."

Sue possessed a streak of persistence. When an area of the country produced no results, she moved on. She said she became friendly with operators, having long conversations with them because they weren't busy at that time of night. They, in turn, tried to help her.

"One night I was picking out little counties or towns around in the lower part of Georgia and the upper part of Florida.[6] I'd pick this town and say, 'I'm looking for Howard Jiggs Brooks.' They'd try to find (him). I kept calling and calling. Finally, this man told me, 'Lady, you've called me six times. I sure hope you find what you're looking for.' But I never did find anything."

Neither did Bobbie. To both, the cause seemed lost.

Not until my grandfather's stroke did my aunts hear, directly from him, what had transpired in Tennessee. I wondered why my grandfather decided to bare his soul when he did. Sue said her dad understood survival of another stroke wasn't likely.

"Do you think he didn't want to die without . . . ," I began to ask before Sue completed my thought.

"Without somebody knowing the truth, I think so," she said, somberly.

On the night at St. John's Hospital when Brooks asked her to listen to his tale, Bobbie said he talked for more than an hour of the days leading up to the January 1931 night he bade goodbye to my grandmother. He told his daughter everything: the bank's failure, the fear he was dying of tuberculosis, the awful business at the cemetery, the getaway plan, the trek to Sayre, Oklahoma, then Corpus Christi, then Sherwood, setting up camp at Spring Creek and, later, deciding to stay in Texas. The man of few words talked and talked and talked, Bobbie said.

"What was your reaction?" I asked.

"It would be like shock," she replied. Her reaction, I'm sure, mirrored my jumbled feelings when I learned details of how my grandfather came to have a second life in Texas. But her experience was wholly different, too. Her dad was a known quantity to her, or so she thought. That unlawful activity played a role in his back story, including the disinterment and mutilation of a cadaver, was unsettling. Sue was as surprised as her sister. She couldn't believe her dad had been involved in such an affair. Freddie was both resolute and stoic about his father's confession. Nothing in the past could diminish his father's image. To him, the important takeaway was the upright, well-liked, hard-working man he had known all his life, not the flawed man who left Tennessee in a hurry.

Bobbie said her father waited until he was home from the hospital before telling his wife because he didn't know how Hootsie would react. "He was afraid she would leave him while he was in the hospital," she said.

To say Hootsie was stunned at the extent of her husband's revelations, is an epic understatement. She knew of another wife and children but had no idea of the appalling details surrounding his hasty exit from Tennessee.

"I guess she knew all along there was something there and she wouldn't never ask. So, I think she was probably hurt because she was not the first one to find out. And I think the only reason I was the first, it was because I was the one there that night," Bobbie said.

Following the 1971 stroke, my grandfather's health improved to a point, but his stamina for physical labor didn't return. Sue and Bobbie could tell a difference when they came for weekend visits. There was no doubt the stroke aged him, but the daughters also looked at him differently because they now knew that he was five years older, born in 1895 not 1900. Brooks was seventy-six, not seventy-one. Something else was cause for concern, too. A measure of paranoia seeped into his life. When Brooks heard a car enter the drive leading to the house, he'd look out the living room window to see who was coming.[7] "If he didn't recognize the person, he slipped out the back door," Sue noted. Paranoia is not uncommon among stroke survivors, but Bobbie said her father's fear was specific. "He was afraid his best friends would come get him," she said.

I was saddened by this revelation. Here was a man who lived the second half of his life in Texas without, for the most part, looking back to see if anyone from the past had tracked him from Tennessee. However, the stroke's effects and his decision to tell what happened all those years ago left him vulnerable. When he said friends might come, I wondered if he was thinking of Irion County friends, or was he thinking of Saltillo friends, friends he hadn't seen in four decades?

Saltillo had been on my grandfather's mind for some time, even before he called Bobbie to his hospital bed to take notes. In March 1971, not quite two months before his stroke, Brooks received word from Howard that my grandmother died of cancer.[8] He broached the idea with Jiggs of returning to Saltillo for the funeral. Afterward, Jiggs would inconspicuously introduce him to my father and aunt, Mary Lou.

The brothers quickly realized how terrible of an idea it would be to bring back to life a man who had been dead for decades and, even worse, to show up on the day of my grandmother's funeral. I'm glad he didn't come, turning a memorial into a circus of raw emotion worthy of a grocery store tabloid. However, my grandfather's consideration of the trip, to risk the life and reputation he had crafted in Texas so he could pay last respects to my grandmother, raised the question of whether he was pondering how to set things right before he died.

Perhaps Boss was planning a covert road trip to see my father and aunt, to visit the graves of my grandmother and his daughter, Margaret Lois. Closing my eyes, I could see him parking his Chevrolet pickup in front of my father's home in Missouri and knocking on his door. What would he say? Would he explain 1931 in detail? Would he just say, "I'm sorry." I wondered how my father would have responded. Or my Aunt Mary Lou.

These are pointless musings because the stroke negated a face-to-face reunion. Instead, he asked for pencil and paper, making Sue and Bobbie the curators of his story.

My grandfather's second stroke occurred on February 5, 1973, a Monday evening.[9] There was a water board meeting that night, and Brooks was getting dressed to leave. One minute he was feeling fine; the next he was prone on the floor, unconscious. A blood vessel burst in the right hemisphere of his brain, but it was much worse than the first stroke. The emergency room physicians and a neurologist stabilized him, but told the family there was nothing that could be done. On Wednesday, he rallied long enough to recognize Hootsie, but returned to a semi-conscious state.

"It was a sad occasion," Bobbie remembered. "You wanted him back, but you knew that if he ever woke up from the stroke he would have been paralyzed and maybe couldn't speak. And we knew he would have been miserable."

My grandfather clung to life for seven days at St. John's. About two in the morning on February 12, a nurse told Hootsie and Bobbie to alert other family members because the end was near. Brooks' breathing was labored, his chest barely rising with each inhalation. Hootsie's sister, Ethel, woke up her pastor and asked him to pray with the family. The Brooks family stood around the bed holding hands. The preacher began a prayer for the soul of Marvin Lester Brooks and my grandfather's chest rose for the last time, but, as Bobbie remembered, "you never heard it come out."

The time of passing was 4:30 a.m. Both of my grandfather's deaths came in the pre-dawn darkness of winter mornings. The first was on a snow-covered state highway in Tennessee. There, he stood in the cold, a fugitive, watching a stand-in corpse be consumed by flames. The second was in a hospital established not long after he was born by a group of nuns doing the Lord's bidding in West Texas. Family surrounded him from head to foot as they said goodbye.

It was a sad time, but not the saddest, in my mind. In the week leading to his death, my grandfather cried out for my grandmother and his children in Tennessee. He called out for his children by name: Margaret Lois, Mary Lou, and Lytle.

He also called for my grandmother.

Sue heard him more than once. "He kept wanting Mary. He said, 'Mary, Mary where are you? Mary, I need you,'" Sue said.

These words of a dying man will forever be on my heart.

MEETING SONNY

MAY 6, 2015: BROOKS

I thought my visit to West Texas so far had provided a good primer on the geography of the region, but I was wrong. This was made pointedly clear as Bobbie's Caddie took us farther west than I had been before, at least via ground transportation. Like many travelers, I've flown across this part of the state several times in an airplane, but I was back on US Highway 67, skimming along on the straight blacktop at sixty miles an hour. My aunts and I were off to see their kid brother, Sonny, who lived in the unincorporated town of Girvin in Pecos County, 129 miles west of San Angelo.

Once we passed through Irion County, mountains came into view, reminding me of the approach to the Cumberland Plateau in Tennessee, a high table of verdant land that bisects the eastern half of the state between Nashville and Knoxville.

The difference was that in this dry region the rising ground was almost treeless. Instead, the turning rotor blades of hundreds of wind turbines spanned the ridges on both sides of the road, standing like giant pinwheels. The supporting shafts rose hundreds of feet into the air, while the blades were nearly two hundred feet in length. They were an impressive sight. They towered above the ridges, their aerodynamic blades nimbly responding to the breath of blue skies.

I saw them come into view first after passing Barnhart, then saw more as we traveled farther west through Big Lake, Rankin and McCamey, towns whose histories are connected to oil exploration and their futures, it seems, are staked on reliable winds.

I wondered what my grandfather would have thought of the sight. I suspect he'd be fascinated with these twirling behemoths. However, being a man of the land, he'd also ponder the veracity of calling a collection of these spinning contraptions a "wind farm." The only mode of farming he knew was the kind that left dirt beneath his fingernails, work that tested a man's mettle. According to the rules of farming he knew, nature was not always a friend. Droughts wilted crops. Floods did equal damage. Livestock acquired diseases. But here in this dry land, where streams of wind were ever present, man had found a way to convert the un-seeable into electricity that lit homes and powered industries.

As we drove on, the landscape became the backdrop for a Hollywood western.[1] Cue the lost, shuffling, whiskered soul crying out for water. Later, I learned we were entering the Trans-Pecos region, part of the Chihuahuan Desert, the largest in North America, stretching from central Mexico north to southern Arizona and New Mexico. The area included the nine most western counties of Texas, counties that were the largest in the state. Together, their land mass of 31,000 square miles nearly matched the size of South Carolina.[2]

"We're about to cross over the Pecos River," Bobbie noted from the driver's seat. "Hang on." She was referring to the region's checkered history in the late nineteenth century when it was said "there were no laws west of the Pecos." This region was a hideout for thieves and spawned the rise (and the legend) of Judge Roy Bean, known as the hanging judge.

As I took in the passing landscape, so different from Middle Tennessee, I wondered how anyone could make a living here. Even the Pecos River worked hard, constantly twisting and turning, forming one hairpin curve after another, as it flowed to the Rio Grande.

Girvin is in northeastern Pecos County.[3] Cattle traders established a settlement here in the 1890s, but growth didn't come until the Kansas City, Mexico and Orient Railway extended its line.[4] By the 1920s, several businesses including a hotel and a saloon had opened. By the end of that decade, following the discovery of oil, Girvin became a delivery point for rigging equipment and supplies and continued to be a hub for ranchers sending cattle to market. In 1929, the town became one of the first in the region to receive electricity after a turbine was installed on the Pecos River to provide power to the oil fields. Girvin homes had electric lights more than a decade before power came to Saltillo, back in Tennessee.[5]

In 1935, Highway 67 bypassed Girvin, and the town's post office moved to the new road.[6] In the boom-and-bust of oil production, Girvin became a casualty. A decade later, trains had no reason to stop there anymore and by 1963, the town's population dwindled to only thirty hearty souls, according to census data. It's about the same today.

"We're here," Bobbie said, easing her car into a gravel lot in front of a cinder block building with a low-pitched tin roof. She pulled into a space near the building's front door. There were a few other cars and numerous pickup trucks already in the lot. Standing beside the car, I looked around and saw this was the only outpost of activity for miles around. The sun hovered directly over us and the air was summer warm, with not a breeze stirring.

Jutting from the left side of the building was a covered outdoor seating area that offered shade from the sun. Several men and boys were seated at tables. They nodded hello. Butting up against the patio on the far left was an interesting sight, a rusty freight car bearing the fading logo of the Santa Fe Railway. But there were no train tracks. It's as if the last time the train stopped in Girvin, the rail car was abandoned as a memento.

The building offered no sign to explain what it was, just a white door that Bobbie opened and then motioned for me to follow.

"What is this place?" I asked her.

"Well, it's a place the family can get together. Sonny's been fixing it up."

A blast of cool air coming out the door got my attention. There was air conditioning, thank God. I let the sisters go ahead of me. They knew everyone and soon enough a chorus of "So good to see you" and "How are you" was heard as Bobbie and Sue were hugged and welcomed. I smiled and scanned the room looking for anyone who looked like a Bingham, but I didn't see a single familiar trait.

Sue motioned for me to come over and she introduced me to Sonny's wife and daughter-in-law. They were very cordial, asking me about Nashville. They pointed out Sonny's children and grandchildren. The welcome mat was out for me, the woman of a thousand questions from Tennessee.

Suddenly, all my searching for a Bingham face among all those Brooks came to an end. Seated in a folding chair sipping water from a bottle was Sonny, and I'll be damned if I wasn't looking at Boss Bingham . . . and my father. I'm sure my mandible clanked as it hit the floor. I couldn't believe what I was seeing. His firm jaw line reminded me of my father's. So did his cheek bones. In Sonny's eyes I saw my grandfather, peering at me with the same laconic pose that I studied so closely in the bank photograph of him taken more than ninety years earlier. Sonny aged like my grandfather, too, a furrowed forehead, cheeks that sank to jowls and a weathered face from being outdoors much of the time.

But he frequently smiled, wide and toothy and accompanied by a chuckle when a granddaughter neared to whisper in his ear.

"It's so nice to finally meet you," I said to him, reaching to shake his hand. It was beyond nice. I wanted to stare at his face longer than is customary in social situations, particularly with a person you're meeting for the first time. I wanted to search for more similarities, to enjoy this moment of connecting dots between the Binghams of Saltillo and the Brooks of West Texas.

Sonny and I moved to a corner of the room to talk. Only later did I realize how unusual this situation was. He's fifty-six. My father, his half brother whom he never met, was born thirty years before him. I was born four years before Sonny. Yet, in the structure of family, he was my uncle.

"If you would, say your name and where you're from," I asked.

"Well, you want the name I go by or the name I was born with?" he replied in a definitive Texas drawl, a smile on his face. I am convinced his blue-green eyes twinkled a bit. When he narrowed them and chuckled, I quickly learned to pay attention. I wondered was this a trait passed to him by his dad, or was I looking at vestiges of Hootsie?

I told him I'd like both names.

"William Lewis Brooks," he said. "I go by Sonny, instead of William and I live in Girvin, Texas, which is nowhere."

His given name was a surprise to me. I thought Sonny was his real name.

"Nah. They let my brother name me and nobody liked it. They went to calling me Sonny and it's been that ever since," he said. Indeed, Freddie did receive the naming rights since he finally had a brother, albeit one that was twenty years younger. It's also true that William Lewis just didn't stick. No one knows who started calling the baby "Sonny," but he has answered to the nickname all of his life.

I enjoyed hearing his voice; it was easy on the ear. Sonny had the habit of occasionally inserting "Like I said," into a sentence, which implied that he was reiterating a point already made, but he usually hadn't. It was just his West Texas way, I determined, of adding emphasis. Did my grandfather speak like that, or have any language peculiarities of his own, I wondered? Did his southern accent become more Texan than Tennessean after living so long in the Lone Star State? My mind was stirring as he talked.

One of Sonny's earliest memories of his dad was tagging along with Brooks in the fields. "I wasn't even six years old before he had me driving the tractor," he said. "I lived in Sherwood. I grew up on the farm and spent all my time in the bushes and on the creeks."

His eyes brightened. "When I was little, Daddy would take me up to where our irrigation pump was and kick my butt out and I'd fish up and down that creek all day long and he'd come back and pick me up in the evenings. I didn't even know how to swim. I could (still) swim across. I'd just grab a log and paddle across, float my way across. That's just the kind of way we grew up."

I was not surprised to learn Sonny earned a living in the outdoors. For almost thirty years he was a state-licensed trapper, dispensing with coyotes, bobcats and an occasional mountain lion that were causing problems for ranchers.

"I can't work inside a building. I'm an outdoor person. I worked the oil field and like I said, I got into trapping. That was like going and playing every day than really working."

Sonny was the surprise baby. According to Sue and Bobbie, their mother, Hootsie, became pregnant when she was forty-four and Brooks was fifty-three (fifty-eight by his Tennessee age).

Bobbie had explained to me earlier that her mother did not know she was pregnant. "She went to see her primary care doctor in San Angelo. He said you're going through the change." However, medicine prescribed for her made her ill. Sensing something was wrong, Hootsie's sister took her to a gynecologist who pronounced her with child, several months along as a matter of fact. The news made Hootsie angry, and Brooks took the brunt of it. "She was so mad at him. For a week, she wouldn't talk to him. Oh, she was so mad," Sue said, chuckling.

"Yeah, she was going through the change, all right," Bobbie added.

When Sonny was born, Sue was married and had a child, Karla, who was eight months old. Meanwhile, Freddie was in college and Bobbie was a junior in high school. The unexpected baby was doted on, though not spoiled. But Sonny learned, as all children do, which parent is the most accommodating, and that was his father, the youngest of the Brooks siblings admitted.

"He never tied my hand as much as Mama did. He always let her do that. Like I said, he was a hell of a daddy. He helped me do anything I did. If I wanted to go fishing, he was taking me," the youngest Brooks noted.

As for having three much older siblings: "It was like having more parents." Sue and Bobbie shared a muted laugh at hearing this. "The closest thing I got to a sister is my niece, Karla," he added. In any other family, I might have to stop to figure out how a man could have a niece who was older than himself, but this is my family and I understood right away.

As a father, Brooks was not a jokester, the son noted, "but he was always pulling stuff." When he and Karla would accompany him out to check fields, "he'd reach out and grab the electric fence, then touch you on the ear. Give you a little jolt. I think he was a lot lighter with me than he was with Sue and them." Sonny recalled one occasion when he and two other boys were caught using chewing tobacco and snuff. "We thought we were being sneaky. We got down to the river and Daddy took us to the Twelve Mile Bridge and kicked me and Charles and Jimmy out and left us there. Before he left, he asked me which one had the chewing tobacco. He wanted some," Sonny said, laughing at the memory. He said that was a long walk home.

Brooks sometimes fancied a good "chaw" or a dip of powdered snuff, a tobacco habit I was unaware of before hearing Sonny's story. I was not surprised to learn his favorite brand was Garrett Snuff, headquartered in Memphis, about a two-hour drive west of his Tennessee hometown.

I turned the subject to what I came to talk about, his father's past. Sonny didn't learn the details of his father's dual life until after the 1973 stroke that killed him. The revelation of a life, and family, left behind in Tennessee made no difference to Sonny.

"It didn't matter one way or the other really, to tell you the honest truth. Like I say, I was always kind of the black sheep. I figured I just took after Daddy." By "black sheep" he meant that he didn't attend college or work in an office like his siblings did. Sonny was happy to be where he was happiest: tracking animals in the scrub, hunting in the woods or fishing in the creeks. Loving the outdoors was a trait of his father that he emulated, Sonny said.

After his father died and the two sides of my grandfather's life began having reunions, Sonny was not inclined to meet any of the Tennessee Binghams who came to Texas. Nor was he interested in visiting Saltillo. "I skipped the country when they came to (San) Angelo. I hitchhiked out to Barnhart," he said. "I kind of remember it, but not that much. I've been married forty years this year and that's been about how long it's been."

On another visit from his Tennessee relatives, Sonny, then a teenager, did meet Bill Bingham, who was Great-Uncle Howard's oldest son. At the time Bill was gathering material for the book he was writing at his father's behest on the Boss/Brooks saga. I told Sonny that I didn't know Bill's approach to telling the Texas part of the story.

"He didn't impress me very much," Sonny said firmly. "He was kind of . . . the opposite way you say you're approaching it. He was kind of wanting to put Daddy over on the bad guy side and I just . . . after meeting him, I never cared about meeting any of the rest of you all. As far as I was concerned when I was born that's when my life with Daddy started and that's all I care to know about him."

But Sonny regretted that he never met one specific member of my Tennessee family.

"I'd loved to have met Jiggs," he said, referring to his uncle, my great-uncle, by his nickname, "but the rest of it, it's just a different world to me."

I took satisfaction in understanding that Sonny wanted to meet his father's brother, to glean information of his dad's early life. He wanted details only a sibling would know, stories of the boys exploring the woods of Hardin County, basking in the freedom of childhood, of forming baseball teams with other town boys and playing games that stretched into dusk, of spending an idle hour on the Saltillo side of the river watching the ferry, weighted down with farm trucks and passenger cars, slowly thread its way across the water. Sonny knew the adult years of his father but recognized the incompleteness of his father's story and that made me like the youngest son even more.

In childhood, kids believe they know everything about their parents. Only when we lose them do we realize there are crevices of our parents' lives that will always be hidden from view. Sonny knew my grandfather better than I ever will, but even so there remained a void. We were on the trail of the same quarry, hoping to add another layer to the portrait of a man dead and gone, but not from our minds.

I learned more about Sonny's family tree. His son has a company that installs the wind turbines like I saw on my drive to Girvin. His daughter hoped to study nursing at Angelo State. I watched as Sonny reclined on the floor, his grandkids piling on top, all of them laughing at the sight they made. He made a fine grandfather, he did.

Before I left, Sonny had a question for me: "Whereabouts in Nashville was he born?" He was referring to his father. I explained that Saltillo, where Brooks was born, was south of Nashville, a little more than a two-hour drive. I told him that I grew up in the same county, but in a different town named Savannah. I mentioned that Saltillo used to be a bustling river boat port and Savannah was the smaller of the two. However, over the decades boat traffic waned because distribution of goods moved to trucks. Savannah became bigger because a new bridge over the Tennessee River was located there instead of nearer to Saltillo.

He absorbed this information. The story sounded familiar, he said.

"Girvin is actually a mile north of here on the railroad tracks. You all came through Barnhart on the way through. Those were two of the biggest shipping capitals of cattle in the world for years. I mean everything from South Texas come up through here," he said, taking a moment to pause. Girvin disappeared, he said, with the railroad. Today, the former prosperous community exists only on paper, kept alive by historians plundering the pasts of Texas ghost towns.

"This is sorry old country out here, but it grows on you. I was raised up on the creek with big trees, but I still love this old country out here. I don't know what there is about it."

Sonny's closing words resonated with me. I felt he was voicing the thoughts of his father for me to hear, expressing an affinity for land, for soil from which all life grows, even in a desert. Indeed, it was good that I met Sonny Brooks. Driving home in Bobbie's Caddie, with the sun setting in the rearview mirror somewhere west of the Pecos, I sensed a new connection to my grandfather, like he was waving at me from afar.

IS JIGGS THERE?

BOSS/BROOKS

With the final digit of the Tennessee number entered on the rotary phone, the spring-powered dial returned to its home position with a snap. Several months after my grandfather died in the winter of 1973, Sue was again on the phone, hoping to contact her lost half siblings and other relatives in Tennessee. Unlike past efforts to accomplish this task, whiling away hours looking at state maps and guessing which small towns to call, this time she knew to look only in Tennessee.

"My name is Bingham, not Brooks," her father told his family as he recuperated from his first stroke.

All those years she had been looking for the wrong last name. It was simple as that. A crucial bit of misinformation which led to dead ends every time. This revelation didn't change her strategy, however. Jiggs, my grandfather's younger brother, remained at the top of her to-be-found list, if for no other reason than his unusual nickname. How many Jiggs Binghams could there be?

Sue heard the operator: "Information, can I help you?" Sue requested numbers for Binghams in Nashville and began calling from the list. Soon enough she heard the familiar chirp of a ringing phone. After a few rings, a male voice answered "Hello." Being a veteran of making these calls, Sue got straight to the point. She told the man that she was in search of Howard "Jiggs" Bingham. There was a moment of silence, followed by a question: "Who are you?"

"I'm Boss Bingham's daughter and I'm looking for Jiggs Bingham," Sue replied.

There was a longer period of silence, a tipoff that, finally, she found someone who knew Jiggs. "He said, let me . . . just a minute, and then he put the phone down. When he came back, he said, here's a phone number."

Sue said she never dialed a number so fast, which is a difficult task on a rotary telephone.

"I had Jiggs on the phone, just like that," she said. When he answered, her words tumbled like water over Niagara Falls. "I told him I'm Billie Sue Brooks and my daddy was L. B. Bingham, Boss. He went by the name of Boss all the time. He had a brother that was called Jiggs and a sister that was called Verna." Her rushed words were met with silence, she said. But there was no click. Jiggs stayed on the line. Sue said several minutes passed before my great-uncle got over the shock of the call and began to answer and ask questions. The pair talked for more than an hour.

This account made me smile. Listening to the story unspool from her memory, I shared her wonder and joy that she had made contact with the one and only Jiggs Bingham.

If the night of my grandfather's departure in 1931 gave birth to The Lie, entrenching my grandmother and other Tennessee relatives into a morass of deceit and shame, then this phone call between a niece and her uncle was the moment the secret's grip on the Bingham family began to loosen.

Sue and Bobbie had many other phone conversations with Jiggs, Aunt Mary Lou, and my father. In May of 1973, not quite three months since their father's death, the Texas sisters traveled to Nashville, and Jiggs toured Saltillo with them, making sure Bobbie crouched on the floorboard at certain points in the tour because Jiggs said she resembled Myrtle, my grandfather's younger red-headed sister. Jiggs didn't want to answer any questions should locals become curious. Bobbie thought ducking out of sight was silly because she didn't think she and Myrtle looked alike, but she complied.

That was the first of numerous surreptitious reunions the half siblings enjoyed into the 1980s. They met every year or so. Sometimes my Tennessee folks traveled to various cities in Texas. The Texas group visited my father at his home in Charleston, Missouri, which is where I first met Sue and Bobbie when I was in college, and they traveled to see my Aunt Mary Lou at her home outside Philadelphia, PA. Some gatherings were large, Sue's kids and Bobbie's kids from Texas getting to know their Tennessee cousins; other reunions were smaller affairs, just the adults. Even Hootsie accompanied her daughters on one trip.

Effort was made by both sides to forge meaningful relationships. The reunions were important to closing the divide between the half siblings, but another significant development was the exchange of letters, particularly between Sue and Bobbie in Texas and my father, Aunt Mary Lou, and Jiggs at their homes in Missouri, Pennsylvania, and Tennessee, respectively. The correspondence flourished in the mid-1970s and continued for more than a decade. In this form of communication, viewed as quaint as a rotary phone in our digitally connected world, the families of Boss and Brooks shared the minutia of their lives: the pursuits and accomplishments of their offspring, misadventures in canning and travails of the weather, too hot, too cold, too rainy or too dry.

Sue, writing to "Aunt Dorothy, Uncle Jiggs and family" on March 15, 1975, consoled Dorothy (Jiggs' wife) on the death of her mother. "I am so sorry. I hope that she did not suffer long." As to her own mother, Hootsie, Sue reported she couldn't slow her down. "(Tonight) she is out square dancing or trying to. Their Singles Club is trying to learn how. I would like to see them. I bet that is some sight," she wrote, adding, "It helps her. She gets pretty lonely."

My Aunt Mary Lou, writing to "Sue and all" on June 30, 1975, reported that the cute family kitten had officially become a cat, "as she killed her first bird, to the dismay of her owners. So now we will have to go out and buy her a collar with a bell to alert the birds, so it doesn't happen again." She also noted attendance at a recent dinner party the previous weekend for all the original homeowners on the block of their subdivision where they had lived for twenty years. "There are only 15 of us (remaining), out of a probable 50," she wrote.

In a July 10, 1975, letter to Pete (my father's nickname) and my stepmother, Helen, Sue lamented her busy schedule: keeping the garden watered, going out of town for a tax seminar (Sue worked in accounting) and ferrying her boys to youth league baseball practices. She told of a thrilling game where "it was the last inning. We had one run ahead and they had the bases loaded when we finally got the last out." Sue also thanked my father for several potato plants he sent home with her following a reunion earlier in the year. "I gave Mama three of the plants and she is very proud of them," she noted.

Inevitably, the content of the letters always turned to the patriarch of the family. This man with two names, Boss and Brooks, was still being figured out. In paragraphs freighted with pent-up emotions my relatives on both sides expressed themselves honestly. They wrote what they didn't have the courage to say in the social setting of a family reunion.

In the March 1975 letter, Sue turned from the mundane to what she wanted to say about her father's affection for his Tennessee children.

"One thing those kids can be sure of (is) their daddy loved them with all his heart . . . He loved them so much that he wouldn't do anything that would hurt them . . . I have always known how much my daddy loved them because I knew how much he loved me and how he would cry, his heart breaking every time they were mentioned, or something happened to remind him of back there." Sue reminded her Tennessee family that her father called out for his first wife and children as he lay dying. "This was something that was so hard for me. I had to keep Mama away when he was like that because I knew how it would hurt her."

Sue also wrote of the day, some months before Brooks' death, when he destroyed the small photos of his Tennessee children that were in his pocket when he left his Saltillo home in 1931. These photos were the only physical reminder of the family he left behind, the same photos that had captured the attention and imagination of his Texas daughters.

"He always kept those pictures, until he was afraid that he was going to be exposed. Then he destroyed them because that was the only thing that could connect him with the past. Oh, how it must have hurt to destroy those pictures," Sue wrote, adding she still possessed the small frame that held the photos of my Aunt Margaret Lois, Aunt Mary Lou, and my father.

In June 1975, just a few weeks after Sue and Bobbie and their families visited my father in Missouri, Mary Lou wrote a three-page letter addressed to Sue, but for all the Texas siblings to read. After introducing her five children, three boys and two girls, born in stair steps from 1955 to 1964, and offering fat paragraphs about their activities from playing baseball in college (Frankie) to wearing braces (Mary Lois) to the rambunctiousness of her youngest, Ronald, nicknamed "Pip," my aunt indicated a change of tone.

"Now, that concludes the easy part of the letter," was her transition line.

Learning of her father's life in Texas rattled Mary Lou to her core. Relatives told me this as I began the search for my grandfather, but it wasn't until I read this June 1975 letter to her Texas half siblings that I understood the depth of her emotions.

"When I talk about my kids, I find it extremely easy. I am finding it is extremely difficult—and that explains the delay in writing (to you)—to adjust to the new events," she began.

"I always knew—I don't know how—that he was alive, and, in my childhood, I daydreamed a million things that could have happened, but never did it occur to me that it was in any way deliberate on his part. I always assumed that he had picked up a passenger and it was the passenger in the car (who was burned) and that (my father) was wandering around with amnesia. And that when he finally did know who he was, he had a family and therefore couldn't come back, but I never dreamed or even thought that he could ever just deliberately leave us and never come back or get in touch with us. Being a parent, myself, I can just not comprehend how a parent could do that. Never a birthday card, never a Christmas card, nothing."

Her damning condemnation of my grandfather's absence leaped from the page. I don't know if my aunt previously voiced these thoughts to anyone other than her husband, Frank, but there's no doubt she was ready to fire her grievances at will. And she did.

"I don't understand how he could have agreed to anything like that, and I know for a certainty that he must have made the plans without my mother's knowledge, as she was a very right/wrong person. There was never any gray area or extenuating circumstances that would make a wrong in any way acceptable. She would never, therefore, have agreed to join him no matter what the circumstances. Nor would she have ever asked him for anything afterward. She lived a life of nothing but problems, never any money, my sister in bed for years with TB and hemorrhaging time after time with no doctor around, me in bed with rheumatic fever and never once did she ever complain or say anything about him but that he was a good father and neighbor. However, I never heard her say he was a good husband. I often wondered why . . . now I know," she continued.

It pains me to read my aunt's words, particularly about my grandmother, but the sad truth is that my grandmother played a significant role in my grandfather's disappearance.

Sue made note of Aunt Mary Lou's strong tone in her next letter to Pete and Helen, my father and stepmother. "I had a letter from Mary Lou on Tuesday, and she is very bitter about her dad," Sue began. "I think there are quite a few of the facts that she doesn't know."

Sue told my father that Mary Lou and Sue's brother, Freddie, "have a lot of the same thoughts, except in the opposite direction. They both feel the other one let their side down. Freddie thinks that since your mother and Jiggs both knew how to contact Daddy that they let him down by not doing so more and Mary Lou feels the other way." Sue offered that Brooks thought it too dangerous to write directly to my grandmother and other relatives in Saltillo.

I'm confident that simple of an explanation wouldn't have been accepted by Aunt Mary Lou.

Sue noted she experienced two bouts of anger and bitterness after learning details of her father's dual life. "Thankfully, Daddy was there to help me the first time and it took the Lord to work it out for me the last time," she wrote, adding that she hoped providence would intercede on Mary Lou's behalf, too.

These letters, laced with raw emotions that still have the power to bring me to tears, were the beginning of the great unraveling. If I managed to pull threads of the Boss/Brooks story that have never been pulled before, it's due in large part to the honesty of these letters. During my journey I have read and re-read them. They have been a path of discernment for which I'm grateful to have as a guide.

And may I rejoice, for at last, this story has letters that were not used as tinder for evening fires. They were saved, treasured and, most importantly, shared.

I note that the writers and receivers of this remarkable string of correspondence were primarily women in the family, but I know the letters circulated among Freddie, Sonny, and my father. The sons were always interested to know what was being said, even if they appeared disinterested.

It's important to point out that no matter what emotional turn the content took, the letters ended with cordiality, with declarations to write more soon. Sue always signed her letters, "Sis."

Even Aunt Mary Lou, having unburdened her heart's lament in the June 1975 letter, ended with a yearning to know more about these Texans with whom she shared a genetic connection. She mentioned a planned gathering at my father's home later that summer.

"Anyway, as of now, unless something drastic comes up (and who knows, when there are five kids involved) we plan to come to Lytle's either the third or fourth week of August," she wrote.

"And if you feel that you would still like to see me then I hope you will be able to come."

STRONG WOMEN

I discovered a poem by Icelandic poet Ingibjorg Haraldsdottir that resonated with me. The poem is well-known, having been translated into dozens of languages since its release in 1983. It's a short work of only fifty-four words and its title is also brief: "Woman." It's a lament and an acute observation of how females are often relegated, by unintentional or deliberate misogyny, to be the ones who clean-up for the men after the males have "dissected, discussed and settled" the problems of the world with a handshake. It's a woman who, as the poem's next to final line has been translated in English, "opens the windows to chase out the cigar smoke."

The men of Saltillo met. On a winter's day in 1931, their conspiracy was executed, and for decades going forward women in my grandfather's life were clearing the air. When I began chasing the Boss/Brooks story in earnest, I considered its purpose was to define the man who disappeared. Having traveled many literal and figurative miles in his footsteps, however, I now understand that the women of this story, those who abetted him, loved him, and missed him, are equally important. In instances, they're more important. I know and appreciate the power of strong women. It has been a surprise and a delight to acquaint myself with several of them on this journey.

My Great-Great-Grandmother Lucy Bingham impressed me. Her husband, Wylie, either died by bushwhack or simply abandoned her in the wilds of southern Arkansas in the mid-1800s with their brood of five sons, the youngest, an eighteen-month-old, who became my great-grandfather. Her tenacity to make her way back to Saltillo and raise her boys is a story worthy of a longer telling.

My Great-Aunt Verna emerged as a strong woman, taking on the job of facilitating Boss's escape from Tennessee, and sending cash to him in Texas during the Depression when her meager salary as a Sears stenographer barely covered her own needs. She also was the communication conduit between my grandmother, Jiggs, and Boss, with letters arriving at her Monroe Avenue address in Memphis before being forwarded to Saltillo or my grandfather's rented post office box in San Angelo.

In his will, my grandfather named Verna guardian of my father and his sisters, placing her into the legal fray with the insurance companies for years to come. One of the cases in which she's named as complainant advanced to the Tennessee Supreme Court, where the high court took her side. Of Verna, Howard always said that my father and his sisters had no braver advocate, but I wonder why she agreed to maintain The Lie, knowing she was culpable in several crimes. If the plot had been uncovered, Verna could have spent years of her adult life at the women's penitentiary, but she never violated her brother's confidence. I found no evidence that Verna ever wrote a single word about the situation. With her death in 1942 at the age of forty, all that she knew was lost.

My Aunt Mary Lou makes the list for reasons much different than Verna. Her father's disappearance when she was five left an indelible mark on her psyche. She was her father's constant companion. She perched on his shoulders as he checked on the livestock. In a page of simple prose written decades before learning her father had lived another life in Texas, my aunt recalled details of that last day with him. "He was going to Jackson today on a business trip and she would miss his goodnight hug and kiss, so when he gave her an extra-long hug and more kisses than usual, she just smiled and thought nothing unusual about it."

The next morning, she wrote, there was "knocking on the door." There were three men at the door. One man said, "The car went off the road," and then added, "Boss was killed."

Mary Lou's prose ends: "the happy little five-year-old would never be completely happy again."

Through childhood and into her young adult years, my aunt inquired often about her father, relatives told me. Inevitably, my grandmother would burst into tears and Mary Lou would retreat. She stopped inquiring of the "black box," a cardboard container holding legal papers, a transcript of one of the insurance trials. After my grandmother died in 1971, my aunt retrieved the box and began her own investigation into her father's disappearance, but she learned little. After being informed of her father's double life when she was forty-seven, her mind was often clouded by bitterness and disappointment.

Aunt Mary Lou sought grace and healing in church. "Every Sunday when we sing 'Let there be peace on Earth and let it begin with me,' I feel sure I can forgive and forget, and then every time I look at any of the pictures of him, I find . . . I just can't forgive. When you go through life wanting so badly to find your father and then find out he could have found you any time he wanted to, you wake up one morning and find there isn't any more use to daydreaming of finding your dream," she wrote Sue and Bobbie in a letter.

My heart ached for my aunt's pain, but I'm proud of her forthrightness about her inability to forgive, even as she developed a relationship with her half siblings in Texas. At the core of her struggle, she just wanted to understand her father's and mother's actions, just as I did.

I also felt a special kinship to her for other reasons. At certain remarks, hand gestures or facial expressions from me, my mother noted, "You are just like your Aunt Mary Lou." She and I also studied business after high school, and we both, expressing our independent natures, moved away from small-town life to Nashville to begin our careers. Aunt Mary Lou died in 2008 about the time my interest in the Boss/Brooks story began to grow. She is not present to read what I've written, but I'm hopeful she would be pleased that it's being told.

I'm also glad to say that the women I now know as Aunt Sue and Aunt Bobbie are happy that I've wanted to know my grandfather. Truly, if not for these two persistent women, my generation of the Tennessee Binghams may never have known that my grandfather did not die in a fiery one-car crash, or that he had a second family, or even the existence of The Lie, a coverup that was otherwise destined to die with those who created it. In 1972, when my grandfather, fearing a second stroke, decided to tell all he knew, Sue and Bobbie used the new information to contact the "first family" and the great thaw began. What once had been forbidden to be discussed was discussed. Once they found us, their generosity to share photos and memories of the former Boss Bingham was as genuine as their interest in learning about their newfound relatives in Tennessee.

Hootsie, Sue's and Bobbie's mother, earned my respect, too. The first time I saw a photo of her the differences between my grandfather's wives were apparent. My grandmother was tall and slim, with her short hair perfectly coiffed and accented by high cheekbones. Hootsie's frame was sturdier, with fuller, darker hair framing a rounded face.

There were differences in disposition, too. Whereas my grandmother was friendly but reserved in the presence of non-family members, Hootsie was outgoing and enjoyed the company of others.

I wondered if my grandfather was attracted to his Texas wife because her sunny temperament lifted his homesick spirits, perhaps even made him laugh. I am sure it was helpful that Hootsie was different from the wife he left in Saltillo.

Learning the truth about Brooks' Tennessee exodus blindsided Hootsie, her daughters told me. What she knew of her husband of thirty-five years was based on subterfuge: a contrived name, a birth date off by five years, and most shocking of all, his participation in crimes, including bigamy. Yet she stood by Brooks, nursing him to health following his first stroke. She loved him and was lonely without him when a second stroke killed him in 1973.

Seeing photos of Brooks and Hootsie, I have feelings of jealousy on behalf of my grandmother. After all, Hootsie took my grandmother's place, but Hootsie, I reminded myself, was an innocent player in my grandfather's second life. All she knew until 1971 was that Brooks had left children behind in Tennessee, a fact that apparently touched the Texas woman. Their mother, the daughters recalled, often showed them photographs of their half siblings that Brooks carried in a pocket the night he left Saltillo. By doing so, she encouraged the curiosity of her daughters, perhaps hoping for a day in the future when all her husband's children could meet one another. If so, her lesson was not lost on Sue and Bobbie. I'm grateful for Hootsie's role in this development. She remained a strong woman despite the loss of her husband and later, the loss of her home to fire. She died on September 17, 1997, twenty-four years after Brooks died and three days after her husband would have turned 102 (by his true birthdate).

While researching my family's story, I discovered a photograph of my grandparents taken while they were dating. They are positioned side by side, Boss on the left and she on the right, her arm draped across his knee. They are at ease: he with a hint of a smile and she with the corners of her mouth held high. What's most striking to me is the expression on her face, how smitten she was of her husband-to-be. How happy she was, a happiness that disappeared in a winter night's wind.

In my view, my grandmother is the strongest woman in this story. She took on the protection of her husband, children, and other family members by playing a role in the disappearance of my grandfather, a role tortuous to bear and contradictory to her beliefs and values. She risked being charged with several felonies, including perjury, but when she faced aggressive investigators snooping around her home or attorneys who grilled her without mercy in court, she remained resolute. I cannot defend her for lying on the witness stand, even though I understand preservation of her family was the motivating factor, but I admire her backbone. My grandmother always carried herself with perfect posture, erect, chin up. I can imagine her walking into the Hardin County Courthouse for trial that way, projecting strength, even as she was likely consumed by dread.

More than three years elapsed between Boss's departure from Saltillo to the settlement of the insurance cases, a period during which her life was scrutinized, her husband's name was denigrated, and her family's resources diminished. She had to tend the livestock and chickens, milk the cow, churn butter, clean the house, wash the clothes and cook, all the while caring for three young children. Added to her burden was the knowledge that she and her husband would never be together again. A reunion would be impossible due to the vortex of legal matters resulting from the demise of the Hardin County Bank.

Her fortitude to tell my grandfather that he was free to begin a new life goes beyond the grain of human nature, but I dare say that wasn't the hardest task she faced. That came when Margaret Lois contracted tuberculosis as a teenager and my grandmother watched as the disease slowly ravaged her daughter's body, leaving her bedridden, plagued by fits of coughing so strong that handkerchiefs were often marked by bright red blood stains. My aunt died two days before Christmas in 1947 at the age of twenty-four.

I began researching my grandfather's disappearance in my forties. By the time I turned sixty, it was clear to me this story was more than a Bingham history. Many of my grandparents' contemporaries, I concluded, were enmeshed in the secrecy. Their descendants deserved a public telling of the Boss story as much as my cousins and I.

However, I was consumed by doubt about my grandmother's judgment. She was a private person. Would she have disapproved of me trying to set the record straight?

My answer came in a dream where she returned to life and the family planned a party to welcome her. I wanted to be by her side every moment so that I could tell her of my plans to write the Bingham story. In the random way that dreams are created, my opportunity to seek her blessing came as we were in a grocery store buying food for the meal. Her reaction was to tilt her head, acknowledging she had heard me. Her expression offered understanding and acceptance. There was no surprise, or objections, just that simple movement of her head.

When I woke up, a river of calm overwhelmed me, as if I had been enveloped by one of her hugs. This was a gift from my grandmother, a way for her to grant me peace in my storyteller role.

About my grandmother, let me add a final observation. Considering the troubles of her life, I am in awe that she never suffered a mental breakdown.

But she didn't.

She just kept opening and re-opening windows to chase out smoke.

MAKING THE CALL

The important role of Joseph C. Lucas, the seventy-year-old man whose body was disinterred and used as a stand-in for Boss, cannot be denied.[1]

Without a body double, my grandfather would have been reported as missing, instead of dead. If no burned body was found in his Chevrolet coupe, there would be no death certificate issued, no claim to death benefits, no headstone in Shady Grove Cemetery. L. B. Bingham would just be a man who disappeared during the Depression.

But there was a body found in the burned-out hulk of my grandfather's car.

Lucas was a few weeks shy of his seventy-first birthday when he died on December 18, 1930. He was buried next to his wife, Roxie Ann, who died in 1919 at the age of fifty-nine. Stone markers, darkened by age, bear their names.

On many occasions I've stood before the tombstone of this man whose body was snatched by my ancestors. My family had long known that Mr. Lucas had not been at rest by his wife's side since mid-January 1931. Lucas was re-buried twenty-five steps away. Standing in front my grandfather's Tennessee grave, all it took was a slight turn of my head to the right and the Lucas headstone came into view. Some of the writing on the Lucas headstone was readable from my grandfather's grave. "Affectionate father and husband," was etched under Lucas's name.

My family's direct involvement in disturbing another man's grave has always been unfathomable to me. How could someone demonstrate such utter disregard for another human being?

One day early in my fact-gathering phases, I experienced a blinding flash of the obvious: the Lucas family didn't know the Bingham secret. I tried to imagine being in their place. If that violation had involved one of my relatives, wouldn't I want to know?

I stalled answering the question. Instead, I again considered the possibility that no grave was disturbed. I have followed this path many times before, hoping to find reasonable doubt that a body was stolen, but this delusion always ends at a funeral home in Jackson where a charred corpse was taken by an undertaker who was also the county coroner. Men from Saltillo viewed the remains and declared it was Boss. The undertaker testified to this in the insurance trials. The men from Saltillo testified to the same.

Beyond this proof, my grandfather's brother, Howard, told of digging up Lucas's body. My grandfather also told his daughters in Texas of the night the borrowed body was consumed by fire.

So, this terrible, egregious, despicable act happened. And my grandfather was the reason.

A phone call had to be made I decided. After all these decades, the Lucas family deserved to be told the truth, but I procrastinated for weeks. Competing thoughts came to mind. Did it really matter after all these years? Wouldn't it be best just to let the Lucas family remain ignorant of what happened? I realized those were the same arguments some of my cousins used to persuade me not to explore my grandfather's disappearance. That convinced me I needed to find Mr. Lucas's surviving kin. I owed him that. The Bingham family owed him that.

But I was anxious, for obvious reasons. How would the Lucas family react? I could envision them being suspicious, shocked, and feeling cheated from having the truth withheld. I imagined there would be crying, perhaps cursing.

Fortunately, it took a few days of searching genealogical websites, obituaries, and phone listings before I found a woman in a neighboring state who I believed was the great-granddaughter of Joseph C. Lucas. The computer sleuthing afforded me time to build my resolve. Even then, I procrastinated, unsure how to explain what happened in 1931 and embarrassed for my family's role. Eventually, my ambivalence and whining grew tiresome, and I committed to calling.

I dialed her place of business, but it was closed. At the beep, I left a message that I'm sure sounded like cryptic ramblings of a mad woman. I said I had information about her family that I thought would interest her and I left my telephone number. A couple of days passed before she returned the call. The phone was on speaker, I could tell, so I assumed others were also listening.

Before telling the Boss story, I made sure that her great-grandfather was Joseph C. Lucas, who was buried at Shady Grove Cemetery in Saltillo.

"Yes," she said. "I remember going to Shady Grove with my mother to place flowers on the grave." The woman was in her seventies and her voice offered a pleasant accent. In another context, two southern women who had just been introduced would have plenty to talk about: food, the weather, raising children. But I didn't know if this phone call was going to remain pleasant, considering the subject.

Taking a deep breath, I launched into the Boss script I had rehearsed. I told her that my grandfather faked his death in 1931 and required a body. Her great-grandfather, having died a month earlier, was chosen and I told her that the body was burned in my grandfather's car. I explained her ancestor's corpse was identified as L. B. Bingham and a funeral was held the next day at Shady Grove, with her great-grandfather being interred in a new grave very close to where he was originally buried.

She seemed to take what I was telling her in stride, listening without interruption. I was out of breath and expected much more of a reaction than she offered.

"That is bizarre and interesting, but how do you know that?" she simply asked.

I told her of the Saltillo men who identified the body, of the funeral director who accepted the men's declaration. I told her that, late in their lives, my grandfather and his brother acknowledged the body theft in interviews with family members.

I could tell she was processing this information. She asked other questions, but absent the anger I feared would erupt. I was catching my breath when she caught me off guard. "You know, he's dead and gone. Those bones are just bones. He's at peace, let it be. No reason to do anything about it—let the dead be dead," she said.

Given the nature of the information that I had just told her, she was incredibly gracious. Before ending the call, I told her I'd be happy to answer any more questions she might have. She thanked me for contacting her.

Her thanks were pleasing to hear, considering my pre-call fretting, but the call was anything but cathartic for me. In fact, now that I had shared my family's decades-old secret, I was awash with guilt and shame, and worse, left in a state of uncertainty about what to do next.

How does one generation atone for the mistakes of a previous one? Is it even possible? Although she expressed no wish to have her ancestor's remains moved, I was uncertain what, if any, action should be taken. Should a small marker, a permanent asterisk, if you will, be placed by my grandfather's Shady Grove headstone explaining that Lucas was reburied there, while my grandfather is really buried in Sherwood, Texas? Or would it be more respectful to do nothing, to not bring attention to the foul act perpetrated by Boss and others?

To let bones just be bones, silent in the ground.

Since my conversation with the descendant of Mr. Lucas, I still have no idea if I should or can do anything to rectify the misleading headstone at Shady Grove.

What I did in the name of transparency, however, was necessary. The Lucas family deserved to know what my grandfather and his peers did in 1931.

In my search for truth, I learned that my grandmother and Great-Uncle Jiggs offered penance to God in their prayers, but I'm unsure their confessions altogether eased their pain. For me, the latter is also true. I wanted confession to lift a burden carried since my college years.

But it did not.

Poor Mr. Lucas.

Perhaps, it's good that he will forever be with me.

Perhaps, thinking of him from time to time will be the least I can do.

LESSONS LEARNED

BOSS/BROOKS

When I began asking questions about my family's complicated story, my goal was to understand why my grandfather disappeared in 1931. I hoped to define the man once and for all. Was he a crook or a scapegoat, a coward or a man of principle, a manipulative schemer, or a man of incredible naivete?

Almost fifteen years after I began interrogating the past in earnest, my grandfather is more alive to me today than at any point since my father summoned me to his Missouri home in 1975 and told me the convoluted truth.

I know that in Texas Brooks was a respected man of the community, honest to a fault, generous to give a helping hand. Upon his death the State Senate issued a memorial resolution, describing Brooks as a man who "endeared himself by word and deed to all he met."[1] In Irion County, he was not too proud to ask for help from neighbors when machinery broke down or if help was needed to harvest a crop.

I know my grandfather loved and was loved. His Texas children viewed him as an accommodating and kind father when they were young and admired his commonsense sagacity when they entered adulthood. I know he acknowledged mistakes and lived with regrets that accompanied them.

In contrast, my grandfather's Tennessee legacy remained a bifurcated narrative. Prior to 1931, he presented as an upstanding citizen and businessman, a farmer who loved the land, a man of faith and a good provider and father. Following the bank's failure, however, Boss was a pariah among many depositors who lost large and small fortunes. They labeled him a crook. His death in a fiery car crash was proof enough that providence had the last word. But others in Saltillo did not speak ill of Boss. Particularly, many of the men in the community with whom he was close remained silent about the bank's failure for the rest of their lives.

Many descendants of my grandparents' contemporaries from 1931 have told me the Boss story was not a subject to be mentioned. In fact, their responses were strikingly similar in tone, something along this line: "We couldn't talk about that." Two examples illustrate this point.

Joe Parker, great-grandson of Dr. Luther Parker, was in his fifties before he learned of the Boss story. "Yeah, they didn't talk about it," said Parker, whose great-grandfather was my grandfather's physician, as well as president of the bank's board of directors.

Standing in the shade of a barn on his property near Saltillo, Joe Parker recalled that his father, Wallace Parker Jr., told him "a lot of people would've, could've went to jail," for what happened in 1931. Joe said he was told that a body had been dug up from the cemetery and burned up in a staged wreck to make authorities believe that Boss Bingham was dead. "The bank was going broke," he remembered his father telling him, and Boss needed to leave "before everything went ka-plooey."

In the 1980s, Joe said that Howard's son, Bill, expressed anger toward the Parkers. Several of my Bingham kin believed Dr. Parker played an outsized role in Boss leaving, an accusation I could not substantiate.

"I overheard Jiggs tell Bill or somebody that the Parkers were your best friends. They are not your enemy. I asked Daddy what did that mean and he didn't say nothing right then, but later on he told me what that meant." Joe said he was told that his great-grandfather was an ally of my grandmother after the insurance trials concluded. "I think he even helped the lady and her children," he said. Dr. Parker's records indicated he remained the family's physician until he died in September 1936 at the age of sixty.

Joe apologized for being lean on details because the narrative his father told him was only a synopsis—highlights about the burned body, Boss's successful getaway and how the insurance companies "hounded'em and hounded'em" using private investigators to search for the head cashier they suspected was still alive.

Jake Boroughs, ninety, long retired and living in Savannah, was six when his family lived near the Bingham farm where his dad, Robert, worked for Boss. During the school year, Boss took Margaret Lois and Jake to school. He remembered my grandfather as a friendly man. "He carried me to school, and her, every morning and bring us back of the evening," Boroughs said.

The spry nonagenarian said his dad and Boss were good friends so it's easy to speculate that Robert Boroughs played a role in my grandfather's departure, but Jake Boroughs said his father never uttered a word about the mystery surrounding Boss Bingham. "I never heard of anything," he said. "I've heard some talk about it since, just lately."

What strikes me about these examples is the force of The Lie as it penetrated generation after generation of those who grew up in Saltillo. When the Boss story was broached, even decades after 1931, only limited facts saw the light of day.

When I began this journey, I so wanted to mark a moment in time that I could unequivocally identify as the tipping point from which all falsehoods flowed. Then I could say, but for this one action the tragedy forever marking the Binghams of Saltillo could have been avoided.

Of course, my family's story is not so easily deconstructed. Where do I even begin to explain what I've learned? Let's start with the bank's failure. That's an appropriate choice because Hardin County Bank is at the center of this story.

From interviews with Howard and my Texas aunts, a common thread of the Boss/Brooks story is that money was lent under the table to several cotton gin owners or three attorneys, take your pick, to invest in the stock market before the 1929 collapse of Wall Street.

Looking at the gains to be made, it's understandable why there was interest.[2] The value of common stock increased by 120 percent—a compound annual growth of almost 22 percent between 1925 and October of 1929. When the market was robust, the bank was repaid with interest. Success inevitably led to other illicit loans, but by the time of former Head Cashier Robert Hinkle's death in May of 1928, the market's volatility became highly problematic, especially for a small institution like Hardin County Bank. When stocks finally tanked and margin calls were issued, that's when the trio of loan holders, whoever they were, couldn't come up with cash to repay their "loans."

This story may be true, but there's no paperwork for these outstanding loans, of course, because they were off-the-books transactions. There's no hint of such loans in the bank audit, either. In fact, all I know with certainty about the failure of Hardin County Bank is found in the reports and testimony of the auditor, Eustace A. Jackson. He noted my grandfather's failure to maintain order of the account ledgers with such specificity that I cannot disagree with Jackson's assessment: Boss was a poor bookkeeper, especially in his years as head cashier. He confused accounts, repeatedly crediting deposits made by one customer to another customer's account. He cashed checks but didn't process them. He allowed more than one hundred accounts to be overdrawn. For some account holders, county tax warrants were marked as paid, but no deposits were transferred to the county's account. Several families believed their mortgages were paid in full only to have the auditor show otherwise.

Finally, there's the matter of his personal checking account, overdrawn by more than $9,000. While my grandfather's lackadaisical recordkeeping is adequately confirmed, the auditor's report offered no details about the charges that created my grandfather's large deficit. In fact, what's missing in the auditor's report, and what I expected to see, is a declaration of thievery, that Boss deliberately converted bank funds to personal use.

That Boss used bank funds for gain was a foregone conclusion early on. Ten days after the bank closed, Elijah W. Ross, lawyer for Hardin County Bank, complained in a letter to D. D. Robertson, superintendent of banks for Tennessee, that Boss had gotten "away with the capital stock, surplus and undivided profits, aggregating at least $20,000."

Proof of robbing the till, however, was never presented at the insurance trials. This is because the bank joined my grandmother in her lawsuits against the insurance companies so the bank could receive a share of the payouts. Consequently, proving that Boss deliberately pilfered the bank's coffers wasn't an issue. Proving L. B. Bingham was dead and buried was the only point of contention.

But when my grandmother and the bank went toe-to-toe in a lawsuit to decide how the insurance funds would be split, lawyers for Hardin County Bank did pursue the question of whether Boss diverted bank resources for his own purposes. In pre-trial depositions, Ross questioned the acquisition of every mule, wagon, tractor, and farming implement used on my grandparents' farm from 1926 until 1931. They also quizzed my grandmother on her spending habits and how her home was decorated, searching for proof of a lifestyle beyond the family's means. But this line of inquiry never resulted in charges that bank funds were used to purchase animals, implements or furniture.

Much more damning was my grandfather's investment in Saltillo Gin Company, which was organized in the fall of 1929. When he left Tennessee two years later, my grandfather owned thirty-two shares of the cotton ginning operation and was secretary and treasurer of the business. Par value was $100 per share so my grandfather's stake in the business was $3,200, a considerable sum for the era.

Of course, Boss didn't have that kind of money. The audit showed that about $1,500 of gin stock purchases were paid for by checks written on his overdrawn account. Due to his position as head cashier, my grandfather concealed the transactions.

The audit revealed he was doing the same for many of the bank's account holders. Among those deposed in May 1933 was Thomas Stanphill, the bank's liquidating agent. Stanphill, under questioning by Grover McCormick, one of my grandmother's attorneys, acknowledged that in 1930 Boss allowed many depositors' accounts to remain overdrawn. "Lot of overdrafts, yes sir," Stanphill said.

McCormick tightened the timeline on my grandfather's $9,700 overdraft, asking if it were true that "practically all of the big overdrafts show up the last six months of Mr. Bingham's activities as cashier of the bank?"

Stanphill acknowledged this was correct. "Yes sir, most of it appears the latter part of 1930."

Based on my grandfather's confessional letter to the bank's board of directors I am certain the final quarter of 1930 was a tense period. The weight of the Depression was keenly felt. Many loan holders, families Boss had known all his life, were slow to pay, or delinquent by several months with little hope of balancing their accounts. Lines of credit disappeared, just as farmers needed cash to buy seed and fertilizer.

So, what does all this tell me about my grandfather's actions?

I returned to trial testimony about the bank ledgers documenting my grandfather's overdrawn account. If he wrote checks in mid-1930 for $1,500 to purchase gin stock, that leaves a balance of a little more than $8,000 of his overage that begs an explanation.

What did he buy with so much money, equal to more than $200,000 in today's economy? The ledgers, which were introduced as evidence in the insurance trials, were sent on to the appellate court in Jackson when two of the insurance companies appealed their losses in county court. Unfortunately, evidence from civil trials was destroyed, likely burned.

I am, again, left to parse court transcripts for answers. Thankfully, they survived the decades.

In deposing Thomas Stahphill, the liquidating agent, my grandmother's lead attorney, Grover McCormick, asked if a large chunk of customer overdrafts and items listed in the audit as "irregularities and omissions" was charged to my grandfather's account?

"You do not charge an official of being a thief because he allows some individual depositor to overdraw his account?" McCormick asked.

"Not necessarily so, no sir," was Stanphill's reply, a reply that left a lot of wiggle room for interpretation. Unfortunately, McCormick did not pursue this line of questioning further, so I am left to ponder if a portion of my grandfather's overdraft is explained by the auditor charging him with the negative accounts of other customers.

Then there's the notion that Boss purposely added the shortcomings of depositors' accounts to his own to protect friends and neighbors and stave off foreclosures for a few months. Several in my Tennessee family believe this is what happened. There's ample evidence from the audit that few of the bank's accounts were in order. Most had not been reconciled in some time, which conveniently worked to the advantage of desperate account holders. As long as my grandfather failed at his fiduciary responsibilities, he temporarily helped his customers, who were also his friends and neighbors.

But without the bank ledgers I've found no definitive proof to sufficiently explain my grandfather's overdrawn account.

Several months before his departure, Boss was warned by Dr. Parker not to allow overdrafts and to be firm with the bank's customers. I don't believe he could follow this order. I recalled my grandfather's admonition to his oldest Texas daughter, Sue, after she told him of plans to apply for a job at a bank. Decades later, Sue clearly remembered her father's words as well as the measured tone of his voice. He told her that she was "too soft-hearted" to handle the pressure of being firm with people down on their luck. "You're just like me," father told daughter. My grandfather apparently did not possess the resolve to put the bank's interest above his concern for Saltillo residents floundering in the failed economy.

Even so, I must acknowledge that my grandfather abused his power as cashier to spend above his means. In particular, the gin stock issue was problematic. Desperate to make things right, I believe Boss made his 1930 cotton crop an all-or-nothing gamble to earn enough to get him out of the hole. Cotton prices had held at sixteen cents per pound from 1926 to 1929, despite the country's worsening economy.[3] Maybe my grandfather believed the commodity market was due to rebound. From a farming perspective, his Hail Mary crop of 1930 was an astounding success. The crop produced almost thirty-five bales, each weighing between 550 and 600 pounds, among the largest yields Boss had ever grown.[4] In a year when cotton brought twenty-five cents per pound, that would have been fortuitous.

His success offered no relief, however, for the market was flooded with cotton. Payouts were pitifully low. He received as high as eleven cents a pound for a few bales; a dime for others.[5] By the time the cotton was shipped to buyers for ginning, the chill of late autumn was thick in the air and Boss, no doubt, grew more desperate. He likely made enough to cover expenses, but not enough to close the floating loan.

Did he truly believe the 1930 crop would be his solution? Did he plant the seed in the spring knowing he was possibly turning Tennessee soil for the last time? Again, I am sitting in the twenty-first century trying to decipher a man's course of action more than ninety years in the past. I repeat the lament of this story once more: there's much I know and much I do not.

What I understand with the highest level of certainty is that my grandfather left town with no more than the $105 that he sent Uncle Jiggs to collect at the bank. I also am certain my grandfather did not leave a stash of cash, skimmed from the till of Hardin County Bank, to keep my grandmother financially afloat. In the wake of his departure, both were destitute, strapped to make ends meet for years to come: he in Texas camping, convalescing by a creek and she in Tennessee, laboring to keep the farm operating while raising three young children and fighting off foreclosure.

After his first stroke in 1971, my grandfather swore to his Texas daughters that he "never took a penny" of depositors' money. In the end, whether he spoke the truth remains a moot point because the lawsuit to divide the insurance proceeds was settled out of court. My grandfather's actions as head cashier never faced the scrutiny of a jury.

Let's move on to the insurance policies. There's no dispute that during his buying spree from 1928 to 1930, Boss used bank funds to purchase numerous policies and to make semiannual payments to keep the policies in force. Illegal? Yes, without a doubt. The question to be answered is "Why did he do this?"

On this issue, consider his letter received by the board of directors on the winter day his burning car was found by a teenaged boy checking rabbit traps. Boss in his own handwriting, informed the board of the considerable insurance on his life. He wrote: ". . . if anything should happen to me, all of it is for the benefit of the people who have money in the bank, as I do hate for anyone to lose on my account."

I am convinced insurance was my grandfather's plan to right the bank, particularly the policies purchased during his time as head cashier. Nothing else makes sense. Of course, because he couldn't afford all the premiums Boss wrote checks on his overdrawn account. This added, no doubt, to his anxiety that should Hardin County Bank fail, his shortcomings would be made public.

To his credit, my grandfather's insurance plan worked, to a degree.

Because of the insurance money, account holders were partially reimbursed for their losses, but my grandfather did not consider other ramifications of the bank's failure. Hundreds of the bank's customers found themselves owing money because their accounts were judged overdrawn. Many of the same customers whom my grandfather helped through his poor bookkeeping were served foreclosure papers. They lost farms, homes, and businesses in the Depression, pushed over the edge by the bank's closing.

I now gladly leave the subject of life insurance, but with one question unanswered. I've often wondered if my grandfather knew the value of the final payout to my grandmother and his children. To reiterate, most of the $27,000 in insurance proceeds were distributed to the bank, with my grandmother's lawyers also receiving a significant portion. My grandmother and her children received $6,869 as their share. Did he think the allotment given to his wife and children was fair? Further, did he ever consider that many account holders lost their homes and family farms to the bank's collection efforts? Did he believe the heartache wrought by his leaving was worth harboring a secret all those years?

Let's now advance to Boss's getaway from Saltillo, the part that has never failed to fascinate my friends when I shared the Bingham story.

I consider it beyond rational thought to believe that only two men—my grandfather, ill from tuberculosis, and Howard—could have exhumed the remains of Mr. Lucas, the stand-in. In the light of day, in weather less inhospitable than a freezing winter night, perhaps two men would be up to the task. On January 13, 1931, however, muscle power was needed: perhaps as many as seven or eight able-bodied men; perhaps as few as five. Certainly, more than two.

Move on to the scene of the burned car and the badly charred corpse found inside. The heat required to consume toes and feet, hands and arms, had to be continuous for more than an hour. Based on what I learned of fire forensics, the job required frequent dousing with an accelerant to methodically burn away any proof that Mr. Lucas was Mr. Lucas.

These two acts, the exhumation and the immolation, are proof that my grandfather's exit from Saltillo was orchestrated. To accomplish these repugnant tasks required co-conspirators, men of the community who were otherwise committed to living an honest and decent life. Boss intersected with these individuals in dozens of ways. They waved at each other as they passed on dusty lanes. Business deals were made face-to-face with a handshake. At school programs, Sunday church services, quarterly Woodmen Camp sessions and midweek meetings at the Masonic Lodge, the orbits of these men tracked the same paths.

When word came there was trouble at the bank, a number of these men volunteered to erase the life of Lytle Boss Bingham and to never talk about that frigid night in the cemetery. Who would do that? Men from Sulphur Well Church, where Boss was a Sunday school leader, are often mentioned. Others believe the lawyers who took under-the-table loans were participants. On a recent late spring day when I was visiting Saltillo, I met a woman who was fascinated that I was writing a book on my grandfather. She didn't ask a question so much as to make a statement. "It was the Masons," she blurted, convinced she was right. Ask enough people in Saltillo and you'll hear all manner of theories.

However, of this I am certain: a contingent of men was there that bitter night, grunting as they lifted the pilfered body from its soggy grave in Shady Grove Cemetery, and held their breath from the smell as they placed it in the car for transport to the burn location. These same men were there on a remote section of State Highway 5 south of Jackson as fuel was poured onto a stolen corpse until the burial clothes were saturated.

A match was struck and the vapors erupted in a roaring blaze, lighting up the dark Tennessee sky.

I wondered if these men regretted their decision to leave the warmth of their homes on that bitter night to do something so foul. Was their participation a payback for Boss keeping them financially afloat with his ill-kempt ledgers? Could these men's care for their friend be the sole reason for their participation in his getaway? I'll never know, but I know they were there and because of what they did and saw, I'm certain they were marked by that January night. The Lie gripped them as forcefully as it held my family.

With a beginning like this, encased in secrecy, is it any wonder that my grandfather's story has been mythologized over the decades, turned into a tale of unrelenting greed or romantic escape or selfless sacrifice, depending upon whatever second- or third-hand information the storyteller cobbled together.

The greatest irony is that the key participant in the conspiracy of The Lie, my grandfather, is the one who couldn't keep the secret. He's the one who broke the chain, unburdening himself to his family after a stroke in 1971. In the same manner, Great-Uncle Howard told family and a few friends about that winter night in 1931. By his death in 1990 at the age of eighty-one, Jiggs had given several lengthy interviews.

My grandmother, on the other hand, took The Lie to her grave. She never told my Aunt Mary Lou or my father that their dad was alive and living under a new name in West Texas. She died in 1971 without acknowledging her role in his getaway or her letter of divorce that she wrote to him. She never told her side. She never explained her feelings. She never divulged the family secret.

When the truth was revealed to my father, he was asked if he was angry at Boss for abandoning the family when he was two. Pete, my father, was a kind man with a wide smile. He was quick to help someone in need and slow to anger. He read the Bible every day and was active in church, serving as a deacon.

But his answer to the question surprised me. No, he wasn't angry at his father, he replied, but if he was going to be angry with anyone it would be with his mother, "because she knew the truth all those years and never told me."

To be clear, my father may have been momentarily disappointed, but he wasn't angry with her, although he surely had cause to be. One of my father's greatest attributes was he understood that grace is a gift given without consideration of worthiness.

Through the years, I have tried to imagine my grandmother's reaction had my grandfather returned to Tennessee late in their lives. Would she have talked to him? Would such a reunion bring comfort or bitterness?

Perhaps my grandmother's grave in Shady Grove Cemetery implies what her reaction might have been. Her funeral was on a windy day in March 1971. I remember the hearse pulling into the cemetery, trailed by cars filled with my family. Her coffin was lowered into the dark earth next to Margaret Lois, her oldest daughter.

When my aunt died from tuberculosis, it was my grandmother's choice to bury her in another section of the cemetery, distant from my grandfather's gravestone. Long before her fatal cancer was diagnosed, my grandmother chose the plot next to Aunt Margaret Lois as her final resting place. In so doing she tacitly acknowledged the falsehood of the tombstone bearing her husband's name. Her final act was a repudiation of The Lie.

Nevertheless, I often think of my grandmother's far-away stare that I noticed as a kid whenever she was in the kitchen, kneading dough or stirring a pot on the stove. As an adult I attributed this to her yearning for happier days in her marriage. Although she let my grandfather go, I am convinced her love for Boss Bingham never waned and this has encouraged me to find love for him, too.

When my brother, Steve, was 14, he asked our grandmother why she never remarried after Boss died. Her reply was telling: "I never met another man who was as good as he was."

Boss did not feel like a grandfather when I began pulling on the hanging threads of the Bingham family history. A grandfather bounces you on his knee, brushes his whiskered face across your cheeks as he holds you tight in a hug. That was my experience from my maternal grandfather, Daddy Joe, we called him. He was a good storyteller and I have fond memories of sitting near the wood stove on cold days listening to him unravel tall tales spun from his imaginative mind. Daddy Joe was six feet tall, his thick hair white as cotton and he possessed an outsized personality. He was a talker and enjoyed meeting people, a perfect combination for running his General Store, which he did in addition to farming. My brother and I visited him often when we were little, visits that we enjoyed immensely. What was not to like? He gave us more nickel candy than was good for our teeth and let us jump in the bins of soybeans at the rear of the store for fun. When we were older, we sometimes picked cotton in his fields, a task I can't say I relished. Sitting on the front porch shelling peas with our grandmother, Mama Scott, was a job I enjoyed more, especially because pea shelling was often followed by a watermelon cutting. Sitting on my maternal grandparents' porch, gripping a half-moon slice of sweet watermelon sprinkled with salt, remains a memory that defines summer to me.

Just as the orange-meated melons that Brooks planted in the cotton rows defined the season for his Texas kids.

In my protracted search to find my lost grandfather, I often felt like Lady Justice holding a scale, Boss on one side, Brooks on the other.

To measure a man this way is problematic. Is he the sum of one persona or an amalgamation of both? It's obvious both displayed admirable qualities as good citizens and hard workers, but it's equally clear both had secretive natures. The scales raised and lowered, never holding in the equal position for very long. It's a maddening cycle and pointless. I wanted to pin a label on my grandfather: absconder, coward, a man who was manipulated. But a case can be made for other tags: an unselfish man, a loving father, a goodhearted soul.

None of these attributes, by themselves, adequately defined the Tennessee banker or the Texas farmer. I often questioned which attributes to apply and which to ignore.

In the end, I didn't . . . couldn't . . . make a choice between them. I abandoned my scale. It was a perpetual motion machine, powered by conflictions of a family history so rare as mine. For me, the scales will be tipping this way for time immemorial.

And I must be satisfied with that, even as I lament the secret-keeping burden deposited on my grandmother and the weighty emotional pain inflicted on my father and his sister, Mary Lou.

Even as I weep that Margaret Lois succumbed to tuberculosis without both her mother and father holding her hands.

Even as my body stiffens, as if the very breath of air was pressed from my chest, when I think of my grandfather calling out for his Tennessee children and wife from his death bed.

I do not regret making this journey. I learned so much about my grandfather that I would never have known, facts that made him come alive, to show the depth of his love. Sometimes, the most obvious facts were hiding in plain sight. Late in the writing of this manuscript I realized that my grandfather, in contriving a new name for himself, chose one that gave him the same initials as my grandmother and his daughters. He became Marvin Lester Brooks. My grandmother was Mary Louise Bingham. My aunts were Margaret Lois Bingham and Mary Lou Bingham. Even by scribbling his new name, he made sure he would not forget his Tennessee roots. I claimed this discovery with joy.

In many ways, my grandfather's departure and the bank's closing signaled the beginning of a changing era for Saltillo. A new bridge over the Tennessee River, which opened one year before Boss departed, gave prominence to Savannah, the county seat, and Saltillo began to falter. The river ferry eventually ceased operating, isolating Saltillo, forcing residents doing business in Savannah to follow the river south until they could cross the wide water.

For anyone who doesn't know its rich history, a stroll through Saltillo today does not reveal its proud past as a prosperous river port town. Only a few of the buildings from my grandfather's day remain. J. H. Allen and Son, where my grandmother bought groceries is no longer open. The site of Dr. Parker's apothecary is a vacant lot. Gone are Grissom's Garage and Gant's Barber Shop. The building that housed the bank and the telephone exchange was torn down decades ago, but not before the bank was transformed for a time into an apartment.

The cotton gin that my grandfather invested in was a bust, closing before the Depression ended. In decades to come, soybeans replaced cotton as the major cash crop.

In the wake of the Saltillo bank's closing, Dr. Parker and others attempted to establish a new bank in 1933 but were unsuccessful. The difficult economic era dampened enthusiasm for the banking business. In the early 1970s, a Savannah bank opened a branch in town but closed it a few years later. Ironically, in 1973, one month to the day after my grandfather died in Texas, a new Hardin County Bank opened for business in Savannah and thrives today. Apparently, investors had no qualms about using the name of a failed bank.

Unchanged is Sulphur Well about two miles southwest of town. When I was a little girl, my father would take my brother and me to the wellhead, which was dug in 1836 by men who were looking for a deposit of salt.[6] Instead, the steady flow of water that streamed to the surface after percolating through layers of sulfur-laced rocks yielded a rotten eggs smell when exposed to air. On our visits to the well my father always brought along a cup to sample the water, which was said to have curative powers, but taking a drink never appealed to me. The water still bubbles forth today from its perpetual source far below the land where my ancestors worked the soil and lived their lives.

Through the decades, big-idea projects for Saltillo were pitched. In 1902, an application was made by three Saltillo entrepreneurs who filed a charter to incorporate the Shiloh Battlefield & Interurban Electric Railway Co.[7] The rail line proposed to carry visitors to Shiloh from Jackson, Tennessee, and Corinth, Mississippi. Saltillo would be the northern hub for the line, bringing thousands through town each year, it was hoped. The electric rail line never progressed beyond an idea on paper.

In the early 1970s, the Tennessee Valley Authority (TVA) seriously considered Saltillo as a site for a nuclear power plant, creating more than 2,500 jobs during construction and hundreds of permanent jobs once the plant went online.[8] One can only imagine the changes to Saltillo had this come true. TVA chose another small river town, Iuka, Mississippi. The multi-billion-dollar project was eventually scrapped, however, along with several other nuclear plants in the federal agency's ambitious but costly nuclear energy plan.

Today, Saltillo is home to about 420 souls.[9] There are retirees from Memphis and other cities who like the slow pace of living near the river and long-timers whose families have lived in Saltillo for generations. A few of my Bingham relatives live nearby, but most have departed, either to careers in bigger towns or to the cemetery, having lived out their lives in the bend of the river.

Former residents return on special occasions such as the annual River Day festivities and reunions at Saltillo High School, which closed decades ago due to school consolidation. Many also return on Decoration Day in May, to place new flowers on the graves of loved ones.

I come to Shady Grove Cemetery to walk among my people, my great-grandparents, aunts, cousins, friends of the family whose names I've heard all my life. Uncle Jiggs is buried there. So is my Aunt Margaret Lois, whom I never knew, and, of course, my beloved grandmother. Buried next to her is my brother, Steve, who died in April 2023, four months after being diagnosed with cancer. I regret he did not live to see this story published.

Their headstones will always be a reminder of 1931, the year my grandfather successfully faked his death. Boss's disappearance, however, brought peace to no one. The stain of The Lie colored the lives of several generations.

I believe my grandfather sacrificed himself for what he believed to be the greater good. A body buried under a gravestone bearing his name kept himself and friends from going to jail, but he lost everything—his family, his livelihood, his own identity—in making that deal with the devil. He created a new life for himself but he could never forget his past, the years before 1931.

My grandmother, meanwhile, pledged loyalty to a lie that robbed her of possibilities in her own life. She had few close friends and her reserved demeanor didn't invite deep relationships beyond family and church. She carried a moral burden until the day she died. I'm certain her prayers sought forgiveness for keeping the secret that separated her children from their father.

I admit to pondering an alternative world, one where Boss went to jail and my grandmother awaited his release. Would creating a new life as an ex-convict be easier in the end compared to the life of separation and shame that echoed through generations of family and friends who aided my grandfather's escape?

I have no idea which side of this equation would yield less pain. Add it to the list of other unanswered questions.

As I near the end of this story, let me note the most valuable lesson I learned from my grandparents was to abhor family secrets. Not every family has a secret as tragic as mine, but all families have disagreements that are ignored, divisions that are never plumbed for hidden truths. Having documented my family's experience, I am committed to honesty and respect in all relationships and to never become a keeper of secrets. I think my father would be proud of me.

When I now look at my grandfather's stoic face in that photograph taken at the bank, I sense a measure of vulnerability and desperation in his eyes, and my heart has a soft spot for him. For years he was a stranger to me, but now I realize that I knew my grandfather better than I thought because I knew his son, my dad. There were many traits they shared—a love for gardening, a desire to be helpful and a respect for the act of forgiveness.

Indeed, forgiveness flows like a stream through the Boss/Brooks story. My father forgave his mother for withholding the truth about Boss and eagerly embraced his discovered family, especially his half sisters. Great-Uncle Howard sought forgiveness by telling his story to his son, Bill, and other relatives. My grandmother's decision to release her husband from their marriage vows implies a forgiveness underpinned by a measure of love I can't fathom. Guided also by deep love was Hootsie, who forgave Brooks for concealing his past. Through prayer my Aunt Mary Lou sought to forgive her father for leaving. It's my prayer that her petitions were heard.

By revealing his past to his Texas family, my grandfather sought forgiveness for his actions in 1931. Boss/Brooks was flawed, but who among humankind is not.

If taking my story public does nothing else, I will be satisfied if this saga is better understood by those from Saltillo, but especially by his many descendants, scattered from Tennessee to Texas and beyond, who are the heirs of my grandfather's story.

My husband and I have a vacation spot on the Florida panhandle. My favorite time to walk on the beach is at sunset when the wide sky offers a palette of expressive hues and the blue and turquoise water breaks for land in ribbons of white foam. Over the years as I labored to find my lost grandfather, I stood barefoot on the shore of the Gulf of Mexico, pondering my discoveries: newfound family, lost and forgotten documents, photos of my grandfather I had never seen, including one of him and my grandmother taken when they were courting.

During these sunset walks, I thought of him camping beside Spring Creek, a tributary that flows into the Concho River, then the Colorado, before emptying into Matagorda Bay on the Gulf of Mexico. I imagined him as a boy fishing in the Tennessee River, a waterway that joins the Ohio and then the mighty Mississippi, moving south in a wide swath past New Orleans until it, too, tumbles into the Gulf.

My grandmother also accompanied me to this soul-stirring place, her voice carried by a sea breeze. Closing my eyes, I saw her face. I felt my hand in hers and the enveloping comfort of a hug.

Now, every time I return to the Gulf, both are with me. The grandmother I knew. The grandfather I found. Facing the lapping waves, my feet baptized by the combined waters of my grandfather's homelands, I stare into the horizon trying to see what I can see.

NOTES

Regarding the insurance trials of May 1932: There were seven trials in five days. Most of the same witnesses testified in all the trials. Their responses often differed slightly from trial to trial based on how a question was framed by the attorneys representing Mary Louise Bingham, Hardin County Bank and the State Department of Insurance and Banking, or by the attorneys representing the insurance companies. When a direct quotation is indicated in the manuscript, the specific trial is named.

ABBREVIATIONS

BINGHAM FAMILY
Lytle Boss Bingham: BB
Howard (Jiggs) Bingham: HB
Mary Louise Bingham: MB
Verna Bingham: VB

BROOKS SIBLINGS
Sue Crow: SC
Freddie Brooks: FB
Bobbie Williams: BW
Sonny Brooks: SB

INSURANCE COMPANIES
Business Men's Assurance Co.: BMA
Modern Woodmen of America: MWA

CHAPTER 1

1. National Weather Service, Memphis, *Climatological Data for Savannah 6 SW, TN.,* January 1931.
2. Information about what happened in the cemetery the night Boss Bingham left Saltillo is attributed to three individuals. SC and BW related what their father told

them after he suffered a stroke in 1971. The sisters were interviewed by the authors in May 2015 and on other occasions. Another account of that night came from HB who was interviewed by Steve Bingham in 1997. HB was also interviewed numerous times by his son, Bill, who was writing a book, *The Story of Boss Bingham*. Several chapters were written in the early 1990s but were never published due to Bill Bingham's death in 1999.

CHAPTER 2

1. Goodfellow Air Force Base, https://www.goodfellow.af.mil/.
2. Testimony from Ewing Griffin, Ulrich Watlington and Sam Watlington in insurance trials, May 1932.
3. Testimony from Carl Thompson and J. E. Holland in insurance trials, May 1932.
4. Shady Grove Cemetery, Saltillo, Tennessee, plot 1910.
5. Testimony of MB in insurance trials, May 1932.
6. Interviews with Brooks siblings, May 2015.
7. Ibid.

CHAPTER 3

1. Benjamin G. Brazelton, "First Settlers of the West Side of the River" in *A History of Hardin County, Tennessee* (Nashville: Cumberland Presbyterian Publishing House, 1885), pp. 27–36.
2. Perry M. Harbert, *Early History of Hardin County* (Memphis: West Tennessee Historical Society Papers, no. 1, 1947).
3. *The Binghams of Saltillo* (Savannah: Hardin County Historian, vol. 7, no. 2, July–December 2011).
4. Ibid.
5. *The Goodspeed History of Tennessee*, (The Goodspeed Publishing Co., 1886, reprinted by Southern Historical Press, 2017), pp. 841–842..
6. Find a Grave, database and images (www.findagrave.com/memorial/153972013 /wylie-morgan-bingham. Accessed June 30, 2021), memorial page for Wylie Morgan Bingham (1831–1867). Find a Grave Memorial ID 153972013, citing Shady Grove Cemetery, Hardin County, Tennessee. Maintained by A. Tate (contributor 48091930) and *Find a Grave*, database and images (https://www.findagrave.com/memorial /112335055/lytle_b-bingham: accessed April 1, 2025), memorial page for Lytle B "Boss" Bingham (14 Sep 1895–15 Jan 1931), Find a Grave Memorial ID 112335055, citing Shady Grove Cemetery #02, Saltillo, Hardin County, Tennessee, USA; Maintained by Roger Gant (contributor 47238378).
7. *The Binghams of Saltillo* (Savannah: Hardin County Historian, vol. 7, no. 2, July–December 2011).
8. Ibid.
9. Ibid.

10. Ibid.

11. US Census Bureau, *Twelfth Census of the United States: 1900*, Schedule 1, Population of Hardin County, Tennessee.

12. Registration records, January 1914 and 1915. Office of the Registrar, Western Kentucky University, Bowling Green, KY.

13. Western Kentucky University Archives, Bowling Green Business University, "UA99/9 Southern Exponent of Business Education, vol. VIII, no. 1," Paper 2798, 1914. http://digitalcommons.wku.edu/dlsc_ua_records/2798.

14. J. Lewie Harman Sr., *Brief Historical Sketch of the Bowling Green Business University*. (Bowling Green, KY: Bowling Green Business University, 1948), pp. 1–7.

15. Ibid.

16. Perry M. Harbert, *Early History of Hardin County* (Memphis: West Tennessee Historical Society Papers, no. 1, 1947).

17. Tennessee State Library and Archives, "Statements of Condition 1922," Hardin County Bank, Saltillo, Tennessee, Department of Insurance and Banking 1916–1999, Record Group 48, Box 4.

18. Marriage license for L. B. Bingham and Mary Brooks, dated Feb. 4, 1916, in Saltillo, Tennessee; found in Ancestry.com, accessed April 9, 2020.

19. US Census Bureau, *Fifteenth Census of the United States: 1930*: Schedule 1, Population of Hardin County, Tennessee.

CHAPTER 4

1. John Olszowka, Marnie M. Sullivan, Brian R. Sheridan, and Dennis Hickey, *America in the Thirties* (Syracuse: Syracuse University Press, 2014), p. 168.

2. Interviews with Brooks siblings, May 2015.

CHAPTER 5

1. Details of the final days and death of Robert Hinkle is attributed to two sources. HB was interviewed numerous times by his son, Bill. SC and BW said their father also spoke of Hinkle's actions in the weeks before Hinkle was found dead of a gunshot wound.

2. "Bank Head Killed in Gun Accident" (Nashville: *The Tennessean,* May 6, 1928), p. 1.

3. Certificate of Death for Robert Hinkle, May 5, 1928 (Nashville: State of Tennessee Bureau of Vital Statistics).

4. *The Agricultural Situation* (Washington, DC: US Bureau of Agricultural Economics, January 1953), vol. 37, no. 1.

5. Ibid.

6. Tennessee State Library and Archives, "Statements of Condition," 1922–1930 Hardin County Bank, Saltillo, Tennessee, Department of Insurance and Banking 1916–1999, Record Group 48, Box 4.

7. Ibid.

8. Ibid.

9. Bill Bingham, *The Boss Bingham Story* (unpublished), "Saltillo" chapter, circa 1980s.

10. Ibid.

11. Tennessee State Library and Archives, "Statements of Condition," 1928 Hardin County Bank, Saltillo, Tennessee, Department of Insurance and Banking 1916–1999, Record Group 48, Box 4.

12. Bill Bingham, *The Boss Bingham Story* (unpublished), "Saltillo" chapter, circa 1980s.

13. Ibid.

14. (Nashville: *The Tennessean*, May 6, 1928), p. 1.

15. US Census Bureau, *Twelfth Census of the United States: 1900*, Schedule 1, Population of Carroll County, Kentucky. Retrieved from https://www.archives.gov /research/census/publications-microfilm-catalogs-census/1900/part-07.html.

16. "Index to Compiled Service Records of Volunteer Union Soldiers Who Served in Organizations from the State of Indiana" database with images Fold3 (https:// www.fold3.com//title/799/civil-war-service-index-cmsr-union-indiana: accessed July 9, 2021).

17. US Census Bureau, *Twelfth Census of the United States: 1900*, Schedule 1, Population of Carroll County, Kentucky. Retrieved from https://www.archives.gov /research/census/publications-microfilm-catalogs-census/1900/part-07.html.

18. Tennessee State Library and Archives, "Statements of Condition," 1928 Hardin County Bank, Saltillo, Tennessee, Department of Insurance and Banking 1916–1999, Record Group 48, Box 4.

19. Testimony of HB at insurance trials, May 1932.

20. John Kenneth Galbraith, *The Great Crash 1929* (New York: Houghton Mifflin Harcourt, 1954).

CHAPTER 6

1. Joseph M. Nance, "Republic of Texas," *Handbook of Texas Online*, accessed October 28, 2024, https://www.tshaonline.org/handbook/entries/republic-of-texas.

2. Terry C. Maxwell, *Wildlife of the Concho Valley* (College Station, TX: Texas A&M University Press, 2013), pp. 1–8.

3. W. J. Latimer, J. A. Kerr, A. L. Gray, et al., *Soil Survey of Hardin County, Tenn.* (Washington, DC: US Department of Agriculture, 1926).

4. C. C. Wiedenfeld, *Soil Survey of Irion County, Texas* (Washington, DC: US Department of Agriculture, 1986).

5. Ibid.

6. Testimony from MB at insurance trials, May 1932.

7. Texas State Cemetery, Biographical entry for Dorsey B. Hardeman, www.cemetery .tspb.texas.gov.

8. Ibid.

9. Fleetwood Ball, "Among the Brethren" (Nashville: *Baptist and Reflector*, July 4, 1929), p. 14.

CHAPTER 7

1. National Weather Service, Memphis, *Climatological Data for Savannah 6 SW, TN.,* January 1931.

2. Ibid.

3. Map of Saltillo prepared by Tennessee Department of Highways and Public Works, 1929.

4. Testimonies of MB and HB at insurance trials, May 1932.

5. Morbidity and Mortality Weekly Report, *Historical Perspectives Centennial: Koch's Discovery of the Tubercle Bacillus* (Atlanta: Centers for Disease Control, March 19, 1982).

6. Tennessee Department of Health website, https://www.tn.gov/health. *Health Department History 1926–1960*, entry for 1930.

7. "Annual Bulletin of Vital Statistics for the Year 1931" (Nashville: Tennessee Department of Public Health, 1932), p. 7.

8. Thomas M. Daniel, *Wade Hampton Frost, Pioneer Epidemiologist 1880–1938: Up to the Mountain* (Rochester: University of Rochester Press, 2005), p. 182.

9. Testimony of MB in insurance trials, May 1932.

10. Testimony of HB in insurance trials, May 1932.

11. Deposition of Dr. L. A. Parker, *Hardin County Bank v. Mary L. Bingham et al,* March 12, 1932.

12. Gary Richardson, *Banking Panics of 1930–31, Federal Reserve History* (Richmond: Federal Reserve Bank, 2020).

13. Deposition of Sinclair S. Dickey, *Hardin County Bank v. Mary L. Bingham et al,* March 1, 1932.

14. Testimony of Dr. Luther A. Parker in insurance trials, May 1932.

15. Testimony of HB in insurance trials, May 1932.

16. Testimony of Dr. Luther A. Parker in insurance trials, May 1932.

17. Testimony of HB in insurance trials, May 1932.

18. Ibid.

19. The handwritten letter by L. B. Bingham was introduced as evidence in each of the insurance trials. Unfortunately, the original was likely destroyed after the cases were adjudicated because evidence in civil trials was not customarily saved for posterity by court officials.

20. Interview by Steve Bingham with Mary Lou Bingham Tirpak, 2006.

21. Testimony of HB in insurance trials, May 1932. SC and BW provided same information in May 2015 interviews.

22. A plan to reunite after Boss reached a western state was spoken of during interviews conducted by the authors with SC and BW, and also in an interview of HB conducted by Steve Bingham.

CHAPTER 8

1. The identity of Joseph Lucas as the stand-in is attributed to SC, BW, and HB, as well as other Bingham family members. Certificate of Death for J. C. Lucas, Dec. 18, 1930 (Little Rock, AR: Bureau of Vital Statistics).
2. John Kenneth Galbraith. *The Great Crash 1929*. (New York: Houghton Mifflin Harcourt, 1954), p. 11–22.
3. Ibid.
4. Testimony of Ulrich A. Watlington in insurance trials, May 1932.
5. Testimony of MB in insurance trials, May 1932.
6. Testimony of HB in *Mary L. Bingham et al. v MBA*, May 1932.
7. Ibid.

CHAPTER 9

1. Purchase dates of life insurance policies from exhibits entered in insurance trials, May 1932.
2. "Audit of Hardin County Bank," Tennessee Department of Banking and Insurance, January–February 1931.
3. Ibid.
4. Ibid.
5. Ibid.
6. Ibid.
7. "Saltillo Bank Short $38,000, Report Shows," (Jackson, TN: *The Jackson Sun*, March 1, 1931), p. 1.
8. Letter from L. A. Parker to D. D. Robertson, Oct. 27, 1930.
9. *McConnell v. Henochsberg* noted in a letter from Memphis attorney John Vorder Bruegge to Elijah W. Ross, May 9, 1932.
10. *McConnell v. Henochsberg*, Court of Appeals of Tennessee, Dec. 6, 1929.
11. "Memphis Cashier Ends Life Today" (Chattanooga: *The Chattanooga News*, Dec. 7, 1926), p. 1.
12. Testimony at trial, *McConnell v. Henochsberg*, Shelby County Chancery Court, Memphis, 1928.
13. Ibid.
14. Ibid.
15. Ibid.
16. Ibid.
17. "American Bank Loss Revealed by Suicide Remains at $300,000" (Memphis: *The Commercial Appeal*, Dec. 8, 1926), p.1.
18. Deposition of Earl Bingham, *Hardin County Bank v. Mary L. Bingham et al*, March 1, 1932.
19. Deposition of Dr. Luther A. Parker, *Hardin County Bank v. Mary L. Bingham et al*, March 1, 1932.

20. "Hardin Cashier Burned to Death as Car Overturns" (Nashville: *The Tennessean*), p. 5.
21. Tennessee State Museum, "New Deal, Banks" (Tennessee4me website, www .tn4me.org). Accessed April 10, 2020.

CHAPTER 10

1. Testimony of Ulrich A. Watlington at insurance trials, May 1932.
2. Testimony of Sam Watlington at insurance trials, May 1932.
3. Testimony of Ulrich A. Watlington at insurance trials, May 1932.
4. Ibid.
5. Testimony of Ewing Griffin at insurance trials, May 1932.
6. "Ewing Griffin Sr., Funeral Home Head Dies at 63 Years of Age" (Jackson, TN: *The Jackson Sun*, Nov. 22, 1953), p. 1.
7. Testimony of Ewing Griffin at insurance trials, May 1932.
8. Ibid.
9. Ibid.
10. Ibid.
11. Ibid.
12. Ibid.
13. Ibid.
14. Ibid.
15. Ibid.
16. Ibid.
17. Testimony of Carl W. Thompson at insurance trials, May 1932.
18. Testimony of Carl W. Thompson, J. E. Holland and HB at insurance trials, May 1932.
19. Testimony of Vanden Griffin at insurance trials, May 1932.
20. Testimony of Carl W. Thompson, J. E. Holland and HB at insurance trials, May 1932.
21. Testimony of HB at insurance trials, May 1932.
22. From www.cremationresource.org. Accessed July 6, 2019.
23. Certificate of Death for L. B. Bingham, Jan. 14, 1931 (Nashville: State of Tennessee Bureau of Vital Statistics).

CHAPTER 11

1. Linda D. Wilson, *The Encyclopedia of Oklahoma History and Culture*. "Sayre," https://www.okhistory.org/publications/enc/entry.php?entry=SA027.
2. Ibid.
3. Interviews with SC and BW, May 2015.
4. "Bus Time Tables" (Jackson, TN: *The Jackson Sun*, Nov. 11, 1930), p. 10.
5. Interviews with SC and BW, May 2015.
6. Will of L. B. Bingham introduced as evidence at insurance trials, May 1932.
7. Interviews with SC and BW, May 2015.

8. "1,500 in Attendance at Convention" (Corpus Christi, TX: *Corpus Christi Times*, March 17,1931), p. 1.
9. Interviews with SC and BW, May 2015.
10. Irion County Museum and Historical Society, *Irion County Texas* (San Angelo, TX: Anchor Publishing Co., 1978), Entry for "The M. L. Brooks Family," pp. 240–241.
11. Leta Crawford, *A History of Irion County*. (Waco: Texian Press, 1966), p. 135.

CHAPTER 12

1. History of Freeman family from interviews with SC and BW. Additional information from family burial records.
2. Interviews with SC and BW, May 2015.
3. Irion County Museum and Historical Society, *Irion County Texas* (San Angelo, TX: Anchor Publishing Co., 1978), Entry for "The M. L. Brooks Family," pp. 240–241.

CHAPTER 13

1. Deposition of E. A. Jackson. *Hardin County Bank v. Mary L. Bingham et al*, April 7, 1932.
2. Ibid.
3. Ibid.
4. National Weather Service, Memphis, *Climatological Data for Savannah 6 SW, TN.*, January 1931.
5. Testimony in deposition of E. A. Jackson. *Hardin County Bank v. Mary L. Bingham et al*, April 7, 1932.
6. Ibid.
7. From inventory of items in the bank to be sold after Hardin County Bank closed.
8. Testimony in deposition of E. A. Jackson. *Hardin County Bank v. Mary L. Bingham et al*, April 7, 1932.
9. Ibid.
10. Ibid.
11. Ibid.
12. Ibid.
13. Ibid.
14. Ibid.
15. Ibid.
16. Ibid.
17. Ibid.
18. Testimony in deposition of Thomas C. Stanphill. *Hardin County Bank v. Mary L. Bingham et al*, April 7, 1932.
19. Testimony in deposition of E. A. Jackson. *Hardin County Bank v. Mary L. Bingham et al*, April 7, 1932.

20. Ibid.
21. Ibid.
22. Letter from W. C. Baker to E. W. Ross, March 11, 1933.
23. Letter from Adrienne Irwin to E. W. Ross, March 16, 1933.
24. Letter from eleven friends of E. O. Edwards, undated, to E. W. Ross, received in March 1933.
25. Affidavit of Arch White, Morris Chapel Community, March 28, 1933.
26. Testimony in deposition of E. A. Jackson. *Hardin County Bank v. Mary L. Bingham et al*, April 7, 1932.

CHAPTER 14

1. Gary L. Tefler, Lane Rogers, and V. Keith Fleming. *U.S. Marines in Vietnam: Fighting the North Vietnamese* (Quantico: Marine Corps History and Museums Division, 1984), pp. 24–30.
2. Letter to US Rep. O. C. Fisher regarding Lance Cpl. Freddie Brooks from Dale Tankersley, Selective Service Board, Midland, TX. Baylor Collections of Political Materials, W. R. Poage Legislative Library, Baylor University, Waco, Texas, July 8, 1967.
3. Correspondence between US Rep. O. C. Fisher, Selective Service Board and Marvin L. Brooks. Baylor Collections of Political Materials, W. R. Poage Legislative Library, Baylor University, Waco, Texas. July 11–October 16, 1967.

CHAPTER 15

1. Motion filed by the Tennessee Department of Insurance and Banking, September 9, 1931.
2. Letter from Solon T. Gilmore to Elijah Ross, March 18, 1931.
3. Letter from George G. Perrin to Elijah Ross, March 30, 1931.
4. Motion from BMA attorney Solon T. Gilmore in *Mary L. Bingham et al v. BMA*, January 26, 1932.
5. Deposition of MB, *Hardin County Bank v. Mary L. Bingham et al.*
6. Letter from R. Neely Jernigan to Charles N. Ward, April 6, 1932.
7. Ibid.
8. Ibid.
9. Ibid.
10. Letter from R. Neely Jernigan to Homer Ballew, April 7, 1932.
11. Letter from Homer Ballew to R. Neely Jernigan, April 13, 1932.
12. Letter from R. Neely Jernigan to Charles N. Ward, April 6, 1932.
13. Ibid.
14. Ibid.

CHAPTER 16

1. National Weather Service, Memphis. *Climatological Data for Savannah 6 SW, TN.*, 1931 and 1932.
2. Court list of insurance policies issued to L. B. Bingham.
3. "Abernathy, Former State Senator, Dies" (Nashville: *The Tennessean*, April 26, 1940), p. 34.
4. "Millard Lee, 78, Services Tuesday" (Jackson, TN: *The Jackson Sun*, March 24, 1958), p. 11. "John A. Shelton" (Jackson, TN: *The Jackson Sun*, October 26, 1965), p. 7.
5. John Trotwood Moore and Austin P. Foster, *Tennessee, The Volunteer State 1769–1923, vol. 3* (Nashville: S. J. Clarke Publishing Co., 1923), pp. 265–266.
6. "Rites Wednesday for W. N. Key, Prominent Attorney" (Jackson, TN: *The Jackson Sun*, July 24, 1963), p. 1.
7. "Judge Jere Galbraith Dies Unexpectedly in Memphis Hospital" (Jackson, TN: *The Jackson Sun*, June 23, 1948), p. 1. "Funeral Services Held Today for Former Mayor of Henderson" (Jackson, TN: *The Jackson Sun*, August 3, 1953), p. 2.
8. Kim Wires, *State of Tennessee v. Lennie Kendall* (Nashville: Tennessee State Library and Archives, Tennessee Supreme Court Records Project, Jan. 8, 2016).
9. "Joseph Ballew Services Set for Tomorrow" (Nashville: *The Tennessean*, March 9, 1972), p. 34.
10. "Veteran Attorney Killed by Truck" (Memphis: *The Daily News*, Dec. 5, 1968), p. 1.
11. "Perry M. Harbert Rites at Savannah" (Jackson, TN: *The Jackson Daily Sun*, Dec. 16, 1959), p. 6.
12. "Savannah Attorney Warren H. Sloan Services Friday" (Jackson, TN: *The Jackson Daily Sun*, March 14, 1968), p. 10.
13. "Ex-Gov. Tom Rye Dies in Paris at 90" (Nashville: *The Tennessean*, Sept. 13, 1953), p. 1.
14. Testimony of MB in *Mary L. Bingham et al. v. BMA*, May 2, 1932.
15. Testimony of MB at insurance trials, May 1932.
16. Testimony of MB in *Mary L. Bingham et al. v. BMA*, May, 1932.
17. Ibid.
18. Testimony of MB in *Mary L. Bingham et al. v. MWA*, May 1932.
19. Ibid.
20. Ibid.
21. Ibid.
22. Ibid.
23. Testimony of MB in *Mary L. Bingham et al. v. MBA*, May 1932.

CHAPTER 17

1. National Register of Historic Places, US Department of the Interior. Nomination form: Old Irion County Courthouse, August 29, 1977.

2. J. Wallace Higgins, *The Orient Road: A History of the Kansas City, Orient and Mexico Railroad* (The Railway and Locomotive Historical Society Bulletin, no. 95, 1956), pp. 10–46.

3. Crawford, Leta. *A History of Irion County* (Waco: Texian Press, 1966).

4. Gunnar Brune, *Major and Historical Springs of Texas.* (Austin: Texas Water Development Board, Report 189, March 1975).

5. Crawford, Leta. *A History of Irion County.* (Waco: Texian Press, 1966).

6. From interviews with SC and BW, May 2015.

7. Gunnar Brune, *Major and Historical Springs of Texas.* (Austin: Texas Water Development Board, Report 189, March 1975).

8. Find a Grave, database and images (www.findagrave.com/memorial/112335055 /lytle-b-bingham. Accessed July 5, 2021), memorial page for Lytle B "Boss" Bingham (September 14,1895–January 15, 1931), Find a Grave Memorial ID 112335055, citing Shady Grove Cemetery #02, Saltillo, Hardin County, Tennessee. Maintained by Roger Gant (contributor47238378).

    Find a Grave, database and images (www.findagrave.com/memorial/33371569 /marvin-lester-brooks. Accessed July 5, 2021). Memorial page for Marvin Lester Brooks (September 14, 1900–February 12, 1973), Find a Grave Memorial ID 33371569, citing Sherwood Cemetery, Sherwood, Irion County, Texas. Maintained by Steve Voss (contributor 46775339).

CHAPTER 18

1. Hardin County Chancery Court order regarding policies issued by Massachusetts Protective Association, June 25, 1931.

2. "Insurance Cases" (Savannah, TN: *The Savannah Courier,* May 13, 1932), p. 1.

3. Member brochure for Modern Woodmen of America, circa 1925.

4. Jere Galbraith reply to MB et al. Regarding request that MWA pay interest on death benefits, July 1932.

5. Ibid.

6. Order affirming the Hardin Chancery Court decisions in *Mary L. Bingham et al. v. BMA* and *Mary L. Bingham et al. v. MWA,* November 1932.

7. Order affirming the Hardin Chancery Court decisions in *Mary L. Bingham et al. v. BMA* and *Mary L. Bingham et al. v. MWA.* February 1933.

8. Letter from D. D. Robertson, superintendent of banks, to E. W. Ross. May 9, 1932.

9. National Weather Service, Memphis. *Climatological Data for Savannah 6 SW, TN.,* June 1933.

10. *"Cotton—Acres Harvested"* (Washington, DC: National Agricultural Statistics Service, US Department of Agriculture, 1928–1933).

11. From interviews with SC and BW, May 2015.

12. *Hardin County Bank v. Mary L. Bingham et al.,* settlement offer, Nov. 30, 1933.

13. D. D. Robertson to E. W Ross, November 1933.

14. Letter from E. W. Ross to Grover McCormick, April 18, 1934.
15. Letter from E. W. Ross to W. H. Key, Dec. 19, 1933.
16. Letter from W. H. Sloan to E. W. Ross, April 21, 1934.
17. Order from Chancellor Tom Rye, May 10, 1934.
18. Ibid.
19. Ibid
20. Ibid.
21. Ibid.
22. Ibid.
23. Hardin County Archives, Requests for distribution of funds relating to *Hardin County Bank v. Mary L. Bingham et al.*, 1935, 1937, 1939, 1943 and 1945.
24. Monthly reports of Clerk and Master C. S. Welch regarding funds held in *Hardin County Bank v. Mary L. Bingham et al.* 1934–1946.
25. Hardin County Archives, Requests for distribution of funds relating to *Hardin County Bank v. Mary L. Bingham et al.*, 1939.
26. Ibid.
27. Order for distribution of funds relating to *Hardin County Bank v. Mary L. Bingham et al.*, April 5, 1938.
28. Testimony of J. M. Bingham in *D. D. Robertson v. J. M. Bingham et al.*
29. Requests for distribution of funds relating to *Hardin County Bank v. Mary L. Bingham et al.*, 1946.

CHAPTER 19

1. Interviews with SC, BW, and FB, May 2015.
2. Texas Historical Commission, Historical Marker 5044, St. John's Sanitorium, San Angelo, Texas.
3. Denise Morris, "St. John's Centennial, A Century of Caring" (San Angelo, TX: *San Angelo Standard-Times,* Nov. 13, 2010).
4. Interview with BW. May 2015.
5. Interview with SC, May 2015.
6. Ibid.
7. Ibid.
8. Interview with HB by Steve Bingham, 1977.
9. Interviews with SC and BW, May 2015.

CHAPTER 20

1. Glenn Justice and John Leffler, *Handbook of Texas Online,* "Pecos County," accessed July 7, 2020, http://www.tshaonline.org/handbook/entries/pecos.

2. Robert H. Schmidt, "Trans-Pecos," *Handbook of Texas Online*, accessed July 7, 2020, https://www.tshaonline.org/handbook/entries/trans-pecos.
3. Glenn Justice, *Handbook of Texas Online*, "Girvin, Tx," accessed July 7, 2020, http://www.tshaonline.org/handbook/online/articles/hng07.
4. J. Wallace Higgins. *The Orient Road: A History of the Kansas City, Orient and Mexico Railroad,* The Railway and Locomotive Historical Society Bulletin, 1956.
5. Karl Dudley. *The Tennessee Magazine,* "Electricity, the Next Greatest Thing," January 2010.
6. Handbook of Texas Online, Glenn Justice, "Girvin, Tx," accessed July 7, 2020, http://www.tshaonline.org/handbook/online/articles/hng07.

CHAPTER 23

1. The identity of Joseph Lucas as the man whose body was disinterred and used as a stand-in for L. B. Bingham is attributed to Howard Bingham in interviews with his son, Bill Bingham, and Howard's great-nephew, Steve Bingham. In addition, SC and BW, the daughters of Marvin Lester Brooks, also identified Lucas.

CHAPTER 24

1. Texas Senate. Senate Resolution In Memory of Mr. M. L. Brooks. Regular Session. (TX, 1973).
2. John Kenneth Galbraith, *The Great Crash 1929* (New York: Houghton Mifflin Harcourt, 1954).
3. Lawrence A. Jones and David Durand, "The Cotton Belt" (Washington, DC: National Bureau of Economic Research, 1954).
4. Deposition of Robert Boroughs in *Hardin County Bank v. Mary L. Bingham et al.,* Oct. 21, 1933.
5. Ibid.
6. Zelma Oneal, "Old Sulphur Well is monument to intrepid pioneers" (Jackson: *The Jackson Sun,* Aug. 26, 1966), p. 6.
7. The Electrical Review, New York, New York. Jan. 4 –June 8, 1902, p. 2.
8. Tennessee Valley Authority, "Impact Statement on Saltillo Site," Section 9. Kent Gardner, "Pre-Civil War Boom Town Awaits Atomic Age" (Jackson, TN: *The Jackson Sun,* July 5, 1973), p. 13.
9. US Census Bureau, *2020 Decennial Census of the United States.* Accessed April 12, 2025. https://census.gov./all?q=Saltillo+town,+Tennessee.

BIBLIOGRAPHY

The Binghams of Saltillo. Savannah: Hardin County Historian, vol. 7, no. 2, July–
    December 2011.

Brazelton, Benjamin G. *A History of Hardin County, Tennessee.* Nashville: Cumber-
    land Presbyterian Publishing House, 1885.

Brune, Gunnar. *Major and Historical Springs of Texas.* Austin: Texas Water Develop-
    ment Board, Report 189, 1975.

Carey, Bill. *Fortunes, Fiddles and Fried Chicken: A Business History of Nashville.* Nash-
    ville: Hillsboro Press, 2000.

Crawford, Leta. *A History of Irion County Texas.* Waco: Texian Press, 1966.

Daniel, Larry J. *Shiloh, the Battle that Changed the Civil War.* New York: Simon &
    Schuster, 1998.

Daniel, Thomas M. *Wade Hampton Frost, Pioneer Epidemiologist 1880–1938: Up to the
    Mountain.* Rochester: University of Rochester Press, 2005.

Foss, Katherine A. *Constructing the Outbreak: Epidemics in Media and Collective
    Memory.* Amherst, MA: University of Massachusetts Press, 2020.

Foster, Austin P. *Counties of Tennessee.* Johnson City, TN: The Overmountain Press,
    1998 (reprinted from 1923).

Fronczak, Paul Joseph and Tresniowski, Alex. *The Foundling: The True Story of a Kid-
    napping, a Family Secret, and My Search for the Real Me.* New York: Howard
    Books, 2017.

Galbraith, John Kenneth. *The Great Crash 1929.* New York: Houghton Mifflin Har-
    court, 1954.

Groom, Winston. *Shiloh 1862.* Washington, DC: National Geographic, 2013.

Gunnell, John. *Standard Catalog of Chevrolet 1912–2003.* Stevens Point, WI: Krause
    Publications, 2011.

Harbert, Perry M. *Early History of Hardin County.* Memphis: West Tennessee Histori-
    cal Society Papers, no. 1, 1947.

Hardin County Historical Society. *Hardin County, Tennessee, A Pictorial History.*
    Paducah, KY: Turner Publishing Co., 1994.

Harman Sr., J. Lewie. *Brief Historical Sketch of the Bowling Green Business University.*
    Bowling Green, KY: Bowling Green Business University, 1948.

Higgins, J. Wallace. *The Orient Road: A History of the Kansas City, Orient and Mexico
    Railroad.* The Railway and Locomotive Historical Society Bulletin, 1956.

Irion County Museum and Historical Society. *Irion County Texas.* San Angelo, TX:
    Anchor Publishing Co., 1978.

Latimer, W. J., J. A. Kerr, A. L. Gray, et al. *Soil Survey of Hardin County, Tenn.* Washington, DC: US Department of Agriculture, 1926.

Maxwell, Terry C. *Wildlife of the Concho Valley.* College Station, TX: Texas A&M University Press, 2013.

McThenia, Tal and Margaret Dunbar Cutright. *A Case for Solomon: Bobby Dunbar and the Kidnapping that Haunted a Nation.* New York: Free Press, 2012.

Morland, Andrew. *Legendary Farm Tractors, A Photographic History.* Stillwater, MN: Voyageur Press, 2003.

Olszowka, John, Marnie M. Sullivan, Brian R. Sheridan and Dennis Hickey. *America in the Thirties.* Syracuse, NY: Syracuse University Press, 2014.

Richardson, Gary. *Banking Panics of 1930–31, Federal Reserve History.* Richmond: Federal Reserve Bank, 2020.

Tefler, Gary L., Lane Rogers and V. Keith Fleming. *U.S. Marines in Vietnam: Fighting the North Vietnamese.* Quantico: Marine Corps History and Museums Division, 1984.

Walling, Molly. *Death in the Delta: Uncovering a Mississippi Family Secret.* Oxford, MS: University Press of Mississippi, 2012.

Ware, Susan. *American Women in the 1930s: Holding Their Own.* Boston: Twayne Publishers, 1982.

Wexler, Laura. *Fire in the Canebreak: The Last Lynching in America.* New York: Scribner, 2003.

White House Conference on Child Health and Protection, final report, 1930.

Wiedenfeld, C. C. *Soil Survey of Irion County, Texas.* Washington, DC: US Department of Agriculture, 1986.

Yafa, Stephen. *Big Cotton: How a Humble Fiber Created Fortunes, Wrecked Civilization, and Put America on the Map.* New York: Viking, 2004.

———. *Cotton: The Biography of a Revolutionary Fiber.* New York: Penguin Books, 2006.

www.ingramcontent.com/pod-product-compliance
Lightning Source LLC
Chambersburg PA
CBHW031459120626
46545CB00005B/1676